READING

BEYOND

WORDS

READING
BEYOND
WORDS

FOURTH EDITION

W. Royce Adams

Jane Brody

Santa Barbara City College

Holt, Rinehart and Winston

Fort Worth   Chicago   San Francisco   Philadelphia
Montreal   Toronto   London   Sydney   Tokyo

Publisher: Ted Buchholz
Acquisitions Editor: Michael Rosenberg
Developmental Editor: Stacy Schoolfield
Project Editor: Mark Hobbs
Production Manager: Ken Dunaway
Art & Design Supervisor: Serena Barnett
Cover Design: Margaret Unruh
Cover Art: Edan Lange / Audrey McCaffrey

Library of Congress Cataloging-in-Publication Data

Adams, W. Royce.
    Reading beyond words / W. Royce Adams, Jane Brody. -- 4th ed.
      p.   cm.
    Includes index.
    1. College readers.   I. Brody, Jane, 1948 -   . II. Title.

PE1122.A33   1991   428.4'2--dc20   90-5300
                                            CIP

ISBN: 0-03-052769-4

Address for editorial correspondence: Holt, Rinehart and Winston, Inc., 301 Commerce Street, Suite 3700, Fort Worth, TX 76102

Address for orders: Holt, Rinehart and Winston, Inc., 6277 Sea Harbor Drive, Orlando, Florida 32887.   1-800-782-4479, or 1-800-433-0001 (in Florida)

PRINTED IN THE UNITED STATES OF AMERICA

1 2 3 4 067 10 9 8 7 6 5 4 3 2

Holt, Rinehart and Winston, Inc.
The Dryden Press
Saunders College Publishing

Preface to the fourth edition

As in previous editions, the chief aims of *Reading Beyond Words* are (1) to focus on teaching students in college developmental reading courses *why* they should and *how* they can become more personally and intellectually involved in their reading, and (2) to provide instructional materials that will develop reading-study skills not only for college survival, but for lifetime use. While many reading comprehension exercises include objective comprehension checks similar to those required in many academic courses, other exercises call for students to summarize, classify, compare, and analyze what they read through writing and discussion questions. Our major objective is not merely improving comprehension skills as measured by multiple-choice questions, but more importantly, to get students involved in a cognitive-affective thinking process.

Nearly two-thirds of the forty-five reading selections in this edition are new or used differently. More chapters and passages taken from textbooks used in history, psychology, sociology, philosophy, literature, personal development, and marriage and family courses are included. While we recognize the need for college reading courses that help students master their textbooks, we feel it is a disservice to limit instruction to those skills alone. Too many subject-matter courses merely require reading for literal recall and memorization, often providing no opportunity for controversy or stimulation of thought. Consequently, we include here many reading selections from a wide variety of sources and activities which we hope will counterbalance and stimulate students to think about complex issues they have not encountered before as well as challenge their present beliefs. In addition, we have enlarged the chapter on reading literature to include poetry as well as fiction, believing that instruction in how to read literature is too often neglected.

The text is structured so that readers can use the chapters as they appear or in any order. In most cases, however, we recommend assigning chapters as they appear. The range of skills and topics can be seen by looking over the Table of Contents. None of the reading selections, which vary widely in reading level, have been altered or selected on the basis of "easy reading," but rather are typical of what college students will encounter in their texts. Answers, except for those used to explain concepts or certain practices, appear in the Instructor's Edition, which can be obtained from your local Holt representative or by writing to the English Editor, Holt, Rinehart and Winston, Inc., 301 Commerce Street, Suite 3700, Fort Worth, Texas 76102.

We have deliberately chosen not to include any timed readings or discussions of reading rate, feeling that it will be a better use of their time for users of this book to concentrate on other aspects of reading skills development. Increase in reading rate generally occurs naturally as one learns the skills presented in *Reading Beyond Words*. However, the number of words contained in each of the nine supplemental readings is provided for those instructors who wish to show their students how to time themselves.

We with to express our appreciation to those who have helped us with their suggestions and comments: Kim Matthews, Mineral Wells College; Donna Farrell, Manatee College; Loraine Threadgill, Community College of Philadelphia; Barbara Henry, West Virginia State College; Julie Colish, University of Michigan, Flint.

Contents

2

Taking notes   49

3

Reading essays

6

8

Reading literature   267

9

Reading the newspaper 306

Additional reading selections   351

Reading textbooks

1

R¹   *Reading beyond words*

In the space below, write what you think the term "reading beyond words" means:

_____

_____

_____

Reading is much more than recognizing words with the eyes. The kind of reading we have in mind is an active process requiring reasoning. It means examining the ideas presented through words and deciding what they mean, rather than simply accepting them. Because much of the reading required of us in grade school and high school consists of reading for facts, memorizing them, and then repeating it all on an exam, we seldom get an opportunity to read critically and think through the ideas presented to us. To read beyond the words means not only to comprehend what the words are saying, but to interpret, question, compare, and evaluate what an author says.

As you work through the text, you will be asked to do a variety of exercises that range from defining how a word is used to interpreting, comparing, and evaluating what you read. You may have trouble with some activities if you are not used to reading critically, but the difficulty will be with the newness of the activity, not with your lack of ability. Thinking about what you read is a skill and a habit that we want you to acquire.

In the **R¹** sections of each chapter in this book, you will be presented with a quotation or cartoon whose meaning requires reading beyond words. Here's your first quotation:

> "Tell me, I'll forget. Show me, I may remember.
> But involve me, and I'll understand."—*Unknown*

In the space that follows, explain what the quotation means and how it applies to you:

_____

_____

_____

_____

R² *Reading actively*

A. Vocabulary preview

Directions: Following are some questions about words and phrases that appear in the reading selection you are about to read. Answer them as well as you can.

1. a quick survey of the chapter: here, *survey* means _____

_____

2. pause and digest what you are reading: here, *digest* means _____

_____

3. the notes seem like hieroglyphics; *hieroglyphics* means _____

_____

4. to eliminate one of the *alternatives* on a multiple-choice test means to

_____

5. *Folk wisdom* refers to what kind of wisdom? _____

_____

6. "Don't beat about the bush" means _____

_____

7. a tendency to procrastinate; *procrastinate* means _____

_____

8. to wait passively means _____

_____

B.   Thought provokers

1. Place a check mark before any of the following items that seem to fit you.

_____ A. I always examine my textbooks after I buy them to see what the preface says, to look over the table of contents, and to look for any aids, such as an index or a glossary.

_____ B. When I start to read an assigned chapter, I usually look it over to see what it is about and how long it will take me to study it.

_____ C. When I study read, I read from one heading to the next, stopping to make certain I understand what I read before going on to the next heading.

_____ D. I can usually keep my mind on reading assignments if I preview them first.

_____ E. When I study read, I make notations and mark key points in the textbook.

_____ F. After I study read, I usually write up notes that summarize the key points of the assignment.

_____ G. I have already looked over this chapter and have a pretty good idea what it is about, what I should look for, and how long it will take me to study read it.

_____ H. I have a pen ready to make notes and answer the questions in this book.

If you checked all of the items above, you're ready to read on. If you didn't mark some items, go back and read them again, doing what they suggest. Remember to follow all those steps the next time you are given a reading assignment in any book.

2. Write a short paragraph in the space that follows on what you personally feel you need to learn about reading textbooks. Your instructor may ask you to share your response.

_____

_____

_____

_____

_____

C.   Reading practice

Directions: Read the following article on how to study and then answer the questions that follow.

How to Communicate with Your Textbook

Dennis Coon

The chapters of this text are designed to help you use the SQ3R method—a valuable study-reading technique introduced over 40 years ago by Dr. Francis P. Robinson. The SQ3R approach is designed to help you (1) select what is important, (2) understand these ideas quickly, (3) remember what you have read, and (4) review effectively for tests. The symbols SQ3R stand for important steps in effective study reading:

Step One: *Survey* = Look over the title and main headings in each chapter before reading in detail. Read captions under any pictures or illustrations. Read any summary statement or review if the chapter has one. This step should be a quick survey, taking no more than two minutes. It gives you an overall picture of what is in the chapter.

Step Two: *Question* = In order to concentrate on the content of a chapter, turn each topic heading into one or more questions. This will increase your interest in what you read, and it forces you to concentrate on ideas and information. The result is an increase in your comprehension.

Step Three: *Read* = The first R in SQ3R refers to read. As you read, try to answer the questions you asked. Read only from *one topic heading to the next*, then stop. Don't go on to another heading.

Step Four: *Recite* = The second R stands for recite. After you have turned a heading into questions and read only to the next heading, you should stop and recite; that is, try to answer your questions and summarize what you've read in your own words. If you can't answer your questions or summarize main ideas, scan back over the section until you can. It can be helpful at this point to jot down important terms and ideas in a brief set of notes that includes the questions you asked. After you have completed one section in this way, turn the next topic heading into a question and then read to the following heading. Again, you should look for answers as you read, and you should recite before moving on. Repeat this process until the entire chapter is read.

Step Five: *Review* = When the chapter has been read completely, look over your notes and check your memory by reciting the answers to questions again. Or better yet, get someone to ask you questions about each topic to see if you can answer in your own words.

Question: Does this method really work?

Experiments show that using the SQ3R method improves reading comprehension and efficiency. Students who haven't learned a reading strategy tend to read straight through an entire chapter and try to remember everything. This approach is only slightly better than not reading at all! It is not wise to read a textbook as you would a novel. You must actively "dig out" information and give yourself a chance to pause and digest what you are learning. A survey prepares you to read effectively by giving you an overview. Questioning maintains your concentration on the subject, and it allows you to read in short "bites." Recitation of what you've read allows you to actively participate in and check up on your learning. Finally, review of the whole chapter ties

together what you have learned and increases your understanding.

Have you ever had the experience of passing your eyes over several pages of a textbook, only to discover that you couldn't remember anything? More than anything else the SQ3R method helps avoid this. That's why it's important that you not keep reading an assignment, but that you stop periodically, recite by taking brief notes in your own words, and review immediately after the entire chapter has been read. . . .

Effective Note-taking

Question: The SQ3R may be good for study-reading, but what about taking notes in class when it's difficult to know what's important?

Effective note-taking requires active listening. Active listeners have a plan to follow. They know that they'll "drift away" on other thoughts if they do not control their attention. Here's a listening-note-taking plan that works for many students. The important steps are summarized by the letters in the word LISAN, pronounced LISTEN (From Carman and Adams, *Study Skills: A Student's Guide for Survival.* 2nd Ed. Wiley 1984).

L = *Lead. Don't follow.* Try to anticipate what the instructor may be going to say. As in SQ3R, try to set up questions as guides. Questions can come from the instructor's study guides or the reading assignments.

I = *Ideas.* Every lecture will be based around a core of important ideas. Usually an idea is introduced and examples or explanations are given. Ask questions such as: What is the main idea of this lecture? What important ideas will help support this?

S = *Signal words.* Listen for words that tell you the direction the instructor is taking. For instance, here are some groups of signal words:

There are three reasons why	Here come ideas
Most important is	Main ideas
On the contrary	Opposite idea
As an example	Support for main idea
Therefore	Conclusion coming

A = *Actively listen.* Sit where you can hear and where you can be seen if you need to ask a question. Be on time. Look at the instructor while he or she talks. Bring questions from the last lecture or from your reading you want answered. Raise your hand at the beginning of class or approach your instructor before the lecture begins. Do anything that helps you to be active.

N = *Note-taking.* As you listen, write down only key points. Listen to everything, but be selective and don't try to write everything down. If you're too busy writing, you may miss important parts of the lecture.

There is something more you should know about note-taking. In a recent study, psychologists Robin Palkovitz and Richard Lore (1980) found that most students take reasonably good notes—and then fail to use them! Palkovitz and Lore discovered that students who missed questions on tests could later find the answers in their own notes. Apparently, most students waited until just before an exam to look at their notes. By then the notes were so old they had lost much of their meaning. If you don't want your notes to seem like hieroglyphics, it pays to review them on a regular basis. And remember,

whenever it is important to listen effectively, the letters LISAN are a guide to better comprehension.

Taking Tests

Question: If I have read effectively and listened effectively in lecture, is there anything else I can do to improve my study skills?

One area that often gives students difficulty is test-taking. Learning the material in a course is only a first step. You must then be able to show what you have learned on a test. Here are some guidelines for test-taking you might consider.

OBJECTIVE TESTS. Objective tests (multiple-choice and true-false items) are often reading tests. They check on your ability to recognize a correct statement among wrong answers or a correct statement against a false one. If you are taking an objective test, try this:

1. Read the directions carefully. Don't assume that because the question has a T or F to circle, or four or five items to select from, that you know what to do. The directions may give you good advice or clues for the test. If the directions are not clear, ask the instructor to clarify them.

2. Read each statement or question carefully. If you have several choices for each item, read them all before deciding the correct answer. You may mark one you think is correct only to find the last choice says "both a and d," yet you only marked "a" as the answer.

3. Skip items you are not certain about. Go through the test answering the ones you do know. If there is time left, go back to the ones you skipped.

4. Eliminate certain alternatives. With a four choice per item multiple-choice test, the odds are one in four that you could guess right. If you can eliminate one of the alternatives, your odds are one in three. If you can eliminate two alternatives your guessing odds are one in two, or 50–50. Those are better odds than pure guessing.

5. There is a bit of folk wisdom that says, "Don't change your answers on a multiple-choice test. Your first choice is usually right." Careful study of this idea has shown it to be false. Students who switch answers are more likely to change from wrong to right than the reverse (Davis, 1975; Edwards and Marshall, 1977). This is especially true if you feel very uncertain of your first answer. When you have strong doubts, your second answer is more likely to be correct (Johnson, 1975).

ESSAY TESTS. Essay questions are often a student's weak spot simply because of poor organization, poor or no support of main ideas, or not writing directly to the question. When you take essay exams try the following:

1. *Read the question carefully.* Make sure that you note key words, such as compare, contrast, discuss, evaluate, analyze, or describe. These words all demand a certain emphasis in your answer.

2. *Think about your answer before putting words on paper.* It's a good idea to make a brief list of the points you want to make in your answer. Just list them as they pop into your head. Then rearrange your points so that you have them organized in the order you want to write them.

3. *Don't beat around the bush or pad your answer.* Be direct. Make a point and support it. Get your list of ideas into words.

4. *Look over your essay for spelling errors, sentence errors, and*

grammatical errors. Save this for last. Your ideas are more important than misspelled words or poor sentence structure. You can work on such problems separately if they affect your grades.

SELF-TESTING AND OVERLEARNING. Many students overlook one of the most direct approaches for improving test scores: When studying, you can arrange to take several "practice tests" before a real one is given in class. In other words, studying should include self-testing by use of flash-cards, "learning checks," a study guide, or questions you have written for yourself. When you study you should say to yourself, "What could I be asked about this?" Ask as many questions as you can and be sure you can answer them. Studying without testing yourself is like practicing for a basketball game without shooting any baskets.

When you prepare for exams, there is something else to keep in mind: Many students underprepare for exams, and most overestimate how well they will do on exams before taking them (Murray, 1980). A solution to both problems is overlearning. In overlearning, study or practice continues beyond "bare mastery" of a topic. This means that you should give yourself enough time for added study and review after you think you are prepared for an exam. . . .

Procrastination

Whether you're on probation or on the dean's list, a tendency to procrastinate is almost universal among college students. Even when procrastination doesn't lead to failure or lowered grades, it can cause much suffering. Procrastinators put off work until the last possible moment, work only when under pressure, stay away from classes and avoid professors, fabricate reasons for late work, and feel ashamed of the last-minute work they do (Burka and Yuen, 1981).

Question: Why do so many students procrastinate?

College work revolves around deadlines and long-range assignments. A tendency to put off work under these circumstances is fairly natural and not limited to school. However, there are some special reasons for student procrastination. Psychologists Jane Burka and Lenora Yuen, who have worked with procrastinators, observe that many students seem to believe the following equation: self-worth = ability = performance. That is, students often equate performance in school with their personal worth. By procrastinating, students can blame poor work on their late start, rather than a lack of ability—after all, it wasn't their best effort, was it?

Perfectionism is a related problem. Students who have very high standards or expectations for themselves may find it hard to start an assignment. Such students seem to expect the impossible from themselves and end up with all-or-nothing work habits (Burka and Yuen, 1981). If you tend to procrastinate, you might find it interesting to list the excuses you've used to avoid studying, and then examine what the excuses tell about your attitudes toward schoolwork.

TIME MANAGEMENT. Burka and Yuen supervise an eight week program for procrastinators at the University of California, Berkeley. Eventually, they say, most procrastinators must face the self-worth conflict; but useful progress can be made by learning better study skills and effective time management. Since we have already discussed study skills, let's consider time management.

A formal time schedule can do much to prevent procrastination and maintain motivation in school. To prepare your schedule, make a chart showing all of the hours in each day of the week. Then fill in times that are already committed: sleep, meals, classes, work, team practices, lessons, appointments, and so forth. Next, fill in times when you will study for various classes, and label them. Finally, label the remaining hours as "open" or "free" times. The beauty of keeping such a schedule is that you know you are making an honest effort to do well in your classes. Not only will you get more done, you will also avoid the trap of thinking about playing when you are trying to work, and worrying about working while you are trying to play. The key to time management is to treat your study times as serious commitments, like class meetings or a job, and to respect your free times as well. By doing so, you will avoid the feeling that you are working all the time, when in reality you are worrying all the time, but accomplishing little.

Motivation

Question: All these study techniques are fine, but what if I'm just not interested in some of the courses I have to take?

It is important to realize that virtually every topic is interesting to someone, somewhere. Although I may not be interested in the sex life of the South American tree frog, a biologist might be fascinated. If you wait for your teachers to "make" their courses interesting, you are missing the point. Interest is a matter of your attitude. No teacher can "make" a course interesting without your help. In fact, many students find that their interest in a subject develops only after they have made an effort to master basic ideas. If you bring an inquiring mind and a positive attitude to your studies, you will find learning exciting, challenging, and interesting. If you wait passively to be entertained, you will find learning a chore. Students and teachers together make a class interesting.

A FINAL WORD. There is a distinction made in Zen between "live words" and "dead words." Live words come from personal experience; dead words are "about" a subject. This book can only be a collection of dead words without your personal involvement. It is designed to help you learn . . . , but it cannot do it for you. You will find many helpful, useful, and exciting ideas in the pages that follow. To make them yours, you must set out to learn actively as much as you can. We think it will be worth the effort. Good luck!

D. Comprehension check

Directions: Answer the following questions. If you cannot answer a question, return to the article and find the answer.

1. What is the reading selection about? _____

   _____

2. What is the main point the author is making? _____

   _____

3. Explain what each of the letters in the study formula SQ3R stand for:

   a. S = _____

   b. Q = _____

   c. R = _____

   d. R = _____

   e. R = _____

4. The author suggests that after surveying a chapter you should read it straight through, taking notes.

   a. True

   b. False, because _____

5. Explain what each letter in the note-taking formula LISAN stand for:

   a. L = _____

   b. I = _____

   c. S = _____

   d. A = _____

   e. N = _____

6. "Your first choice for an answer on a multiple-choice test is usually right."

   a. True

   b. False, because _____

7. Procrastinators usually

   a. put off work until the last moment.

   b. work only under pressure.

   c. stay away from classes and avoid professors.

   d. make up reasons for late work.

   e. all of the above.

8. Explain what is meant by a "formal time schedule." _____

   _____

9. Why, according to the author, do some students find learning to be a chore?

   _____

   _____

10. What does the author mean by saying you must "set out to learn actively"?

    _____

    _____

E.   Vocabulary check

Directions: Write the letter of the best definition for each italicized word in the blank by its number.

_____   1. *survey*   a. submissive; not active

_____   2. *hieroglyphics*   b. comprehend; understand

_____   3. *SQ3R*   c. a study-reading formula

_____   4. *passive*   d. to put off

_____   5. *digest*   e. to carefully examine or investigate

_____   6. *alternative*   f. one of the possible choices

_____   7. *overlearn*   g. setting high standards and feeling disappoint-
                                       ment when not achieved

_____   8. *procrastinate*   h. illegible symbols

_____   9. *bare mastery*   i. minimum of understanding

_____ 10. *perfectionism*   j. studying and reviewing after you think you
                                       understand

Check your answers with your instructor.

R³   *Reading skills check*

A.   Organization of textbooks

In **R²** you read an article entitled "How to Communicate with Your Textbook." One of the points it made was that students should survey or explore each chapter in their textbooks before doing any reading assignments from them. It's also a good idea to survey your textbooks to become more familiar with what they contain. A good reason for getting acquainted with your textbooks is that you will be spending several weeks reading from them. It is important to see the book as a whole: where it begins, where it is going, where it ends, and what aids are in it to help you with each reading assignment. So you need to put to use those five steps mentioned in the article for surveying your texts.

As an example, let's say you just bought the required textbook for a United States history class you are taking. The first of those five steps is to study the title. Here is the title of the book you bought:

From Columbus to Aquarius: An Interpretive History

Volume 1

Study the title carefully and answer the questions:

1. What historical periods will it cover? _____

_____

_____

2. To what does "Aquarius" refer? _____

_____

_____

3. What is an interpretive history? _____

_____

_____

Provided you know the key words in the title, you can get some idea of the book's coverage and purpose. You need to know that Columbus's voyages and discoveries took place in the late fifteenth century (1492). To understand the reference to Aquarius you need to know that besides being a constellation and an astrological sign, *Aquarius* can mean "the Age of Aquarius," which refers to contemporary times. You also need to know that *interpretive* means the history reported will be interpreted or presented the way the author thinks events and actions should be understood. In effect, the title is telling you the history covered will be roughly from the age of Columbus to the present and could contain some interpretation of history with which other scholars disagree. Notice also that you bought Volume 1, which means this book is just the first volume of a set and might not cover everything the title suggests.

The second step in surveying your textbook is to turn to the table of contents in the book and compare its coverage with what the title suggests. Try answering these questions about the table of contents on the next page.

Contents

Textbook excerpts in this chapter come from the book From Columbus to Aquarius: An Interpretive History *by George E. Frakes and W. Royce Adams. Copyright © 1988 by the authors.*

1. Where in U.S. history does this volume begin: _____

_____

_____

_____

2. Where in U.S. history does the book stop? _____

_____

_____

_____

3. What aids does the book contain? _____

_____

_____

_____

4. What can you expect to learn from this book? _____

_____

_____

_____

   Now, at least, you know that the volume you have to read begins with America's first settlers and covers American history up to 1900, the end of the reconstruction period after the Civil War. This volume, then, does not cover everything the title suggests; obviously, that comes in another volume or so. As to study aids, you know now that Chapter 2 has suggestions for reading the book (at this point you may wonder why it is not Chapter 1), it has three appendices containing important U.S. documents, and it has an index. This book has no glossary of terms, which means you may need some outside help if the book doesn't clearly present the historical terms.

   The third textbook survey step is to read the preface or introduction. Read the "Preface" to the history text which appears on the next page.

Preface

This book is written for students of varying reading ability and historical interests. We hope to present America's past in such a manner that the reader will both enjoy and understand his historical legacy. Our book starts with the Pre-Columbian period and follows chronologically to the "Age of Aquarius" .... We include information about racial minority groups, with particular emphasis upon native American Indians, Blacks, and Mexican-Americans (Chicanos).

In *From Columbus to Aquarius: An Interpretative History* we attempt to blend contemporary research in the field of reading skills with acceptable historical scholarship. This book was prepared with concern for the needs of all students, including those who struggle through reading assignments. To a large extent we avoid technical language, but when technical terms are used, we explain them. For ease of reading, we provide easy-to-read type, marginal aids, introductory preparational reading materials at the start of chapters, such as statements of purpose and guide questions based on the SQ3R (Survey, Question, Read, Review, Recite) study formula, plus space in the margins for note taking. Brief chapter chronologies are provided for the student in order to present a sense of time and cause-and-effect relationships. These chronologies are not to be memorized but are intended to serve as overviews that highlight important events. Important historical documents, such as the Declaration of Independence and the Constitution, are included in a double-text manner in the appendix so that archaic prose can better be understood.

The second chapter is devoted to reading and study techniques. Whether or not this chapter needs to be read by the student can be determined by taking the test on the content of Chapter One. Chapters are short so that a student can complete the reading of a chapter without becoming exhausted.

We are hesitant to suggest how an instructor could best use this book. As teachers, we know there is no one single approach, no one right way to teach anyone or anything. We know from correspondence and discussions with colleagues that most teachers use the chronological approach to history. Some teachers prefer a topical approach. We believe that, by the use of chapter subheads, this book can be used both ways.

We would like to thank a number of persons whose help was vital in

. . . [no need to read on; it's just a bunch of names and not important to you at this point.]

Now that you know more about the book, answer these questions to prove it to yourself:

1.   What is the purpose of the book? _____

_____

_____

_____

2.   What are some features that make the book different from other history textbooks? _____

_____

_____

_____

3.   How is the book organized? _____

_____

_____

_____

If you had trouble with these answers, go back and look at the preface again. The answer to the first question is in the first paragraph: Its purpose is to deal chronologically with American history from the Pre-Columbian (before Columbus) period to the present in an interesting manner for students of various academic backgrounds. The second question is answered in the second paragraph: a blend of reading skills research with historical research, an avoidance of technical terms when possible, easy-to-read type, study guide questions, chapter chronologies, and so on. The third question is answered in both Paragraphs 2 and 3: The order is chronological, chapters are fairly short, historical documents are in an appendix, and the second chapter deals with reading and study skills. All this information will be useful to you when you begin study reading assignments from the text itself.

The fourth step in surveying a textbook is to look for an index and glossary. Checking the table of contents, you see there is an index. The advantage of having an index is this: Suppose you are studying for a midterm. You have read about six or seven chapters by now. Your instructor has alerted you to the fact that an essay question on the causes of the Revolutionary War might appear on the test. Where would you find information to review? Use the index below to find the answer.

Answer: _____

Did you notice that several causes are listed under American Revolutionary War? Basically, pages 86–87 will discuss the economic causes, political

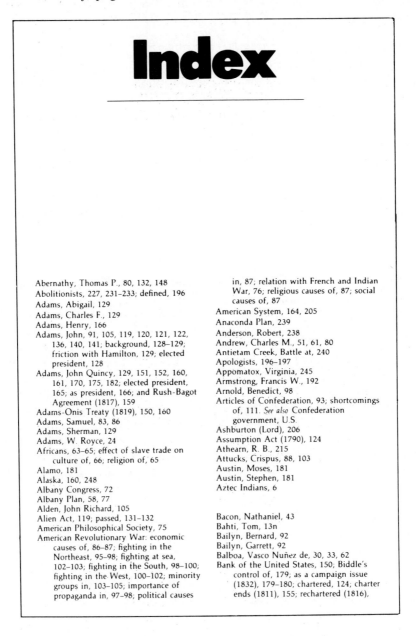

Index

causes, religious causes, and social causes. In other words, to write a good essay exam answer, you should study pages 86–87 and be able to discuss each of those four causes. The index can lead you right to the place to study.

In addition, suppose that you were reading about the abolitionists during a reading assignment and you became interested enough to want more information. By using the index, where in the book could you find more information on abolitionists?

Answer: _____

More information appears on pages 227, 132–233, and 196, where the term is defined. The definition on page 196 would be especially helpful when reviewing for a test. An index, used wisely, is a time saver both for finding new information and reviewing.

Checking the table of contents again, you see there is no glossary listed for this book. But if you remember what the preface said about using as few technical terms as possible, you probably won't need one. Besides, you can use the index to look up the pages where names and terms are discussed and defined within the text itself.

The fifth and last step in surveying is to flip through the book to get an idea of the way each chapter is structured. A look at a typical page shows you this:

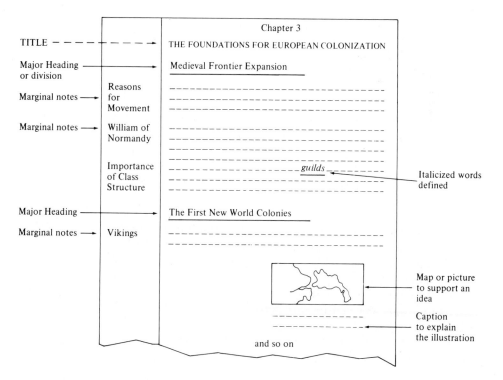

Most textbooks attempt to give you an organizational pattern by using major headings to call your attention to key points. Subheadings or marginal notes provide you with an idea of the supporting points. Italicized words are usually used when a new word is first used or is defined in the glossary. A new major heading calls your attention to the fact that the author is now going to switch to a new point.

The five-step survey just presented may seem time-consuming, but it is not really so. A 15- or 20-minute session getting familiar with your textbook pays off in time saved later. The result will be easier and better learning.

Organization of chapters

Obviously, not all textbook chapters are alike. That is the reason for surveying them *before* beginning a reading assignment. The few minutes it takes—and that is all it should take—help you prepare yourself for reading by turning your attention from other things and focusing it upon the content of the chapter.

Here in brief are the five steps to surveying a chapter. You will be asked to use them later in this chapter:

1. Read and think about the title of the chapter.
2. Read any summaries at the beginning or end of the chapter.
3. Read any questions at the end of the chapter to use as reading guides.
4. Skim over the chapter to see if you can read it in one study session or whether you should break the chapter into two or more reading sessions.
5. Read all the headings, subheadings, marginal aids, and captions under pictures or illustrations.

Doing these steps for any textbook will reveal the chapter's organization, help you decide how best to study it, and help you concentrate better as you read so that your mind won't wander.

B.   Vocabulary tip: dictionary review

Many people use a dictionary only for spelling information or definitions of words. A good dictionary, however, contains much more. Take some time to look at the front and back matter in a dictionary. Most dictionaries include good explanatory notes on how the dictionary is organized, lists of abbreviations used, brief articles on the history of language, dialects, and language usage. The list of abbreviations and their meanings is particularly helpful when you look up a word.

While there is some difference in the way dictionaries list words, most follow a pattern similar to this:

1. The main entry is usually in bold type; if more than one spelling is given, the first one listed is considered the most acceptable.
2. The pronunciation, including accent marks, is usually in parentheses; a brief pronunciation key generally appears at the bottom of the page, but sometimes you need to refer to the larger guide that appears at the beginning of the dictionary.
3. The part of speech is abbreviated (n. for noun, v. for verb, adv. for adverb, and so on) since a single word can often be used as different parts of speech, depending on its contextual usage.
4. The etymology, or history of the word, is usually in brackets, showing the origin of the word and its change into the English language.
5. The various definitions are included, frequently synonyms, sometimes antonyms, sometimes pictures or illustrations.

Once you understand how the dictionary is organized, it shouldn't take more than 20 or 30 seconds to look up a word. At the top of each page appear guide words. The first word is the first entry word on the page and the second word is the last entry word on the page. For instance, if the top of the page has *inflict/inhale*, you know that only words that fall alphabetically between *inflict* and *inhale* will be listed on that page. If you were looking up the word *ingest* then you would scan that page for the word. If you were looking up *inherit*, then you would skip that page and read the guide words at the top of the next page.

When you find the entry word you want, read all the definitions. See which one best fits the meaning of the word in context. Then say the word aloud. Hear how it sounds. If you need to do so, consult the pronunciation key to figure out what the symbols mean.

Learn how to change the word to different parts of speech. For instance, *value* can be a noun (My ring's value has increased) or a verb (I value my ring). You can also change the word to *valued, valuing, valuable*, and so on. Learn as much as you can about the word once you have bothered to look it up.

Here is a dictionary entry. Use it to answer the questions that follow.

EXERCISE 1

guide (gīd) *n.* **1.** One who shows the way by leading or directing, esp. a person employed to guide a tour, group, etc. **2.** Any sign or mark that serves to direct. **3.** An example or model to be followed. **4.** A book or manual that serves to instruct or direct. **5.** Any device that acts as an indicator or regulates the motion of something.—*v.* guided, guiding **1.** To show the way to; conduct; lead; direct. **2.** To direct the course of; steer. **3.** To manage the affairs of; govern. [< OF *guider*, to show the way.] —**guid′er** *n.*

1. The ribbons tied to the tree branches *guided* us along the ski trail.

A.   What part of speech is *guided?* _____

B.   What number definition best fits the way the word is used in the
     sentence? _____

C.   Replace the word *guided* in the sentence above with a word from
     the definition. _____

2. History will show that the President's actions were responsible for *guiding* us into war.

   A.   What part of speech is *guiding?* _____

   B.   What number definition best fits the word as used in the sentence?

        _____

   C.   Replace the word *guiding* in the sentence above with a word or
        phrase from the definition without changing the meaning. _____

        _____

        _____

3. My compass was my only *guide.*

   A.   What part of speech is *guide* here? _____

   B.   What number definition best fits the word *guide* as used here? _____

   C.   What is the origin of the word *guide?* _____

        _____

4. Write a sentence using the Number 4 definition under *n.* (noun).

   _____

EXERCISE 2

   As a way of becoming familiar with dictionary use, answer these questions, using any available dictionary.

1. What is the difference between *neurotic* and *psychotic?*

   _____

   _____

2. What is the difference between *sensual* and *sensuous?*

   _____

   _____

3. How many definitions are there for the word *run?* _____

4. From what language does *adroit* originate? _____

5. What is a synonym for *garish?* _____

6. In the TV series and movie *Star Trek*, the spaceship was called the U.S.S. *Enterprise*. Which definition for the word *enterprise* best fits the reason

   for giving the "starship" that name: _____

7. Look up the italicized words in the following sentences. Replace the words with a one-word definition or short phrase given in the dictionary.

   a. Jerry was *baffled* by the mysterious phone call.

      _____

   b. The mother's *callousness* toward her child's plea was shocking.

      _____

   c. Sally has had to *surmount* many difficulties.

      _____

   d. The lecture was *illuminating* to me since I knew nothing about orchids.

      _____

   e. The leaves of the cabbage were folded *compactly*.

      _____

f. His *facetiousness* was lost on the instructor, who was attempting to be serious.

_____

8. What is the title of your dictionary? _____

    When was it published: _____

Discuss your answers in class.

C. Overlearning new words

Words you know now and use often are words you have *overlearned*. In other words, you are so used to them they come up automatically when you want to speak or write. You need to develop a larger vocabulary by over-learning more words. The best way to do that is to make flash cards for words you want to overlearn and practice them daily. Here is an example of a flash card you might make on a 3 × 5 card for the word *discrepancy:*

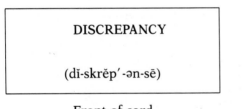

DISCREPANCY (dĭ-skrĕp′-ən-sē)

Front of card

Print only the word and the phonetic spelling on the front.

def.	disagreement between facts or opinions
syn.	difference
sent.	There is a discrepancy between their stories.

Back of card

On the back, you should have at least the definition; when possible a synonym; and a sentence using the word in context. You may want to use a thesaurus to find familiar synonyms and antonyms to help you remember the word.

As you go through the chapters in this book or any others, make cards for words you want to overlearn. Do not try to learn too many at once—maybe 10 words a week. Each week, add your new cards to your stack of old cards. Every day, go through your stack of cards and put the ones you know in one group and the ones you do not know in another group. Study the group you do not know until you think you have them. Then mix up your cards and go through the whole stack. If you do this activity daily, soon you will have overlearned many new words you can use and recognize in reading.

Take time now to go back through this chapter and select a few words to overlearn. Make flash cards for those words and show them to your instructor.

R⁴   *Reading applications*

Application 1.   Surveying a chapter

Directions: A chapter from the history textbook you surveyed in R³, *From Columbus to Aquarius,* is reprinted on pages 27–41. Apply the steps you learned about surveying a chapter and answer the following questions:

1. The title of the chapter is "The Destruction of the Western Indians."

   What specific tribes will you read about? _____

   _____

2. Is there a chapter summary? _____

3. What study aids are supplied as a guide for you to use as you read? _____

   _____

   _____

4. What types of visual aids are provided? _____

   _____

5. What do you learn about this chapter from reading the headings, subheadings, and marginal comments?

   _____

   _____

   _____

6. Is there a bibliography of books on this subject provided in case you wanted to read more on the subject?

   _____

   _____

   _____

7. Could you read this chapter in one study session, or would you divide it up?

   _____

   _____

   _____

   Even though you haven't read the chapter yet, you know more about what you will be reading. Your attention is now focused on the chapter's contents. If you looked over the chronological events listed at the beginning, you know that the historical time line you will be reading about ranges from the 1860s to 1890s. While there is no chapter summary, you are provided with a "Your purpose" section and a "Concentrate" section that offer a type of summary as well as some questions for you to answer as you read. Paying attention to the headings and subheadings provides you with such names as Cheyenne and Arapaho, Red Cloud and the Oglala Sioux, Crazy Horse, Sitting Bull, Chief Joseph and the Nez Percé, to name a few. You also notice there are maps and pictures to aid the presentation of information of this period of history. A bibliography of books on the subject is provided in case you want to read more or are assigned a report on some aspect of this historical period.

   Only you know if you can read a chapter of this length in one sitting or need to divide it up. If you did a good survey of the chapter, your mind is now ready to read more closely, using all the aids you know are there to help you get the most from your study reading.

   Now you are ready to study read.

Application 2.   Study reading the chapter

Directions: Now study read the chapter that you just surveyed, "The Destruction of the Western Indians," on pages 27–41. Follow the steps recommended in the SQ3R formula.

Chapter 5

The Destruction of the Western Indians

Chronology

Here are some events which occurred during the time span discussed in this chapter.

1864	Sand Creek Massacre
1866	Army Trespasses on Sioux Territory and Builds Fort Phil Kearny;
	Secretary of War W. W. Belknap Forced to Resign over Indian Trading Post Scandals
1874	Colonel Custer Ignores Treaty and Invades the Black Hills
1876	Battle of Little Big Horn (Greasy Grass);
	Apache War (1871–1886);
	Second Sioux War (1875–1876)
1877	Nez Percé War (Chief Joseph);
	Crazy Horse Bayoneted in Back at Fort Robinson
1878	The Cheyenne's Long March from Reservation Land to Their Home
1879	Cheyenne Forced to Return to Reservation
1881	Indian Right's Association Formed;
	Protests Against Indian Policy
1887	Dawes Act Gives Some Indian Rights;
	Sitting Bull Ends His Tour with Buffalo Bill's Wild West Show
1890	Ghost Dance War, Battle of Wounded Knee;
	Death of Sitting Bull
1891	Lands of the Sauk, Fox, and Potta Watomie in Oklahoma Are Opened to White Settlement

56

57   THE DESTRUCTION OF THE WESTERN INDIANS

1892   Cheyenne-Arapaho Reservation of 3 Million Acres Is Opened
1893   Cherokee Lands Are Opened to White Settlement
1894   Buffalo Practically Extinct from Mass Slaughter

Your purpose in reading this chapter is to become aware of the following points in more detail:

1. The same Congress that was working for equality and integration of the Negro in the South after the Civil War did its best to segregate the Indian from the white man's culture.
2. As settlers continued to move westward, the government continued to break treaty after treaty with the Indians, exhibiting a type of white supremacy attitude.
3. Examples of Indian policy during the westward expansion are found in the treatment of the Plains Indians, in particular, the Cheyenne, the Sioux, and the Nez Percé.
4. The Dawes Severalty Act of 1887, which was intended as an Indian civilization measure, really helped to cause the destruction of the Plains Indians' way of life at that time.

Concentrate on the following questions as you read:

1. Why did the U.S. government make and then break so many treaties with the Indians?
2. What were the reasons behind the Sand Creek Massacre? the Fetterman Massacre?
3. Why was the Dawes Severalty Act not effective?
4. How did the destruction of the buffalo cause the destruction of the Plains Indians?
5. Why is Crazy Horse a hero to the Sioux Indians?

Suggestion: As you read this chapter, consider what America might be like today if the treaties with the Indians had not been broken. What would you have done differently if you had been involved in Indian affairs during the westward movement?

The Treatment of the Plains Indians

Movies and television have made the "Wild West" a place and a period where the good guys get the bad guys, thus paving the way for women and children to settle peacefully amid the building of ranches, farms, businesses, schools, and churches. But this period, like most periods, was also one of prejudice, greed, recklessness, ecological waste, and violence of all kinds. Many *white eyes* (an Indian term for white man) seemed to hold a superior attitude, similar in some ways to that of Adolph Hitler's belief in a master race.

58   THE EVOLUTION OF MODERN AMERICA

Myths of Western History

During this era of white supremacy, there were many tall tales developed about romantic, brave, and strong fur traders, mountain men, gunslingers, cavalrymen, gold miners, and cowboys. Equally misleading tales were also invented about the American Indian—tales which helped create and perpetuate attitudes and feelings among whites that, for them, justified the destruction of the Plains Indians' cultures and civilizations. More often than not, the Indian was thought of as a bloodthirsty savage, a heathen who ran around half-naked, wearing paint, scalping people, and burning wagon trains. The proud historical account of the development of the West (and there certainly are things to be proud of) sometimes hides not only the destruction of the Indian cultures but also the destruction of much of the American environment itself.

Continuing Indian Problems

The attitude and treatment of the Indians, some of whom had been moved to the Plains with the promise they would never be asked to move again, stems from the reasons people were moving West. Many white settlers of the West were willing to work long and hard hours to change the plains, but most did so with the hope of quickly getting rich. To some pioneers, anything needed was taken, anything in the way was destroyed. Water, trees, minerals were used up with no thought for the future. In the same way, land was taken from the Indian with no real concern for his rights.

Prior to the Civil War, the Indians had made several treaties with government officials, but soon learned that "white man spoke with forked tongue". It seemed to the Indian that as soon as he moved to a new *eternally guaranteed* territory or made peace with the whites, he would be asked to move again. More and more frequently, Indians found themselves being cheated or tricked by corrupt officials of the Indian Bureau. Trappers, hunters, gold prospectors, and army deserters continually trespassed on Indian land. When prospects of wealth were found on Indian territory, pressures were put on Congress and government officials to open it up for exploitation. The rest of this chapter shows only four of many examples of the Indian policies during the westward movement: (1) the treatment of the Cheyenne and Arapaho, (2) Red Cloud and the Oglala Sioux, (3) Crazy Horse, the Indian hero, and (4) Chief Joseph of the Nez Percé.

THE CHEYENNE AND ARAPAHO

About the time of the Civil War outbreak in the Southeast, the Arapaho and Cheyenne Indians were forced to move off land in the Colorado territory that had been given to them *forever* only ten years before (see Figure 5-1). During that ten-year period, the Cheyenne and the Arapaho kept the peace, even though miners were building the city of Denver on their land; stage coaches and pony express riders made roads through their lands; a chain of forts was built; and telegraph wires were strung. When the Cheyenne and the Arapaho were asked to give up all claim to the buffalo-filled land they needed for existance, the idea was rejected by most of the chiefs and braves. The idea of ownership of land was not the same to the white man as it was

59   THE DESTRUCTION OF THE WESTERN INDIANS

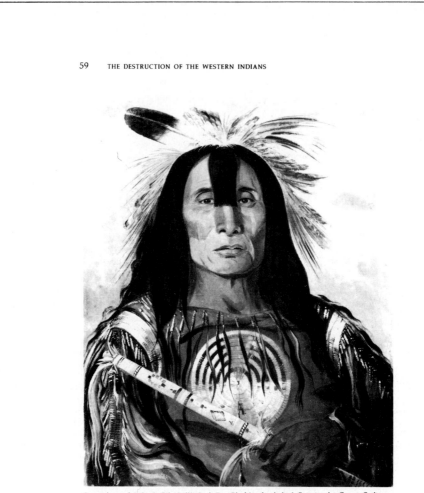

Stu-mick-o-sucks, the Buffalo Bull's Back Fat, Blackfoot head chief. Painting by George Catlin.

to the Indian. The Indian was willing to share and use the land so as not to disturb the balance of nature. When the white man built on land where buffalo roamed, killing buffalo, stripping the land with no thought of replenishing what he used, the Indian went on the warpath.

Indian Need for Buffalo   The buffalo was a necessary part of the Plains Indian's life. It provided him meat, and skin for moccasins, mittens, shirts, leggings, and dresses. The sinew was used for thread and bow strings. Bones were used for tools, horns for cups, and the stomach was used as a canteen. Even the tongue was

60   THE EVOLUTION OF MODERN AMERICA

Figure 5-1 *Distribution of western Indian tribes and major battles: 1860–1890*

used—as a hairbrush. If the buffalo was to survive it needed that land to roam and to graze.

In the 1860s, when the western movement to the Plains began, it is estimated that there were about fifteen million head of buffalo. Within twenty years, the buffalo became almost extinct. The primary reason for their slaughter was to feed the railroad workers. During this time, it became a popular fad to hunt buffalo because of the demand in the East for mounted buffalo heads and buffalo rugs to decorate walls and floors. In the 1860s, a buffalo hide sold for a dollar. They were so scarce by 1894 that robes were being sold for as much as $175 each. With this wanton slaughter, the Indians who previously roamed the Plains and whose way of life revolved around the buffalo, found themselves starving.

Chief Black Kettle   In the 1860s, one of the Cheyenne chiefs, Black Kettle, was convinced, by the Commissioner of Indian Affairs, Colonel A. B. Greenwood, that a new treaty would allow Black Kettle's people to retain their land rights and freedom to hunt buffalo. Black Kettle accepted the terms of the treaty in good faith and Colonel Greenwood gave him a United States flag, telling Black Kettle that, "as long as the flag flew above him no soldiers would ever fire

61   THE DESTRUCTION OF THE WESTERN INDIANS

**The Plot to Kill
the Cheyenne**

upon him." A little over a year later, four prominent white citizens, including the governor of the Colorado territory, John Evans; an Indian agent named Samuel Colley; and Colonel John Chivington, an ex-Methodist minister and leader of Colorado volunteers, plotted to drive the Indians from Colorado and "to kill Cheyenne whenever and wherever found."

**Sand Creek
Massacre**

On November 28, 1864, Colonel Chivington made final plans for a massacre of Black Kettle's people, who were camped at Sand Creek, Colorado, (see Figure 5-1) and who thought they were under the protection of the existing treaty. When some of the officers said that they were unwilling to join in the Colonel's plans, he was quoted as angrily stating, "Damn any man who sympathizes with Indians! I have come here to kill Indians, and believe it is right and honorable to use any means under God's heaven to kill Indians."

Slaughter

About sunrise the next morning, Chivington's force of over seven hundred men lined up on two sides of the Indian camp and began their surprise attack. Robert Bent, an unwilling member of Colonel Chivington's party later said,

I saw the American flag waving and heard Black Kettle tell the Indians to stand around the flag, and there they huddled—men, women and children. . . . I also saw a white flag raised. These flags were in so conspicuous a position that they must have been seen. . . .

The attack was overly cruel. Bent also reported:

There were some thirty or forty squaws collected in a hole for protection; they sent out a little girl about six years old with a white flag on a stick; she had not proceeded but a few steps when she was shot and killed. All the squaws in that hole soon afterwards were killed. . . . Everyone I saw dead was scalped. I saw one squaw cut open with an unborn child. . . . I saw the body of White Antelope with the privates cut off, and I heard a soldier say he was going to make a tobacco pouch out of them.

When it was over, 105 Indian women and children and 28 men were dead. Most of the Cheyenne braves were away hunting buffalo.

Black Kettle managed to escape, but afterwards he was rejected by most of the surviving Cheyennes as their leading chief. The new leader, Leg-in-the-Water, told an emissary who had been sent to make another try for peace: "The white man has taken our country, killed all of our game; was not satisfied with that, but killed our wives and children. Now no peace." The followers of Leg-in-the-Water joined with the Arapaho and the Sioux and the combined forces continued to revenge the dead at Sand Creek.

Black Kettle and his few followers headed South below the Arkansas River. In the summer of 1865, government officials wanted to make another treaty. This time they needed Black Kettle's signature because he had signed previous treaties which the government now wanted to dissolve. Since Denver was located on Cheyenne and Arapaho land, the land titles drawn up by the whites were in doubt. So on October 14, 1865, Black Kettle and other

62   THE EVOLUTION OF MODERN AMERICA

Result of the Sand Creek Massacre

head men of the southern Cheyennes signed the new *peace treaty*. The massacre at Sand Creek and Black Kettle's questionable signature thus gave the white man the Colorado territory. Most of Black Kettle's people did not honor him as chief any more and to them the treaty was not valid.

The End of the Old Cheyenne Nation

After the loss of Colorado and neighboring areas, the northern Cheyennes and the southern Cheyennes were confined to a small area in the Oklahoma territory. Not used to the climate or the poor food, many of the Indians died of disease and hunger. In the summer of 1878, Chiefs Dull Knife and Little Wolf illegally led what was left of their people—300 northern Cheyenne men, women, and children—on a long march home to Montana. In one of the most dramatic marches in history, this small band of people fought off 13,000 army troops and marched more than a thousand miles until they reached their northern homeland. But Washington officials ordered them to return, under an armed escort, to the Oklahoma territory. Refusing to give in, the Cheyenne were locked up and the army tried to starve them into obeying. On January 9, 1879, an escape attempt was made, 64 Indians were killed, and about 110 escaped, of which 78 were later recaptured. This example shows how many of the Cheyenne, or as they were often called by those who knew them, *the beautiful people,* were destroyed in the white man's movement west.

RED CLOUD AND THE OGLALA SIOUX

When the westward movement of whites began to increase, after the Civil War, the Plains Indian tribes were in their way. Construction on the Union Pacific Railroad cut directly across Indian reservations. Miners often ignored reservation boundaries. Settlers, ranchers, and miners crossed Indian territory following a wagon route that John Bozeman had blazed from the Platte River to the Montana Mines (see Figure 5-2). The government offered gifts and supplies to the Indians for permission to use the Indian land, and some of the tribes agreed, but Red Cloud, Chief of the Oglala Sioux, refused. He did so because the chief did not trust the white man after the Sand Creek massacre, and because the land was some of the best Indian hunting grounds.

The Bozeman Trail

The government went ahead with the building of Forts Phil Kearny, in Wyoming, and Fort Smith, in Montana, even though the Sioux had signed no treaty. Red Cloud and his followers knew they could not fight against the firepower of the soldiers' rifles and big guns when they themselves were armed only with a few guns and bows and arrows. But Red Cloud, with the aid of the Cheyenne and the Arapaho, managed to keep the soldiers confused for two years by his fighting tactics.

Army Trespassers

The Indians made life difficult for the whites by constantly hitting and running. They made travel on the Bozeman trail difficult and dangerous. They invented schemes that would draw the soldiers out of the fort and separate them into small groups—then the Indians attacked them.

An example of the sort of tactics Red Cloud used occurred in December, 1866. Ten young Indians were selected to pretend they were attacking a small band of soldiers out cutting wood for Fort Phil Kearny. When the sound of

63   THE DESTRUCTION OF THE WESTERN INDIANS

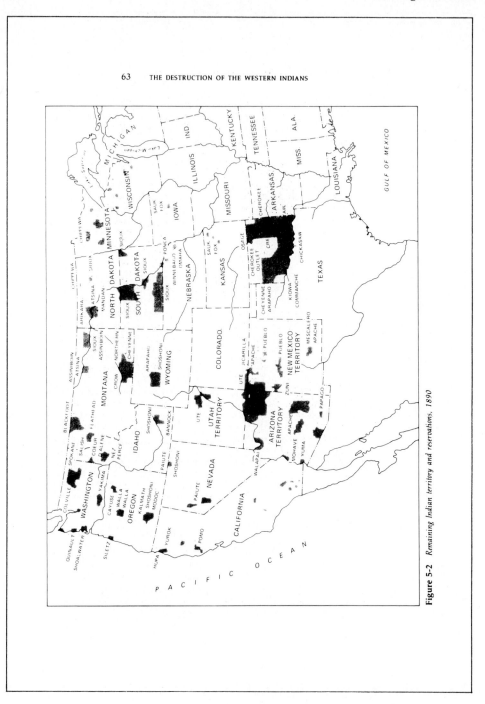

Figure 5-2 *Remaining Indian territory and reservations, 1890*

gunfire was heard, a company of soldiers was sent from the fort to aid the woodcutters. As soon as the soldiers were out of sight, another group of Indians under the command of Crazy Horse, a young Sioux tribal chief, acted as though they were going to attack the fort. As the soldiers fired from the fort, the Indians scattered about acting as though they were frightened but actually they were cutting off the trail of the company of cavalry that had left the fort. The Indian decoys at the wood wagons pretended to be chased

The Fetterman Massacre

by the cavalry led by Captain William J. Fetterman, but the soldiers were led toward Peno Creek where two thousand Sioux, Cheyenne, and Arapaho were waiting on both sides. The horse soldiers were boxed in and all eighty-one men were killed. This fight was called the Fetterman Massacre.

This type of fighting made the Bozeman road almost useless and the government finally gave in to the Indians. In November, 1868, Red Cloud signed a peace treaty at Fort Laramie, Wyoming, and the forts were temporarily abandoned. In this treaty with Red Cloud, the Sioux were given the Black Hills of South Dakota as part of their reservation. Called *Paha Sapa,* the

Indian Wars Continue

area was considered sacred by the Indians. However, in 1874, a column of troops under Colonel George Armstrong Custer ignored the treaty and invaded the Black Hills. It is believed he was ordered to find gold in the area and spread the word about it until a gold rush developed. Soon hundreds of white civilians were pouring into the Indian's sacred land. When the Indians threatened war, the government offered to pay for the land but the Sioux refused to sell. The government then ordered the Sioux onto reservations and voided the tribe's title to the Black Hills. In March, 1876, General George Crook was sent to round up the Indians, but the battles that were fought gave victory to neither side. The Indians got away and the soldiers gave up because of the cold weather.

CRAZY HORSE, THE INDIAN'S HERO

When the treaty signed in 1868 was broken by the whites, Red Cloud tried to keep peace among the tribes of his nation and some of the Sioux came to feel that Red Cloud had gone the way of the whites. Some Sioux called Red Cloud and his followers Hang-Around-the-Fort people. Among those Sioux who felt this way was a young Indian who had shown much bravery at the Fetterman Massacre, Crazy Horse.

Crazy Horse's Youth

As a boy, Crazy Horse was called Curly because of his curly brown hair. He was slender and more fair skinned than most Indians. As was the custom among the Sioux, each boy must have an older man teach and train him in hunting, riding, fighting, and spiritual matters. Curly's teacher was a wise man and a good warrior named Hump. The young brave learned from the older man how to shoot the bow, throw the lance, and shoot a gun. He became an excellent horseman, but more important, Hump taught Curly respect for all people as well as his own people.

How He Got His Name

When he was a young man, Curly had a vision, which is the reason his name came to be changed to Crazy Horse. Black Elk, a Sioux who knew Crazy Horse, says in his autobiography:

65   THE DESTRUCTION OF THE WESTERN INDIANS

... he [Crazy Horse] became a chief because of the power he got in a vision when he was a boy.... Crazy Horse dreamed and went into the world where there is nothing but the spirits of all things.... He was on his horse in that world, and the horse and himself on it and the trees and the grass and the stones and everything were hard, made of spirit, and nothing was hard, and everything seemed to float. His horse was standing there, and yet it danced around like a horse made only of shadow, and that is how he got his name, which does not mean that his horse was crazy or wild, but that in his vision it danced around in that queer way.

A War Leader

Crazy Horse developed followers because of his vision and his belief that he could not be killed in battle. When he went into a fight, he always put himself in danger but was never wounded in battle. Indeed, once he was wounded in an accident and once again by one of his own men in a quarrel over a woman. Crazy Horse strongly believed that his vision meant he was destined to help his people.

Reasons for Leadership

When Red Cloud seemed to give in to the wishes of the whites, many Sioux turned to Crazy Horse as their leader, though he was not officially a chief. His followers loved him because he was concerned with his people and not with gaining wealth or popularity. He refused to accept many gifts or to own many horses, a sign of wealth. He often went without food when it was scarce. It is reported that he was a person who often liked to be alone, but was ready with a joke or a good story when his people needed their morale lifted.

Crazy Horse's Successes

Crazy Horse was an excellent warrior. He planned his attacks well and often defeated bands of soldiers who had more firepower than his Indians had. As the Indian nations began to fall under the soldiers' power, Crazy Horse became a symbol of pride and power and hope to those who followed him. At the age of 35, when forced to return to a reservation, he was betrayed by some jealous friends of Red Cloud and was "accidentally" bayoneted in the back by a nervous soldier on guard duty at Fort Robinson in 1877.

Memorialized

Even today, Crazy Horse stands as a symbol of pride and hope for many Indians of all tribes. At the time of this writing, a sculptor named Korczak Ziolkowski is carving and blasting with dynamite a 500-foot high and 600-foot long monument to Crazy Horse on Thunderhead Mountain in South Dakota. The monument will show Crazy Horse riding a horse as he saw in his vision and will be larger than all four heads of the presidents carved on nearby Mount Rushmore.

The Indians Combine Forces

"Don't Take Any Prisoners"

The northern Cheyenne and the Sioux joined forces on the Little Bighorn River. The orders of the chiefs were, "Don't take any prisoners." On June 25, 1876, in the famous Battle of Little Bighorn, the combined tribes (under the command of Crazy Horse, Sitting Bull, and other tribal leaders) killed General George A. Custer and 264 of his men. In spite of this victory, by the next fall, many of the Sioux were forced to surrender or starve because the

66   .THE EVOLUTION OF MODERN AMERICA

Indian forces disbanded rather than remaining united. Sitting Bull and a few of his tribe escaped to Canada under pursuit of soldiers seeking vengeance for the Little Bighorn battle.

Sitting Bull

Because they were not British subjects, Sitting Bull and his pursued followers were denied land in Canada. In addition, his people were starving and freezing during the cold winters. Promised a pardon by the U.S. government, Sitting Bull and 186 of his remaining tribe returned on July 19, 1881, only to be taken prisoner and held at Fort Randall. But he found that he was famous. Newspaper men came to interview the "Killer of Custer." Many chiefs and warriors came to visit and ask his advice about selling their land or signing treaties. Always, Sitting Bull advised them not to sell.

In 1883, Sitting Bull was released from prison and sent to Standing Rock in the Dakota territory. He became a thorn in the side of the government men who wanted to turn the Indians into *civilized* men. The Indian Bureau appointed a man named James McLaughlin to head the agency at Standing Rock with orders to destroy the culture of the Sioux and to destroy Sitting Bull's influence over his people, but McLaughlin had little effect on Sitting Bull's popularity. In fact, his popularity grew so much that he was invited to attend the ceremony for the driving of the last spike in the Northern Pacific Railroad. The Secretary of the Interior even authorized a lecture tour of fifteen American cities for Sitting Bull. He was so well liked that William Cody signed him up for his famous Buffalo Bill's Wild West Show.

The Dawes Act

In 1887, Sitting Bull was invited to go to Europe on tour with Buffalo Bill, but decided he was needed at home because more land grabbers were at work. The government planned to cut the Sioux reservation into six smaller reservations and leave nine million acres open for white settlers. The Dawes Severalty Act, passed by Congress that year, was intended to put an end to tribal life and convert the Indian to the white man's way of life. Each head of an Indian family was given 160 acres of land which could not be sold or disposed of for twenty-five years. If an Indian accepted the land and gave up tribal life, he was granted citizenship. The Dawes Act assumed falsely that the Indian could easily adapt to white ways. The results, of course, were disastrous to the Indian's social structure. By 1934, the white man had taken 86 million acres of the 138 million acres given to the Indians under the Dawes Act.

Ghost Dance and Attempts to End Indian Culture

One of the ways the white man tried to *civilize* the Indian was by attempting to put an end to the Ghost Dance, a ceremonial of a belief that was very similar to the Christian concept of the Messiah. The white do-gooders failed to recognize the Ghost Dance as essentially Christian in concept and convinced the Indian agents that the dancing would be harmful to the Indian. In an attempt to arrest Sitting Bull and put an end to the ceremonial dancing, Sitting Bull was accidentally shot and killed by a friend trying to defend him. Shortly after the death of Sitting Bull, in December of 1890, a senseless slaughter of three hundred Indian men, women, and children occurred at Wounded Knee Creek, South Dakota. Many historians mark this event as the end of the Plains Indian, but as recently as 1973, modern

67   THE DESTRUCTION OF THE WESTERN INDIANS

Pine Ridge Reservation at Wounded Knee, South Dakota, 1883

Sioux Indians staged an armed confrontation with federal officers at Wounded Knee as a symbolic protest against what they feel are injustices to contemporary Sioux (see page 287 for more detailed coverage).

Wounded Knee campaign, burial of the dead

Chief Joseph and the Nez Percé

The Last Great Indian War Leader

The Nez Percé lived in the Oregon and Idaho territory. The name means pierced nose, so named by French trappers because some of the Indians wore shells in their noses. When the Lewis and Clark expedition of 1805 went through the Nez Percé land, the Indians supplied the explorers with food and watched the expedition's horses while the men traveled by canoe to the Pacific shore. For seventy years after that, the Nez Percé proudly claimed that they had never killed a white man. Though some records dispute this claim, the Nez Percé, on the whole, were peaceful toward whites until the 1870s, when these Indians were provoked into fighting for survival.

Once again, the white man's desire for land and gold was to destroy still another Indian civilization. In 1863, a treaty that the Nez Percé signed, but did not understand, took away three-fourths of the Indians' land. The treaty left them with only a small reservation in Idaho. Some of the Indians refused to leave their old homes and, in 1873, petitioned President Grant for permission to stay. Grant gave his permission, but two years later, changed his mind. The reason appears to be that too many white settlers were putting pressure on the government for the land. In 1875, Grant changed the order and, in 1877, sent the army to move the Indians to their reservation.

President Grant Breaks His Promise

Chief Joseph

Under the leadership of Chief Joseph, the Nez Percé peacefully started toward the reservation territory, but some angry warriors slipped away one night and killed eleven white men. The army, outnumbering the Indians two to one, learned of the eleven murders and attacked the Nez Percé. Under the skillful leadership of Chief Joseph, his men managed to kill one-third of the army troops and escape into the mountains. Combining his tribe with that of Chief Looking Glass, Chief Joseph led the Nez Percé over 1,300 miles in an attempt to escape to Canada or at least get away from the army troops pursuing them.

Battles were constant during the long march. For months, Chief Joseph, Chief Looking Glass, and fewer than three hundred warriors and four hundred women and children kept the entire Northwest Army on the move. However, General Miles managed to surround the Nez Percé and called for a truce, offering to return them to the reservation with no more bloodshed if Chief Joseph would surrender. Believing General Miles, Chief Joseph surrendered, only to find that the white soldier was not to be trusted.

More Broken Promises

Chief Joseph and his people were shipped, in cattle cars, to Fort Leavenworth, Kansas, where they were held as prisoners of war. Almost a hundred Indians died of malaria or heartbreak before they finally were shipped to a reservation in Oklahoma. Joseph was permitted to visit Washington where he pleaded his case, but all he received was sympathy and kind words. The Nez Percé Chief told government officials:

> . . . Good words will not give my people good health and stop them from dying. Good words will not get my people a home where they can live in peace and take care of themselves. . . . It makes my heart sick when I remember all the good words and broken promises. . . . You might as well expect the rivers to run

69   THE DESTRUCTION OF THE WESTERN INDIANS

backward as that any man who was born a free man should be contented when penned up and denied liberty to go where he pleases.

No one listened, and Joseph was sent back to the Indian territory in Oklahoma where he stayed until 1885. Some of the Nez Percés were permitted to go to their reservation in Idaho that year, but Chief Joseph was considered too dangerous and was sent to a reservation in Washington where he died in 1904. The doctor on the reservation claimed the cause of death was "a broken heart."

These accounts are just a few of the destructive occurrences during the movement west. John Collier, a twentieth-century reformer, wrote that the government's treatment of the Indian was based on

... corruption that did not know it was corrupt, and which reached deep into the intelligence of a nation. It was such a collective corruption that dominated the plains Indian record and nearly the whole Indian record of the United States.

Between the years 1864 to 1890, the states of Nebraska, Nevada, Colorado, North and South Dakota, Washington, Montana, Idaho, and Wyoming were added to the Union at the expense of wiping out several Indian civilizations. It is ironical that in the same period, the same American army was protecting the rights and property of the newly freed Blacks. There were in this period, of course, many Indian sympathizers, but seldom were they able to stop the movement to destroy the Indian's way of life. Even the attempts to help the Indian were often based on ignorance of what the Indian really was and what he needed. Instead of trying to understand the Indian and his culture and instead of trying to work out means for coexistence, the white man thought he could make the Indian adapt overnight.

The Indian's tragic experience during westward movement has been overlooked and oversimplified in many of our history books. Far too often, the government's record in the thirty years after 1860 was one of deception, double dealing, and death. Often the Indian leaders trusted the whites, only to learn that official policies and treaty rights were changeable, usually to the disadvantage of the Indian. When Indians did fight for their shrinking land on the Great Plains and in the Rocky Mountains, they were considered by most whites to be savages. The appeals for fair treatment went unheard. This is not one of the most pleasant chapters in American history. Today, the white man continues to pass *helpful* laws which are based on an ignorance of what the Indian wants and needs. More will be said about this in later chapters.

Interesting Reading

NONFICTION:

Beal, Merrill. *"I Will Fight No More Forever": Chief Joseph and the Nez Percé War.* Seattle: University of Washington Press, 1966.

70   THE EVOLUTION OF MODERN AMERICA

Berthrong, Donald J. *The Southern Cheyennes.* Norman: University of Oklahoma Press, 1963.

Brown, Dee. *Bury My Heart at Wounded Knee.* New York: Holt, Rinehart and Winston, 1970.

Grinnell, George B. *Blackfoot Lodge Tales.* Lincoln: University of Nebraska Press, 1962.

_____. *The Cheyenne Indians: Their History and Ways of Life.* Lincoln: University of Nebraska Press, 1961.

Hoebel, Adamson. *The Cheyennes: Indians of the Great Plains.* New York: Holt, Rinehart and Winston, 1960.

Josephy, Jr., Alvin M. *The Indian Heritage of America.* New York: Alfred A. Knopf, 1968.

Neihardt, John G. *Black Elk Speaks.* Lincoln: University of Nebraska Press, 1961.

Olson, James C. *Red Cloud and the Sioux Problem.* Lincoln: University of Nebraska Press, 1965.

Sandoz, Maria. *Crazy Horse.* Lincoln: University of Nebraska Press, 1961.

Stands-in Timber, John *et al. Cheyenne Memories.* Lincoln: University of Nebraska Press, 1972.

Utley, Robert. *The Last Days of the Sioux Nation.* New York: Yale University Press, 1963.

Vestal, Stanley. *Sitting Bull, Champion of the Sioux.* Norman: University of Oklahoma Press, 1957.

FICTION:

Fall, Thomas. *The Ordeal of Running Standing.* New York: Bantam, 1971.

Norman, John. *Ghost Dance.* New York: Ballantine, 1970.

Application 3.   Study reading check

Directions: To check how well you study-read the chapter, answer the
following questions.

1. Some historical accounts of the development of the West fail to discuss
   the way the Indian cultures were treated.

   a. True

   b. False, because _____

2. The mass slaughter of the buffalo helped bring about the end of the
   Navaho and Apache lifestyle.

   a. True

   b. False, because _____

3. Colonel John Chivington was among the few whites who tried to help
   Black Kettle and his Cheyenne people.

   a. True

   b. False, because _____

4. Crazy Horse got his name because of his fearlessness in battling army
   soldiers.

   a. True

   b. False, because _____

5. The Dawes Severalty Act of 1887 was intended to put an end to Indian
   tribal life and convert the Indian to white man's ways.

   a. True

   b. False, because _____

6. Often Indians signed treaties with the government even though they had
   no idea of land ownership.

   a. True

   b. False, because _____

7. Chief Joseph, outnumbered by the army two to one, led his small band of people over 1,300 miles before they were tricked into surrendering under false promises.

   a. True

   b. False, because _____

8. The government's treatment of the Indian was based on "corruption that did not know it was corrupt."

   a. True

   b. False, because _____

Application 4.   Writing a short essay answer

Directions: On a separate sheet of paper, write a short essay answer to one of the following questions based on the purposes given for reading the chapter.

1. Discuss some of the reasons the U.S. government made and then broke so many treaties with the western Indians.
2. Explain the intent of the Dawes Severalty Act of 1887 and why it was not effective.
3. Use one of the following to discuss the Indian policies during the westward movement:
   a. Red Cloud and the Oglala Sioux
   b. Crazy Horse
   c. Chief Joseph and the Nez Percé

Application 5. Surveying practice: a textbook

Directions: The best reading application we can recommend for this unit is to get out of this book and apply the methods you learned in it to other books you are using in other classes. If you do not have a textbook you can use because of the types of classes you are taking, go to the library and check out a textbook for some subject you are interested in: health, psychology, auto mechanics, business education, or anything else. If you are not sure the book you selected is a textbook, ask the librarian. Or borrow a textbook from a friend or your instructor. Following are the applications we want you to try on another textbook. When your answers are complete, show them to your instructor.

1. Name of textbook: _____

2. What does the preface tell you about the content and organization of the text?

   _____

   _____

3. What does the "Introduction" or "To the Student" say about the text that will help you or prepare you to read the text? _____

   _____

   _____

4. How is the book organized, according to the table of contents? (Units? Chapters? Glossaries? Index? Appendix?) _____

   _____

5. Write a short paragraph describing the contents and coverage of this textbook to someone who has never seen it. _____

   _____

   _____

   _____

   _____

   _____

   _____

NAME _____ SECTION _____

Application 6.   Surveying practice: a chapter

1. Name of textbook: _____

2. Number and title of chapter from the text: _____

3. How many major headings does the chapter contain? _____

4. How is the chapter organized? (Major headings, subheadings, marginal

   notes, summaries, questions at the beginning or end?) _____

   _____

   _____

5. How long would it take you to read the chapter? _____ Where
   would you break up the chapter for short reading breaks and comprehension checks?

   _____

6. Does the vocabulary look easy or difficult? _____

7. Write three or more questions you want to answer as you read the chapter.

   _____

   _____

   _____

   _____

NAME _____ SECTION _____

Application 7.   Summarizing what you have learned

At the end of each chapter in this book you are asked to summarize what you have learned in the chapter, usually (a) about yourself, (b) about skills you can apply to your study reading, and (c) any questions you have that need answering. Good summaries contain the most important information presented but organized in a meaningful way and stated in your own words. Look upon writing summaries as an opportunity to master what you have read, to make certain you understand the information presented, and to explain what you've learned in your own words.

While there is often no "answer key" to compare against your summary answers, there are some guidelines to follow in writing good summaries so that you don't just dash off the first things that come to mind. For instance, if you are going to summarize what you learned about yourself, don't be vague; be as specific as possible. Here's an example:

> While reading Chapter 1, I realized that I need to spend more time surveying or previewing before I read my textbook assignments, that I shouldn't be afraid to mark up my own textbook, and that I need to make reading notes after I have completed the reading assignment. I also realize that I need to plan my study time better by making out a schedule and sticking to it.
>
> The most important skills I can apply to my own study reading is the SQ3R approach, Surveying, Questioning, Reading, Reciting, and Reviewing. After applying Applications 5 and 6 to my history textbook, I see how the SQ3R method will help me prepare to read, to concentrate better, and to make certain I understand what I read. The idea of reading a chapter summary first, or looking at the questions at the end of a chapter as a way to focus on the content makes sense to me. Reading from heading to heading and stopping to mark or take notes before trying to understand more information will help keep my mind from wandering.
>
> There are two questions I have to ask of the instructor: What's the best dictionary to get? Should the third R in SQ3R be done orally or in writing?

Notice how the summary covers all three points. The student states four areas of studying that she needs to improve upon. Specific skills are mentioned that the student found helpful and can use. The two questions that are still unclear are written so that they can be answered the next time the class meets or during a visit to the instructor's office.

If you are asked to summarize what you read, then ask these questions:

1.   What or who is being discussed?
2.   Is one thing being compared with another?

3.   Is a process being described? If so, what are the steps involved?
4.   Is there a chronology involved with one thing happening after another?
5.   Did something occur that caused something else to happen?

For instance, if you were asked to summarize the selection you read in this chapter, "How to Communicate with Your Textbook" by Dennis Coon, you could start by asking yourself the questions above. Two of the five questions need to be answered, in this case, Questions 1 and 3. The SQ3R study system is being discussed, and since it is a process, your summary would need to explain the process and each of the five steps involved.

On the other hand, if you were asked to summarize the chapter you read, "The Destruction of the Western Indians," Questions 1 and 5 would help you summarize. In this case the treatment of the Plains Indians is discussed and you would need to summarize the reasons the Indians were treated as they were and what the results of such treatment were. The type of summary needed, then, is based on the type of material being read. Try applying those questions to what you have read the next time you are asked to write a summary but given little direction.

Now, here are the directions for summary writing in regard to this chapter.

Directions: On a separate sheet of paper, summarize what you have learned from reading this chapter (a) about yourself, (b) about skills you can apply to your study reading, and (c) any questions you still have that need answering. Turn this in to your instructor when finished.

Taking notes

2

R¹ *Reading beyond words*

Below is a Doonesbury cartoon strip. Read it and then answer the questions that follow.

1. Explain the cartoon strip.

   _____

   _____

   _____

2. What is Garry Trudeau saying about education?

   _____

   _____

   _____

3. Is Trudeau on the side of the students or the professor?

   _____

   _____

   _____

4. Explain your reaction to the cartoon.

   _____

   _____

   _____

R² *Reading actively*

A. Vocabulary preview

Directions: Using the dictionary entries provided, define the italicized words in the sentences below as best you can.

1. Many lectures will be wasted unless you recognize this danger and strive to *avert* it.

   a·vert (ə-vurt′) *v.* **1.** To turn away: *avert one's eyes.* **2.** To ward off; prevent. [<Lat. *avertere.*]—**avert′ible** or **avert′able** *adj.*

2. In some courses, taking notes is virtually *imperative.*

   im·per·a·tive (im-per′-ə-tiv) *adj.* **1.** Expressing a command, request, or plea; an imperative sentence. **2.** Having the power or authority to command or control. **3.** Obligatory; mandatory. [<LLat. *imperativus.*]— **im·per′a·tive** *n.* —**im′per·a·tive·ly** *adv.*

3. The lecturer presented a *host* of new facts and ideas.

   host¹ (hōst) *n.* **1.** One who entertains guests. **2.** Biol. An organism on or in which a parasite lives.—*v.* To serve as host for [<Lat. *hospes.*]
   host² (hōst) *n.* **1.** An army. **2.** A great number. [<Lat. *hostis,* enemy.]

4. The *implications* are obvious.

   im·pli·cate (im′pli-kāt) *v.* -cat·ed, -ca·ting. **1.** To involve, esp. incriminatingly. **2.** To imply or suggest [Lat. *implicare.*]—**im′pli·ca′tion** *n.*

5. Sometimes the framework of the lecture itself constitutes, *tacitly,* many ideas.

   tac·it (tas′it) *adj.* **1.** Not spoken: *tacit consent.* **2.** Implied by or inferred from actions or statements. [Lat. *tacitus,* p.p. of *tacere,* to be silent.] —**tac′it·ly** *adv.* —**tac′it·ness** *n.*

6. Avoid the mistake of writing the *converse* in place of the statement actually made.

con·verse[1] (kən-vurs') *v.* **1.** To engage in conversation. **2.** To interact with a computer on-line.—*n.* (kän-vər-sā'shən) Conversation. [< Lat. *conversari,* to associate with.]

con·verse[2] (kon-vurs') *n.* The opposite or reverse of something.—*adj.* (kon-vurs', kon'-vurs). Opposite; contrary. [< Lat. *conversus,* p.p. of *convertere,* to turn around.]—conversely (kən-vurs'lē) *adv.*

---

7. Accuracy and completeness are *facilitated* by using some system of shorthand.

   fa·cil'·i·tate (fəsil'i-tāt') *v.* -tat·ed, -ta·ting. To make easier; assist. [< Ital. *facilitare.*]—fa-cil'i-ta'-tion *n.*

---

8. *Rote* copying of notes is virtually pointless.

   rote (rōt) *n.* **1.** Memorization usu. achieved by repetition without understanding. **2.** Mechanical routine or repetition. [ME.]

---

9. See if you can make the apparently *disparate* data fit.

   dis·pa·rate (dis'pər-it, di-spar'-) *adj.* Completely distinct or different; dissimilar. [Lat. *disparatus,* p.p. of *disparere,* to separate.]— **dis'pa·rate·ly** *adv.* —**dis·par'i·ty** (di-spar'-i-tē) *n.*

B.   Thought provokers

1. Based on the vocabulary preview of words from the selection you are about to read, what do you think it will be about?

---

2. Do you take good study notes? ＿＿＿＿＿ What makes you think so?

＿＿＿＿＿＿＿＿＿＿＿＿＿＿＿＿＿＿＿＿＿＿＿＿＿＿＿＿＿

＿＿＿＿＿＿＿＿＿＿＿＿＿＿＿＿＿＿＿＿＿＿＿＿＿＿＿＿＿

3. Do you really believe that taking good notes is important? ＿＿＿＿＿
   Why?

＿＿＿＿＿＿＿＿＿＿＿＿＿＿＿＿＿＿＿＿＿＿＿＿＿＿＿＿＿

＿＿＿＿＿＿＿＿＿＿＿＿＿＿＿＿＿＿＿＿＿＿＿＿＿＿＿＿＿

4. Have you ever been taught how to take good notes? ＿＿＿＿＿ If so,
   where?

＿＿＿＿＿＿＿＿＿＿＿＿＿＿＿＿＿＿＿＿＿＿＿＿＿＿＿＿＿

5. After taking notes, what should be done with them? ＿＿＿＿＿＿＿

＿＿＿＿＿＿＿＿＿＿＿＿＿＿＿＿＿＿＿＿＿＿＿＿＿＿＿＿＿

＿＿＿＿＿＿＿＿＿＿＿＿＿＿＿＿＿＿＿＿＿＿＿＿＿＿＿＿＿

＿＿＿＿＿＿＿＿＿＿＿＿＿＿＿＿＿＿＿＿＿＿＿＿＿＿＿＿＿

C.   Reading practice

Directions: Before reading the following selection from a personal development textbook, survey it. Then, in the space below, write down what you learned from your survey and any questions you hope to answer as you read.

Survey comments: ＿＿＿＿＿＿＿＿＿＿＿＿＿＿＿＿＿＿＿＿＿＿＿＿

＿＿＿＿＿＿＿＿＿＿＿＿＿＿＿＿＿＿＿＿＿＿＿＿＿＿＿＿＿＿＿＿＿

＿＿＿＿＿＿＿＿＿＿＿＿＿＿＿＿＿＿＿＿＿＿＿＿＿＿＿＿＿＿＿＿＿

＿＿＿＿＿＿＿＿＿＿＿＿＿＿＿＿＿＿＿＿＿＿＿＿＿＿＿＿＿＿＿＿＿

Now read the selection from *On Becoming an Educated Person.*

VIRGINIA VOEKS

PROFITING MORE FULLY FROM LECTURES

During four years of college, you will hear some 1,800 lectures. Many of these lectures will be wasted. They will, that is, unless you recognize this danger and strive to avert it.

How could you make lectures worthwhile? Let us put the question differently: How could you be changed by a person's talking to you for an hour? Suppose you already knew all the facts he presented. Even then you could be changed: You could be seeing new relationships from the particular contexts in which he introduces those facts. You could be getting leads on sources of information. You could be exploring ideas which had not occurred to you before he spoke. You could be developing a somewhat different and more comprehensive picture of the world. All of these and more you could be doing. Sometimes, though, we do none of them and leave the classroom almost unchanged.

Whenever we leave a class-meeting unchanged, we have squandered a bit of life. This section points a way to living that part of your life more fully.

1. *Sit as near the front of the classroom as is comfortable for you.*

Ease in concentrating and understanding can be greatly influenced by your position in the classroom. If currently your attention wanders, shift to a different part of the room. Try sitting near the front. The many inevitable noises are not as distracting there nor do they blur as many words and phrases. You understand the words better and therefore can understand the ideas better.

For many students, sitting near the center of a room has resulted in better learning (as measured by high grades) than sitting near the back of a room or on the aisles. Perhaps the majority feel more secure when surrounded by their colleagues than when on the fringes.

2. *Before class begins, get set for that sort of class.*

You do not have to lose the first ten minutes of each class while trying to get organized. You can become oriented toward that class before the hour begins. For example, you can go over your notes from the previous day's meeting just before the class begins. Or you can review the reading assigned for that day. Both of these help you "get in the mood" for that class.

Classes taken at 1:00 or immediately after lunch seem to cause trouble. One is apt to be distracted, particularly disoriented, and sluggish. The blood and oxygen are not zipping to the brain in optimum quantities but going instead to the digestive tract in larger-than-usual proportions. This is fine for digesting lunch, but not much help to thinking. With some students this phenomenon is so pronounced they tend to go to sleep—more so in one o'clocks than usual.

If you are such a student, try eating early in the period available for lunch, eat a light snack, and then eat again after classes are finished. And take especial care to spend the last few minutes before class getting prepared for that class. If the course is a difficult one or particularly important to you, postpone lunch.

3. *Should you take notes?*

Much needless confusion has resulted from assuming this question has one best answer equally applicable to all lectures. That simply is not the case.

As you know, things classified under the same heading may differ greatly. Golf and bowling are both sports but not all the activities necessary for skill in one are desirable in the other. Keeping your eye on the ball is fine for golf, but it does not improve bowling. So it is with studies. *You must modify your procedure in accord with the particular course you are taking and the particular skills you are trying to acquire.*

In some courses, taking many notes is virtually imperative; in others, a few notes will suffice. When the lecturer repeats the textbook, probably no notes are necessary. That material already is accessible. At the other extreme, when the lecturer presents a host of new facts and ideas, many notes may be necessary in order to deeply understand the material or even to understand it at all.

In lectures, as in reading, do not be lured by a plausible, graceful presentation into believing you already know and understand the material and so need no notes. "Understanding" the ideas while a skillful lecturer is presenting them is one thing; understanding them when alone is something quite different.

4. *To profit fully from some courses, many notes are essential.*

Anything important which is clearly expressed can be remembered by attentively listening to it once or at least so we seem to believe. The belief is encouraged by some conversations which contain little we had not previously known. The belief is further fortified by radio advertisements, and speeches filled with over-simplifications and repetitions. Such material we can remember, of course, without notes. But not all lectures are like those conversations, advertisements, and speeches. Would you remember most of the material from a complex book, after reading it once as fast as you could? Such a feat you might deem miraculous. Yet that is what many of us attempt with lectures! We feel strangely disappointed when we do not understand and recall in detail a lecture heard but once. Why do we try to do with lectures what we know cannot be done with books?

There is nothing magical about converting words from visual stimuli into auditory ones. When new-to-you, complex ideas and a wealth of condensed information are presented in a lecture, do not expect to recall the material, far less understand its implications, from hearing it once. Such accomplishments require reviewing and reflective study. In order to have the materials you need for this reviewing and study, take notes on such lectures.

5. *Make written notes of everything which strikes you as ridiculous, or which conflicts with your present desires or beliefs.*

Material which conflicts with your desires or beliefs is particularly apt to be overlooked, misconstrued, or forgotten. Many experimental data demonstrate that phenomenon. For example, a large number of college students listened to a ten-minute speech on the New Deal. Immediately thereafter, they took an objective test on that material. A questionnaire had shown that some of these students favored the New Deal, and that others were opposed. Both groups remembered best the parts of the speech which fit their own views. The pro-New Deal students answered correctly significantly more questions based on the pro-New Deal facts than those based on the anti-New Deal facts. The anti-New Deal students correctly answered significantly more of the questions based upon the anti-New Deal portions than upon the pro-New Deal portions. Three weeks later the students were given a second test on the speech. By then, their tendency to remember accurately only those facts harmonizing with their beliefs was even more pronounced than it had been immediately after the speech. The implications are obvious.

Deviant ideas or facts (and they may be facts, not opinions) are not only difficult to remember, they are difficult to understand without thinking about them. Clearly, you cannot think about something unless you can remember it. This behooves us to make careful, detailed notes of anything we do not believe.

6. *Record at least some of the details of the lecture, as well as the "general idea."*

The basic ideas are meaningless (even when remembered!) and lack significance except in terms of the details they imply. Jotting down some of the illustrations, for instance, clarifies the main idea and helps fix it in your memory by showing a few of its implications.

Record the details of any experiments given. Again this increases the meaningfulness of the "main" points. Such notes are valuable too if later you wish to pursue the subject further, or get to wondering what sorts of evidence exist for some viewpoint.

7. *Try to get the framework of the lecture, as well as what you construe to be the main and minor points.*

Oftentimes some of the main points are not statements, but are implicit in the particular ways in which the materials are integrated. In other words, the framework itself constitutes, tacitly, many ideas. This does not mean there is only one way to organize facts. It means more nearly the opposite: There are many ways to organize facts and the organizations themselves have meanings. After class, try integrating the material in new frameworks of your own creation.

8. *Be accurate.*

In taking condensed notes, do not omit such words as "usually," "sometimes," "very," or "somewhat." Omitting such words changes the basic meaning of the sentence. Avoid also substituting "is" for "tends." Such a substitution radically changes the whole sentence and its implications.

Avoid the common mistake of writing the converse in place of the state-ment actually made. The converse is an interchange of the subject and pred-icate. For example, suppose the lecturer says: All hostile aggression stems from frustration. Do not write: Frustration always results in hostile aggres-sion. That could be false, while the original statement was true.

When several conditions are listed as being necessary for some speci-fied outcome, be certain to record them all. If the lecturer states that $2 + 5 + 8 = 15$, getting down in one's notes that $2 + 5$ gives 15 is not merely incomplete; it is downright wrong and highly misleading.

Accuracy and completeness are facilitated by using some system of shorthand. You can devise your own system. Use symbols and abbreviations you already know, supplemented by ones of your own creation. For exam-ple, abbreviate common words by the first few letters, use contractions, and leave out unnecessary vowels. Use the same abbreviation for the same word each time. Do not bother about writing complete sentences. In taking notes, the trick is to do as little writing as possible while still getting down as many of the facts and principles as possible.

9. Jot down reminders of questions which occur to you during class.

Jot down reminders also of any disagreements you may have. During the lecture is not opportune for following up these questions, for almost certainly you would miss hearing some subsequent ideas. But after class, try to answer your questions.

10. When first learning to take notes, most people have difficulty in writing and listening at the same time.

This difficulty does not last forever. With practice of the two skills (note-taking and attentive listening), you can easily do them simulta-neously. You can learn this even as many people, after much practice, have learned to knit and converse well at the same time. First practice the two skills separately; then practice them combined.

11. After taking notes, what should we do with them?

Rote copying of notes is virtually pointless. Reworking notes has great value. Rewrite parts that are legible the next hour, but will be illegible the next day. Fill in gaps. Add points you still remember but did not have time to record during the lecture. These things can best be done shortly after the lecture.

Then, answer the questions you have noted in the margin of your notes. Find examples of the facts and principles presented. Ideally, use your notes in the ways suggested in connection with studying books.

Suppose, after taking notes, you never looked at them. Taking them still would not have been a waste of time. For one thing, you would have started building skill in note-taking, and that skill is indispensable in some situations for fully utilizing the opportunities afforded for becoming edu-cated. In addition, the mere act of writing something enables many people to remember it better even though they do not look at their notes again.

12. During class, be active.

Be as responsive and attentive as you can be. Listen with the intent to understand and remember the material presented. . . . In many other ways too, you can be active and growing. You can be developing skill in seeing the meanings of material by looking for examples or other applications of the material presented, by answering to yourself the questions raised by your teacher or classmates, by comparing other people's answers with your own, by trying to anticipate how the lecturer will develop a point. You can be re-examining old beliefs and looking at your world through new eyes. You can be following the ideas as well as the words of the lecturer. There is much you can do and learn during lectures.

13. Before devising counter-arguments, be certain you understand the ideas being presented—especially if they differ from your own.

It is these strange, new viewpoints and facts which furnish you with bases for new actions . . . for new interests . . . for new ways of looking at old problems . . . for new conceptions of the world. And these, in turn, are the bases for growth.

You did not enter college hoping to end the same as you began. You hoped to change. So when someone presents a fact or opinion very different from what you believe, note it with care. After class think about it, discuss it with your friends, try to understand it and see in what senses it is true. When you are sure you understand the material, try to think of counter-arguments. Then see if you can devise some way to make the apparently disparate data fit.

Following these steps can lead the way to you becoming an educated person.

D.   Comprehension check

Directions: The following questions are similar to those frequently asked on quizzes. If you need help for some answers, return to the reading selection and find them.

1. During four years of college, about how many lectures will you attend?

   a. 2000

   b. 1800

   c. 1600

   d. 1400

2. According to the author, whenever you leave a class meeting unchanged, you have squandered a bit of life. To get the most from lectures, which of the following should you do while listening?

    a. take notes

    b. devise counter-arguments

    c. look for new relationships presented on information you already know

    d. get leads on sources of information related to the lecture

    e. all of the above

3. Which of the following is *not* a reason for sitting near the front of the classroom?

    a. Noises are not as distracting.

    b. It is easier to hear the lecture.

    c. The instructor will begin to recognize your face.

    d. Studies show grades are lower among students who sit in the back.

    e. None of the above.

4. Classes taken at 1:00 or immediately after lunch seem to cause trouble.

    a. True, because _____

    _____

    b. False, because _____

    _____

5. Which of the following statements is *not* true?

    a. You should take notes for all lectures.

    b. Make written notes of everything that seems ridiculous or which conflicts with your present beliefs.

    c. Record at least some of the details of a lecture as well as the general idea.

    d. Jot down reminders of questions that occur to you during class.

    e. Be as attentive as can be.

6. Anything important which is clearly expressed can be remembered by attentively listening to it once.

    a. True, because _____

    _____

    b. False, because _____

    _____

7. The author presents the results of a study wherein a large number of college students were tested on a ten-minute lecture discussing the New Deal. The results showed that

    a. some students did not need to take notes.

    b. students who took notes did better than those who didn't.

    c. facts and ideas are difficult to remember without notes.

    d. ideas or facts different from our own are difficult to remember and harder to understand.

    e. none of the above.

8. Which of the following are suggested for devising a note-taking system?

    a. Be accurate in what you write down.

    b. Devise your own system.

    c. Use symbols and abbreviations.

    d. Don't try to write complete sentences.

    e. All of the above.

9. What does the author mean by "reworking" notes?

    _____

    _____

    _____

10. What should you do with ideas that are different from your own?

   _____

   _____

11. On a separate sheet of paper, (1) write a summary of the reading selection that contains the main points being made, and (2) compare those points with the main points in the chapter from Coon's textbook on pages 5–10.

E.   Vocabulary check

Directions: In the blank by its number, write the letter of the best definition for each of the italicized words.

_____	1. *avert*	a.	repetition
_____	2. *imperative*	b.	suggestions; hints
_____	3. *host*	c.	prevent
_____	4. *implications*	d.	obligatory; mandatory
_____	5. *tacit*	e.	opposite
_____	6. *converse*	f.	assist
_____	7. *facilitate*	g.	composes; makes up
_____	8. *rote*	h.	a great number
_____	9. *disparate*	i.	inferred from actions or structure
_____	10. *constitutes*	j.	dissimilar

R³   *Reading skills check*

Some instructors give you one or two weeks of reading assignments from your textbook at once. They expect *you* to budget your reading time.

Because you know you cannot read and remember everything, you should, as we have said, try to divide your assignments into short reading sections. You have to judge how long it will take you to do each part. Do not try to read an entire chapter in one gulp. Take your time and concern yourself with only one part. When you are certain you understand that part, then go on to the next. Our minds like to wander. Our attention spans are short. So if we try to read only parts of an assignment, then stop to ask ourselves what we have just read, or take some notes to help aid comprehension, we are actually controlling our minds. That is why it is better to read from one heading in a chapter to the next and then stop. Think about what you just read. If there is a "fuzzy" area, go back and reread that part. Then read from the new heading to the next. Then stop and think again about what you read and make some notes. Doing so focuses attention on the content, and the result is better comprehension and control over mind-wandering.

Our minds cannot remember everything, especially as time goes by. What we read and understand one day we forget or lose three or four weeks later. That is why it is important to take some type of notes. This section is going to present you with three methods of note taking: how to make notes in your textbooks, how to take notes in your class notebook, and how to "map" a chapter of notes on one or two pages. You can decide which one method or combination is best for you and the type of textbook you are reading.

A.   Marking your textbooks

First let's consider how and why to make notes in your book. You can come up with your own way of marking your text, but make certain you *do not* just underline items you think are important as you read. If you do, you will be marking many passages that will be of little use, especially when you review during study periods and before a test. You need a system.

Here's a good way to make and take notes in your book.

1. Read from heading to heading or a short passage and then stop. Do not do any marking as you read.
2. After you have read the section, go back and underline the main ideas of each paragraph, plus a few key phrases that support the main idea.
3. Circle or draw boxes around special terms or new names.
4. Abbreviate points you wish to remember in the margin. You also might write down any questions you want to ask the instructor at the next class meeting.
5. Write a summary of that section in short, abbreviated phrases. Writing a summary is the most important part. It forces you to become actively involved in what you read. It is a form of recitation that will help you remember the material better.

Avoid the temptation just to mark a book as you read or to skip writing a summary. Just marking passages does not mean you understand the material. Marking selectively and writing summaries, however, does force you to think more closely about what you have read.

If an assignment is very long (20–30 pages), don't try to mark every paragraph. Be selective. That's why it is important to read from one section or heading to another, then to stop and take notes on the key points.

Here is an example of a marked textbook passage. Read both the passage and the notes and markings. This passage is a good example of the most helpful type of marking:

Short- and long-term memory

Short-term memory

Naturally, everything seen or heard is not held in memory. *Selective attention* (discussed in Chapter 4) determines what information moves from sensory memory to a second storage system called **short-term memory** (**STM**). STM also holds information for brief periods of time, but longer than sensory memory. STM is sometimes called the *working memory,* because it is the system used when dialing a phone number, remembering a new name, or adding a column of numbers (Atkinson and Shriffrin, 1971).

Short-term memory can only hold a limited amount of information, and once information is removed from STM it is permanently lost. Generally this loss is an advantage. If most short-term memories were not lost, our minds would be cluttered with names, dates, telephone numbers, arithmetic sums, and other useless trivia (Miller, 1964). As you may have noticed when dialing a phone number, STM is severely affected by any *interruption or interference* (Adams, 1967). You've probably had this experience. You

(Review Chap 4)
Sensory memory =
1st stage

STM = 2nd storage
sys.

def -
STM = working
memory

Advantage to
STM — less
clutter

Problem with
STM — forget
too quickly

look up a telephone number and walk to the phone repeating the number to yourself. You dial the number and get a busy signal. Returning a few minutes later, you find that you must look up the number again. This time as you are about to dial, someone asks you a question. You answer, turn to the phone, and find that you have forgotten the number.

Long-term memory

Information that is important, useful, meaningful, or novel may be transferred to a third memory system called (long-term memory) (**LTM**). Long-term memory seems to be based on a separate system in the brain since it permanently records information and has a practically unlimited storage capacity. Evidence for this fact comes from the work of (Wilder Penfield) a neurosurgeon who has found that vivid memories are brought out when the human brain is stimulated with an electric needle (Fig. 10–7). (A description of Penfield's work is found earlier in the "Chapter Preview.") Penfield reports that one patient heard familiar music so clearly that she thought a record player had been turned on nearby. Penfield believes that the nervous system retains a record of a person's past that is like "a continuous strip of movie film, complete with sound track" (Penfield, 1957).

> LTM = 3rd memory system, holds useful info.
>
> LTM = Separate system unlimited storage
>
> W. Penfield's evidence
>
> ← Reread when finished
> <u>Summary</u>: three stages of memory — sensory, STM, and LTM. STM is working memory, brief. LTM holds meaningful info., permanent.

No two sets of markings would be the same, but notice that there is no overmarking; the notes bring out only key points and connections with information in other chapters. The summary is brief but contains the key elements in the passage.

Now, what if you don't want to mark your textbook, because you want to sell it at the end of the course? Although it is *best* to mark right in the book, you could buy some 5- x -8-inch note cards and keep your notes on a card. Then, at the end of each section, paperclip the card to the page. This method is less convenient, and cards can become bulky or get lost, but you might want to try it.

EXERCISE

Following is another short passage from a textbook. Read it, and then mark it as you were just shown.

Mnemonics—memory magic

Various "memory experts" entertain by giving demonstrations in which they memorize the names of everyone at a banquet, the order of all the cards in a deck, long lists of disconnected words, or other seemingly impossible amounts of information. These tricks are performed through the use of **mnemonics** (nee-MON-iks). A mnemonic is any kind of memory system or aid . . .

Mnemonic techniques are ways of avoiding *rote* learning (learning by simple repetition). The superiority of mnemonic learning as opposed to rote learning has been demonstrated many times. For example, Bower (1973) asked college students to study 5 different lists of 20 unrelated words. At the end of a short study session subjects were asked to recall all 100 items. Subjects using mnemonics remembered an average of 72 items, whereas a control group using simple or rote learning remembered an average of 28.

Stage performers rarely have a naturally superior memory. Instead, they make extensive use of memory systems to perform their feats. Few of these systems are of practical value to the student, but the principles underlying mnemonics are. By practicing mnemonics you should be able to greatly improve your memory with little effort.

The basic principles of mnemonics are:

1. Use mental pictures.

There are at least two kinds of memory, *visual* and *verbal*. Visual pictures or images are generally easier to remember than words. Turning information into mental pictures is therefore very helpful (Paivio, 1969).

2. Make things meaningful.

Transfer of information from short-term to long-term memory is aided by making it meaningful. If you encounter technical terms that have little or no immediate meaning for you, *give* them meaning, even if you have to stretch the term to do so. (This point is clarified by the examples below.)

3. Make information familiar.

Connect it to what you already know. Another way to get information into long-term memory is to connect it to information already stored there. If some facts or ideas in a chapter seem to stay in your memory easily, associate other more difficult facts with them.

4. Form bizarre, unusual, or exaggerated mental associations.

When associating two ideas, terms, or especially mental images, you will find that the more outrageous and exaggerated the association, the more likely you are to remember it later.

Share your notes in class. Discuss which notes and markings are most helpful for spaced review studying and review before a test.

B.   Reading notes and lecture notes

Sometimes it's convenient to keep your study reading notes and your class lecture notes together. When an instructor assigns a chapter from the textbook and then lectures on additional information not in your book, consider dual note taking. That means you divide a page from your notebook to handle both.

First, you should get a regular three-ring looseleaf notebook that takes $8^{1}/_{2} \times 11$ inch notebook paper. A looseleaf allows you to shift pages around, tear out unwanted sheets, or insert fresh pages. Take the notebook to all your classes and wherever you study. Start your notes for a new chapter on a new page in your notebook. Do not write on the backs of pages. This system will allow you to remove pages and spread them out for study. A good set of notes, reviewed frequently, often means the difference between *real* learning and *wishful* learning.

Here is one way you could divide your page to accommodate both reading notes and lecture notes (see illustration on page 69). Notice that the page is divided into three parts. The left side is for your reading notes, the right side for lecture notes, and the bottom for summaries, reactions, and connections between reading and lectures. Of course, you could change these divisions any way to fit your own courses.

The important thing is to try not to write down everything you read or hear in the lecture. As we explained about marking your textbooks, you should be selective. Write down in phrases or abbreviations the main ideas and some points that support the main ideas. Record important names, dates, or figures that are connected to the main ideas. Write down page numbers you want to reread when you review or study your notes. The notes are yours, so only write down things that will help you recall what you read and hear. As before, do not try to write notes until *after* you have read a passage from heading to heading or heard enough to grasp an idea.

You can remove notes such as these from your notebook and spread them out on a table for review or in preparation for a test. But notes are no good in themselves. They are only as good and as helpful as you make them.

Review suggestions for lecture note-taking (LISAN) on pages 6–7 and in this chapter.

C. Mapping a chapter

Another note-taking method is called *mapping.** Mapping is a convenient way to place all your notes for an entire chapter on one or two pages. This method has two major purposes: (1) It forces you to find the main ideas and supporting details for the chapter you are reading, and (2) it provides you with an easy-to-understand set of notes for review. Just before a test, you can go over your notes and review an entire chapter by reading your map for

*M. Buckley Hanf, "Mapping: A Technique for Translating Reading into Thinking," Journal of Reading (January 1971), pp. 225–229.

	Reading Notes	**Lecture Notes**
○	Record only main ideas and important details. Make page references for review. Abbreviate. Do not write on back of pages.	Do not try to write everything. Listen for key points and signal words: (a) there are three reasons why (b) for example (c) however (d) therefore Abbreviate when possible. Date each set of lecture notes.

Summary, reactions, connections between reading and lectures.

that chapter instead of rereading your book, wondering why you drew lines under certain passages, and flipping through all the pages in the text.

This method is a bit difficult to get used to, but don't let that keep you from trying it. The advantage to mapping is that you cannot do it until after you have actually surveyed a chapter and noticed its organization and contents. Then you have to read the chapter well enough to be able to condense all the information into a one-page "map."

Here's how to do mapping. You already know this chapter has four R sections, so we will use it as an example. The number of sections is the first thing to know for your map. In the center of a regular sheet of notebook paper, you write the title of the chapter. Around the title you draw some kind of shape that has four corners, such as a box or rectangle. The four corners represent the four major sections. Here's an example, but your four-corner design could be different:

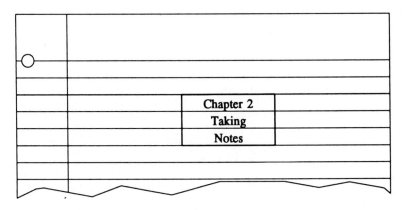

Next, you take the headings of the four major sections of this chapter and make a line or branch for each of them. Now your map should look something like the illustration that follows.

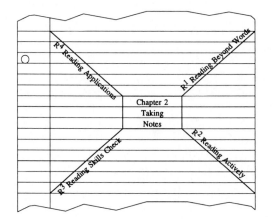

Now you have shown the four major parts of this chapter. You are ready to supply their main points. As you read, you can supply what you think are important details. Your map for this chapter—if you were doing it up to this point—would look something like the illustration below:

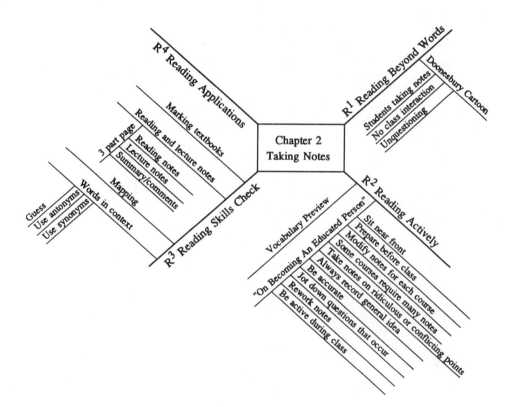

Notice that R³ and R⁴ are printed *under* the lines from the box. This position allows room to write in the spaces without writing upside down. This drawing is a "map" of what we have covered so far in this chapter. In other words, you can look at this page and get a picture of this chapter. Of course, it's best to use your own words or to write down what *you* want to remember. Then your key words will trigger or recall to your mind the main points when you review.

Some longer chapters require more than one page; some sections in a book are so detailed they require a page of their own. But usually you can reduce a chapter to a page or two for quick review. It saves rereading and forces good reading and concentration in order to make a map.

EXERCISE 1

As you finish reading this chapter, complete the R⁴ section of the map above. If there is not enough room, do it on a separate sheet of paper.

EXERCISE 2

Directions: Using the completed map below, of a chapter on the digestive tract, answer the questions that follow.

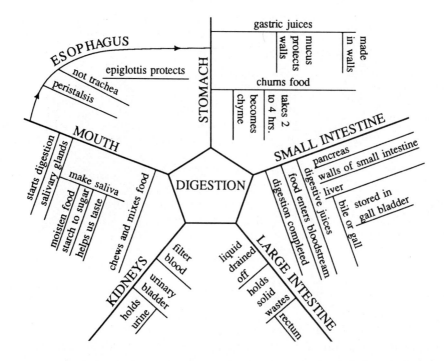

Reprinted with permission of Joan E. Heimlich and the International Reading Association.

1. Assuming that the major branches of the map each represent a section of the chapter, into how many sections is the chapter divided? _____

2. Name each section of the chapter:

_____

_____

_____

_____

_____

3. Why do you think there is a connecting arrow labeled "Esophagus" between the branches "Mouth" and "Stomach"?

_____

_____

_____

4. If you were reviewing for a test on the digestive tract, under what heading in the chapter would you find information to review on the following items?

a. salivary glands: _____

b. pancreas: _____

c. peristalsis: _____

d. gastric juices: _____

e. digestive juices: _____

5. Study the map carefully. Then, on a separate sheet of paper, use the map to write an explanation of how the digestive system works when we eat something.

D.   Vocabulary tip: words in context

The English language consists of more than 500,000 words, but most of us use only 30,000. You do not have to be a mathematical wizard to figure that as you read college materials, you will encounter thousands of unfamiliar words. So what can you do? If you answered, "Buy a good dictionary," you're on the right track. You should have a good dictionary; however, you should also know strategies to identify unfamiliar words, which may save you a trip to the dictionary. You can

1. guess the word by using clues in the sentence, and
2. learn to identify word parts such as prefixes and suffixes and use them as clues.

In this chapter, we are focusing on the first method, guessing at the unfamiliar word.

When you have a lot of reading to do, guessing can save you time. Many times the way a word is used in a sentence (the word's context) gives a clue to the word's meaning. Sometimes unfamiliar words are actually defined for us by the way they are used in a sentence. For instance, notice how you can guess at the meaning of the word *narcissistic* in the following sentence:

> *Narcissistic* people, those who adore themselves, sometimes find loving others difficult.

The clue here is the phrase "those who adore themselves." So *narcissistic* has to do with loving or admiring oneself beyond the norm.

Here's another example:

> Sheila was extremely *impudent;* I've never seen a student be so rude to a teacher.

The clue here is *rude.* We can guess that *impudent* has something to do with being rude or ill-mannered.

Notice how the word *jargon* is defined for us in this sentence:

> The doctor's use of jargon, that is, the technical language he used, kept me from understanding what he was talking about.

The phrase "the technical language he used" actually defines jargon for us. In this case, jargon refers to the technical language used by doctors, although the word actually refers to a special language of any field.

Another way we can figure out a word's meaning in context is to look for words that mean the opposite of the unknown word in the sentence, antonyms. (Notice how the word **antonym** is defined in the previous sentence.) Here is an example of an indirect definition of an unknown word:

> Although the crowd seems *placid* now, the people could easily become a raging mob.

By stating that the crowd could become a raging mob, we can guess that *placid* means calm or peaceful, something opposite from raging.

See if you can figure out the meaning of the word *gaunt* in this sentence:

Her husband was *gaunt*, but she was obese.

Of course, if you don't know the meaning of *obese,* you'll have to head for a dictionary. But if you know it means very heavy, you can guess that *gaunt* must have to do with being thin.

Here's another example. What's the meaning of *objectionable* in this example:

Lynn loves eating snails, but Julie finds them *objectionable.*

If Lynn loves snails, but Julie doesn't, we can assume that *objectionable* means the opposite and Julie doesn't like them.

EXERCISE 1

Directions: In effect, learning to use context clues is part of reading beyond words. Try guessing the meanings of the italicized words in the following sentences. Write down your guess in the blanks provided.

1. His lectures are *lucid,* which makes it easy to take notes.

   lucid: _____

   _____

2. He had no real *incentive* for studying, so he failed the test.

   incentive: _____

   _____

3. She provided *ample* evidence of her need for financial support, and was *granted* a scholarship to continue her education.

   ample: _____

   _____

granted: _____

_____

4. The instructor asked her to *clarify* a confusing comment she had written.

   clarify: _____

   _____

5. The *transition* was always hard for him. He had to change schools when he was seven, when he was nine, and again when he was eleven.

   transition: _____

   _____

6. His close *scrutiny* of the essay paid off. He discovered when he looked it over that he had omitted his conclusion.

   scrutiny: _____

   _____

7. She is *susceptible* to the ideas of others. She believes almost everything anyone tells her.

   susceptible: _____

   _____

8. The government gave money to help them purchase homes outside of the city. This system of *subsidized* housing caused the population of the city to drop.

   subsidized: _____

   _____

9. At some prisons, officials understand the prisoners' need for love and understanding, so they allow overnight *conjugal* visits.

   conjugal: _____

   _____

10. The *proponents* of nuclear power wanted to see the demonstrators jailed.

    proponents: _____

    _____

11. Her *provocative* smile got her more men than she could handle.

    provocative: _____

    _____

   Sometimes an additional clue can help you to guess at the meaning of unfamiliar words. We call these clues signal words. Signal words are words such as:

   but, however, nevertheless, despite, even though, in spite of, although, whereas, yet

Often words like these signal a conflicting idea. Read this example:

   His schedule was *hectic,* but he managed to go out for basketball.

You can guess that *hectic* probably means "hasty, confused, or busy." The word *but* helps you figure it out. This sentence could also read:

   Even though his schedule was hectic, he managed to go out for basketball.

EXERCISE 2

   Directions: In the following sentences, try defining the underlined words by noticing their context, and indicate what the signal words are:

 1. His speech was *concise;* nevertheless, he said all that needed to be said.

    concise means: _____

    _____

    the clue word is: _____

2. He is *prone* to talk too much, yet he kept quiet during the meeting.

   prone: _____

   _____

   clue word: _____

3. Although Harry is usually *inept* at sports, he surprised the coach by winning the race.

   inept: _____

   _____

   clue word: _____

4. Despite her *ingenuity*, she was unable to find the reference she needed.

   ingenuity: _____

   _____

   clue word: _____

5. She *craved* a Porsche, but all she got was a moped.

   craved: _____

   _____

   clue word: _____

6. The first drink he gave me was weak, but the second one was really *potent*.

   potent: _____

   _____

   clue word: _____

7. My dog usually greets me with *fervor,* but today she didn't even get off the floor when I came home.

fervor: _____

_____

clue word: _____

8. June wasn't making enough money to live on, so she took another job to *augment* her income.

augment: _____

_____

clue word: _____

Enough for now. You'll be doing more of this in other chapters. Using context clues to figure out the meaning of a word is a crucial reading skill, but it will not always reveal the meaning of a word. Sometimes it does not help, such as in the sentence, "The girl looked peevish." Peevish could mean beautiful, dull, sharp, bored—any number of things to someone who did not know the meaning. In following chapters you will learn other methods of vocabulary building that will, together with context clues, aid your reading.

R⁴ *Reading applications*

Application 1. Marking a history textbook

PART A

Directions: Following is an introduction to a history book. Read it and apply the marking techniques you learned in **R³**. You may want to review pages 63–65 before you begin.

Introduction

TO THE STUDENT

Unlike many American history textbooks, this book includes a good deal of information about minority groups such as native American Indians, Blacks, and Mexican-Americans (Chicanos). Thus, we hope to provide you with not merely a short history of our country, but with information you may not have found in other history textbooks.

For a great many readers the question, "Why read history?" lies either in the back of the mind or at the tip of the tongue. Historians, when asked this question, usually offer reasons such as these:

—to understand the past so that we can function intelligently today.

—to understand how our country functions and how to keep from repeating the mistakes of the past.

—to seek an understanding of our national character and to understand the variety of cultures that make up America.

But what do such remarks really mean?

We read history for many reasons, but let's be honest here. Most students read history because it is required in school. As teachers, we have heard students complain that their textbooks are boring and unrelated to their real interests. We have tried, with the assistance of community college students, to write a book that presents history in a way that is neither boring nor difficult to read.

As students, you should be on your guard with this or any other book in history, social sciences, or humanities courses. Authors have opinions that sooner or later influence what they write. You should check out the opinions in this or in other books so that your opinions will be as close to the "truth" as possible and not just those of the textbooks you read. In matters of opinion

ix

X   INTRODUCTION TO THE STUDENT

and historical interpretation, the best you or even the professional historian can hope for is well-reasoned judgments which often are described as the *truth.*

There are other and better reasons for reading history besides the fact that it is required. Studying history can enlarge our understanding of ourselves and others. History explains to a large extent why we are what we are today. It explains why we think the way we do, why we look the way we do, and why we have many of the problems we have. While reading history doesn't always provide us with the answers to present problems, it does show us what other men have thought and tried, and why they succeeded or failed. Properly understood, history can help us progress toward a better world. Reading history is not only relevant to *today,* but vital to our personal *futures.*

The key to understanding history is the word inside it: *story.* The reading of history is the reading of the longest, most exciting, most sensual story there ever was. While we cannot take part in Columbus' voyage of 1492, or join in the first Thanksgiving dinner, or be the first man to set foot on the moon, through books we can be a part of each of these events. Books on history become our time machine, taking us practically any place we want to go. Indeed, history provides the key for reasonable men to understand the present and to predict the future.

Henry S. Commager, a famous historian, once wrote, "A people without a history is like a man without memory: each generation would have to learn everything anew—make the same discoveries, invent the same tools and techniques, wrestle with the same problems, commit the same errors." What he is saying, in other words, is that it is not history itself that is important, but what *use* we make of it. We believe that the answers to the problems America faces today can best be solved when we understand our country's past, its failures and its successes.

One final comment. Reading history, or any subject for that matter, is not simply a process of reading words on the page and memorizing some facts and details for a test. Reading is a matter of becoming involved, of thinking or reacting, and of questioning what is read. The pleasure and advantage to reading history lies not in the history itself, in many cases, but in the personal meaning gained from it. The meaning obtained from the reading of history depends on how the subject and the textbook are approached. We have provided you with study-reading guides that will work; however, we cannot provide you with an interest in history. That is something you will have to develop on your own, with the help of your instructor and, we hope, this book.

PART B

Directions: To see how well you read and marked the previous textbook selection, answer the following questions without looking back.

1. What information is this textbook supposed to contain that many other history textbooks do not?

   _____

   _____

   _____

2. Why, according to the authors, do most students read history?

   _____

   _____

3. Against what, as students, do you need to be on guard when you read?

   _____

   _____

4. State two of the several reasons given for studying history.

   a. _____

   _____

   b. _____

   _____

5. The authors claim it is not history itself that is important but _____

   _____

   _____

   _____

6. The authors claim that reading is a matter of

   a. becoming involved in what you read.

   b. thinking or reacting to what you read.

   c. questioning what you read.

   d. all of the above.

Check your answers with your instructor.

Application 2.   Taking notes from a sociology textbook

Directions: Apply the SQ3R study technique to the following chapter from a sociology textbook. As you read from heading to heading, take notes on a separate sheet of paper. You will be asked to use your notes later.

STEPHEN J. BAHR

CHOOSING A MATE

In recent years, mate selection has become more autonomous in many countries of the world. Increasingly young people have freedom to choose their mate without direct influence from their parents. Social conditions in many countries in Asia and Africa are changing to allow greater choice in mate selection (Murstein, 1980). For example, in the Soviet Union a large majority of marriages are love matches (Ferevedenstev, 1983). In China and Japan the number of arranged marriages is diminishing, particularly in urban areas (Engel, 1984).

In a system of free mate selection, what are the characteristics that influence the choice of mate? Why are two people attracted to each other and how does their relationship develop? Why do some relationships continue while others are terminated? These are age-old questions that are difficult to

---

answer. Nevertheless, romantic attraction is influenced by identifiable social characteristics. There are stages of progression that characterize the development of intimacy in many couples. In this section we will review what is known about the development of romantic relationships.

Homogamy theory

Perhaps the most common explanation for romantic attraction is the homogamy theory or "birds of a feather flock together." According to this theory we tend to be attracted to someone who is like ourselves.

A substantial amount of research is consistent with the theory of homogamy. Hill, Rubin, and Peplau (1979) studied 220 couples in the Northeast, 103 who had broken up and 117 who had stayed together. They found dating partners who were similar in age, educational plans, and intelligence were more likely to stay together. Differences in interests, backgrounds, sexual attitudes, and ideas about marriage were common reasons given for breakups.

People tend to marry others who are similar with regard to age, race, IQ, education, socioeconomic status, and religion (Murstein, 1980). There is also evidence that marriage partners tend to have similar interests, values, and personalities. Sternberg (1986) found that similarity is an important ingredient in the development of love relationships. People are more likely to develop relationships with and marry people who are similar to themselves, and they tend to be happier in those relationships than couples who are less similar.

Chambers, Christiansen, and Kunz (1983) found that similarity of physical features may also affect mate selection. They took pictures of both partners of newly married and engaged couples. Judges were asked to try to match couples and to consider facial features as well as general body build and coloring of hair, skin, and eyes. The judges were able to match couples much more frequently than would be expected by chance. Chambers *et al.* concluded that similar physical appearance is one factor in the formation of interpersonal relationships.

There are several possible ways that individuals may become similar physically to their spouses. It may be the result of a narcissistic tendency to marry someone like yourself. Perhaps people feel attracted to and choose someone who resembles a parent. Whatever the mechanism, their findings suggest that homogamy theory works not only for values and personality traits, but also for physical features.

Complementary need theory

Another explanation of mate choice is Winch's (1958) complementary need theory. Although Winch acknowledged that sociocultural characteristics may determine a field of eligibles, he maintained that complementary personality traits are a major determinant of romantic attraction. For example, Winch hypothesized that a person who is nurturant will be attracted to a person who needs to be nurtured. Similarly a strong, dominant personality may be attracted to one who is more submissive. The basic idea of Winch's theory is that two people will be more compatible and develop romantic attraction if they have complementary personality traits. Some have labeled this the opposites attract theory because the matching traits are on opposite ends of a continuum, that is, dominance and submissiveness.

Winch (1967) found some support for three different types of complementariness: (1) nurturance-receptiveness; (2) dominance-submissiveness; and (3) achievement-vicariousness. Kerckhoff and Davis (1962) found some evidence that complementary needs operated after initial homogamous filtering. However, in a number of other studies no support was found for complementary needs as a basis for mate selection (Murstein, 1980; Winch, 1967). Overall, there is little support for the idea that people are attracted to and marry someone with a complementary personality. In fact, the evidence suggests just the opposite, that we tend to be attracted to someone with personality characteristics similar to our own.

However, there is some evidence that individuals with feelings of personal inadequacy are more likely to be attracted to someone with complementary traits. For example, individuals high in self-acceptance tend to be similar to their spouses in personality whereas individuals with low self-acceptance tend to be less similar to their spouse (Murstein, 1980). This suggests that some people may seek a mate who compensates for their deficiencies.

Filter theory

Theories of homogamy and complementary needs are too simplistic, in that they do not adequately deal with the development of a relationship over time. Kerckhoff and Davis (1962) attempted to capture the dynamic nature of mate selection by combining homogamy and complementary needs into a two-stage process called the filter theory. They hypothesized that social similarity and value consensus are important early on, but that complementary needs are important later in the development of a relationship. According to their theory homogamy acts as an initial filter and couples who do not have similar social characteristics and values will tend to break up.

Dating partners with similar values will move to the second filter which is complementary needs. If they do not have complementary needs they will tend to break up, even if they have similar values. Thus, according to Kerckhoff and Davis, both value consensus and complementary needs are important for the development of a relationship.

The filter theory of Kerckhoff and Davis was important because it integrated homogamy and complementary need theories, and it viewed mate selection as an ongoing process. However research has not supported the complementary need aspect of Kerckhoff and Davis' theory (Murstein, 1980; Winch, 1967).

Stimulus-value-role theory

Murstein (1970, 1971, 1980) developed a process theory of mate selection called the stimulus-value-role theory. He maintains that attraction depends on the exchange of assets and liabilities that each person brings to the relationship.

In his theory three types of variables influence the relationship. In the *stimulus* stage, attraction is based on good looks, social skills, reputation, and mental abilities. Individuals are drawn to each other based on an equitable exchange of these characteristics. In the *value* stage couples assess their attitudes and values regarding marriage, sex, and life to determine if they are compatible.

The third stage is an assessment of *role compatibility*. It is an examination of how self and partner will perform in various marital roles, including provider, housekeeper, sexual partner, and child trainer. Each person has expectations regarding the various roles in marriage, and in this stage there is an assessment of how well they anticipate that their expectations will be met.

Research supports many aspects of the stimulus-value-role theory. Murstein (1980) found some support for thirty-three of thirty-nine hypotheses relevant to his theory. Partners who passed through the stimulus and value stages tended to be similar in physical attractiveness and values. Degree of perceived similarity was related to self-acceptance; those with high self-acceptance were more likely to perceive that their partner was like themselves. Individuals who successfully passed through all three stages were likely to cohabit or marry. Physical attractiveness, value similarity, role compatibility, self-acceptance, and sex drive were all found to be related to mate choice.

There was evidence of a bargaining process in which personal assets and liabilities are assessed and equity is sought. Murstein (1980) found that the degree of choice in mate selection depends on the number of personal assets and liabilities. Real choice occurs only among those with many interpersonal assets and few liabilities. In the bargaining, individuals with limited assets or many liabilities often settle for each other rather than really choosing each other.

There is some question about the exact sequence of the stages in the stimulus-value-role theory. Murstein (1980) acknowledged that the three sets of variables may all operate during the courtship process, although he maintained that each set of variables operated primarily at one stage.

Lewis' theory of premarital dyadic formation

Lewis (1972) reviewed existing literature on mate selection and identified six pair processes that he hypothesized operate in a fixed developmental sequence (called the theory of premarital dyadic formation). The first stage is the process of perceiving similarities. According to Lewis, perceived similarities is a necessary condition for further development of a relationship. When couples perceive that they are similar they tend to feel positive about each other and are likely to become more involved. If they perceive that they are dissimilar in values, interests, or personality they will probably discontinue the relationship. Thus, perceived similarity is important as a selection-rejection mechanism at the early stages of dating relationships.

The second stage of relationship development is the process of achieving pair rapport. In this stage there is an attempt to communicate and develop rapport with the other person. Unless people feel that they can talk to their dating partner the relationship will tend to be unsatisfying and will probably be dissolved. Ease of communication appears necessary for early dating relationships to continue.

The third process, according to Lewis, is the development of self-disclosure. After couples perceive that they are similar and develop some rapport, they tend to become more open and disclose themselves to each other. Self-disclosure tends to be reciprocal in that as one person discloses the other is more likely to disclose.

The fourth stage is the development of role taking. When people disclose themselves, others are able to understand their perspective and role take more accurately. Research has confirmed that role-taking accuracy is correlated with the stage of involvement in a relationship. Lewis suggests that role-taking accuracy operates as a selection-rejection mechanism at later stages of dyadic involvement. If one is not able to role take accurately or empathize with the other person, happiness will decrease and misunderstanding will result. On the other hand, if one feels that the other is able to empathize and see things from his or her point of view the relationship is more likely to continue and develop.

The fifth stage in the process is achieving interpersonal role fit. This is a process of fitting two personalities together. It includes identifying personality similarities and differences and the extent to which the two people will be able to work together. Adequate role fit depends on achieving some consensus on the division of roles. Perceiving how you and your potential partner will fit together in earning the money, making decisions about spending money, having and raising children, and caring for the house are all important role decisions. As a couple achieves a reasonable consensus on who performs various role tasks, they are more likely to stay together. Other research has shown that conflicts between role expectations and actual role performance influence marital satisfaction (Bahr, Chappell, and Leigh, 1983; Burr *et al.*, 1979; Rollins and Calligan, 1978).

The final stage in relationship development is the process of achieving dyadic crystallization. During this stage the two partners form an identity as a couple, establish boundaries with the outside world, and increase their commitment and involvement. They begin to function as a dyad and view things more in terms of we rather than me.

Lewis hypothesized that these six stages are sequential and that development of one stage does not occur until the previous stage is completed. That is, usually couple rapport will not be developed until the partners perceive that they are similar and self-disclosure tends to occur only after they develop some rapport. Self-disclosure is necessary before role taking will be accurate, and role-taking ability is needed to determine role fit. Only after two people perceive that they have role compatibility will they gain an identity as a couple.

Lewis' theory is consistent with much existing research and appears logical. Lewis (1973) tested his theory on ninety-one dating couples over a period of two years. The data supported the theory particularly for the middle stages of the model. Pair rapport affected development of self-disclosure, which influenced role-taking accuracy which was significantly related to later development of role fit. Although similarity of perception was not strongly related to pair rapport and role fit did not have a strong influence on dyadic crystallization, there was some support for both processes. Overall, Lewis found support for twenty-nine of thirty-five hypotheses derived from his theory.

The research of Shea and Adams (1984) supports Lewis' theory in that they found a positive relationship between self-disclosure and the development of romantic love. Hill *et al.* (1979) found that dating couples that did not break up tended to have similar values and role compatibility, findings that are consistent with the theories of both Lewis and Murstein.

Lewis' theory of premarital dyadic formation could be used in a variety of ways. His six stages might be useful in evaluating dating relationships. For example, one could determine the degree to which a given couple has completed the six processes. One would predict that dating couples who do not complete each process are more likely to break up than couples who do. One might counsel others not to become engaged or marry unless they have obtained a reasonable degree of self-disclosure, role-taking accuracy and role fit.

Examining these six processes might provide clues as to why a given relationship is not progressing or dissolves. Lack of development at one stage may explain why many dating couples break up, even though they may be compatible in many ways. Lewis' theory suggests that feelings of attraction depend on intimacy as well as on practical concerns such as division of labor and role fit. A pair may be very similar in social characteristics, but if they are not able to self-disclose, the relationship is likely to break up or be unhappy. Even if they have high self-disclosure and high role-taking accuracy, they are likely to run into difficulties if they do not have adequate role fit. Furthermore, psychological problems or inappropriate social skills may preclude adequate development at a given stage and lead to the breakup of a dating relationship. For example, a fear of intimacy or the inability to express individual feelings would inhibit the development of self-disclosure and role-taking accuracy.

The theory would predict that couples who have short courtships and do not establish all of these processes would have less happiness and a greater chance of divorce. Finally, the theory could be used to examine the marital dissolution process. It is possible that couples go through these six stages in reverse order during the process of alienation that precedes divorce. The extent to which alienation is a deterioration of these six processes needs to be explored.

Application 3.   Mapping textbook chapters

PART A

Directions: In Chapter 1, you read a chapter from a history book, "The Destruction of the Western Indians," pages 27–41. Using what you learned in **R³** about mapping, map the chapter about Indians on a separate sheet of paper. You will be asked to use your map later.

PART B

Directions: You have already taken notes on the selection "Choosing a Mate" that you read in Application 2, pages 83–88. Now, on a separate sheet of paper, map the chapter. You will be asked to use your map later.

Application 4.   Testing your note taking ability

Directions: Pick *one* of the following questions and answer it as directed.

1. Using only your map of the chapter "The Destruction of the Western Indians," answer the following question. When finished, attach the map you used to your answer and turn them in to your instructor.

   Question: Why did the U.S. government make and then break so many treaties with the Indians? Provide some examples of broken treaties.

2. Use either your notes or your map for the selection "Choosing a Mate" and answer the following question. When finished, attach your notes or map that you used to your answer and turn them in to your instructor.

   Question: Define the five theories which attempt to explain why we choose the mate we do and identify which one is most accepted. Explain the value of the theories.

Application 5.   Summarizing what you learned

Directions: On a separate sheet of paper, summarize what you have learned from reading this chapter (a) about yourself, (b) about skills you can apply to your study reading, and (c) any questions you still have that need answering. Turn this in when finished.

Reading essays

3

R¹   *Reading beyond words*

Directions: In the spaces below, write what you think the following quotation means:

A.   "Children enter school as question marks and leave as periods."—Neil Postman

_____

_____

_____

_____

_____

_____

Directions: The following is a quote from a graduation speech that actress Isabel Sanford ("The Jeffersons") gave at Emerson College in Boston. Summarize what she is saying in one sentence if you can.

B.   "I think the most important part of a college education isn't so much what you learn academically, but what you learn about life—and about yourself—during your four years at school. You grow up so much during that time. You enter college young, somewhat naïve and willing to learn. You leave four years later, older, wiser, and about $40,000 in debt. You have been through a lot."

_____

_____

_____

_____

R² *Reading actively*

A. Vocabulary preview

Directions: Below are some phrases that appear in the article you are about to read. Answer the questions about the italicized words as best you can.

1. "name a *contemporary* of the medieval poet Chaucer": What does *con-*

   temporary mean here? _____

   _____

   _____

2. "a *pronounced* inequality in the social structure": The word *pronounced* is not a verb here, but an adjective. What is it saying about inequality?

   _____

   _____

   _____

3. "people in *former* times": Does *former* mean before or after now?

   _____

4. "we read about *plunging* reading levels": Does *plunging* mean reading

   scores are going up or down? _____

5. "a problem that is becoming more and more *manifest*": Is this problem

   getting worse or better? _____

6. Use the dictionary entry to find a definition that best fits the italicized word in each phrase that follows:

en·dem·ic (ĕn-dĕm′ĭk) *adj.* Prevalent in or peculiar to a particular locality or people. [<Gk *endemios,* dwelling in a place.]

a. "The problem is *endemic* to private schools as well as public. . . ."

_____

im·pov·er·ish (ĭm-pŏv′ər-ish) *v.* **1.** To reduce to poverty. **2.** To deprive of natural richness or strength.—**im·pov′er·ish·ment** *n.*

b. "not confined to schools in *impoverished* communities"

_____

af·flu·ence (ăf′l̄oo-əns) *n.* Wealth; abundance. [<L *affluere,* to flow to.]—**af′flu·ent** *adj.*—**af′flu·ent·ly** *adv.*

c. "one of the most *affluent* areas"

_____

con·spic·u·ous (kən-spĭk′ȳoo-əs) *adj.* Prominent; remarkable. [<L *conspicere,* to look at closely, observe.]—**con·spic′u·ous·ly** *adv.*— **con·spic′u·ous·ness** *n.*

d. "make *conspicuous* use of them"

_____

ram·pant (răm′pənt) *adj.* **1.** Extending unchecked; unrestrained. **2.** *Heraldry.* Rearing on the left hind leg with the forelegs elevated, the right above the left, and usually with the head in profile. [< OF *ramper,* to climb.]

e. "Ignorance (not stupidity) is *rampant* on college campuses."

_____

B. Thought provokers

Directions: Answer the following questions in the spaces provided.

1. Do you think your last school did a good job preparing you for your education now? _____ Why? _____

   _____

   _____

   _____

2. Read the title of the article that follows. What distinction do you think the writer will make between ignorance and stupidity? _____

   _____

   _____

   _____

3. What do you think is the difference between ignorance and stupidity? Give some examples if you can. _____

   _____

   _____

   _____

4. What subjects do you think you know a great deal about? _____

   _____

   _____

   _____

C.   Reading practice

Directions: Read the article and answer the questions that follow.

BRUCE BAWER

IGNORANCE (NOT STUPIDITY) IS RAMPANT ON COLLEGE CAMPUSES

1   One day recently, a colleague of mine asked her undergraduate English class to name a contemporary of the medieval poet Chaucer. No one had an answer, except one student. His reply: Robert Frost. I was not amused. Perhaps I would have been if such students were the rare exception. But they are not. College students today, by and large, are amazingly lacking in important knowledge, and it's no laughing matter.

2   In my own English classes, ignorance (yes, ignorance—which is *not* the same as stupidity) becomes obvious during the discussions into which our reading leads. When we talked in one class about "A Modest Proposal" by Jonathan Swift, for example, it came out that all or most of the students were unaware that Ireland had ever been governed by England. This knowledge, far from being arcane, is vital to any attempt to make sense out of the present crisis in that part of the world. In another class, when we read "Shooting an Elephant" by George Orwell, nobody had the slightest idea where Burma was.

3   One time, the assigned reading was a piece by historian Bruce Catton comparing Ulysses S. Grant to Robert E. Lee. The class was confused by this passage:

4   "America was a land that was beginning all over again, dedicated to nothing much more complicated than the rather hazy belief that all men had equal rights and should have an equal chance in the world. In such a land Lee stood for the feeling that it was somehow of advantage to human society to have a pronounced inequality in the social structure."

5   After some discussion, the root of the confusion became apparent: My students could not understand that in 1865, some Americans did not consider it self-evident, as Thomas Jefferson did in 1776 and as we do today, that all human beings are created equal. I tried to explain to them that this indeed was the case, and was in fact a major cause of the Civil War, but they would have none of it. They simply had never known enough history to realize that people of different centuries often live by different philosophies. They were like those Renaissance artists who painted the Madonna

in 15th-century Venetian costume, innocent of the fact that people in former times had not always lived and thought exactly as they did.

6   Now, if I were dealing with simpletons, none of this would bother me profoundly. But my students are not simple-minded. Most get good marks in their major subjects, and many intend careers in medicine, engineering, law. Far from being "slow," they are intelligent, and on their way to becoming the "leaders of tomorrow." But they do not have the knowledge that a college student, let alone a leader, ought to have. Their minds are capable of understanding concepts and facts, but many concepts and facts that I consider vital to their becoming well-informed, responsible citizens have never been presented to them. They know their trigonometry and calculus, but they have never heard of Thoreau, and many aren't sure who came first, Lincoln or Washington. They score better than I ever could on a chemistry test, but return blank stares when I ask which countries the United States fought in World War I.

7   Why does this problem exist? Mainly because the primary and secondary schools have never done their jobs. We read nowadays about plunging reading levels and college-board scores, about people suing their high schools for failing to cure them of illiteracy; a while back, in a cover story, *Time* magazine examined teachers who are themselves too ignorant to teach, a problem that is becoming more and more manifest in the nation's schools. The problem is endemic to private schools as well as public, and is not confined to schools in impoverished communities. Indeed, most of the undereducated minds in my classes come from Long Island, one of the most affluent areas in the nation.

8   Placing the blame, unfortunately, doesn't remove the problem. And it *is* a problem, which makes teaching noticeably more difficult. Because my students are critically unaware of vital areas of knowledge, there are only two things I can discuss with them as a group, two areas to which I can turn for analogies and illustrations when trying to make a point in the classroom: rock music and TV.

9   When taking a test for a scholarship in high school, I wondered why there were questions probing my knowledge of art, music, literature, geography, history. It wasn't until I became a teacher that I learned why general knowledge was so important. The fact is simply that a student with a wide range of knowledge learns better. He does this not because he is brighter than someone without his range of knowledge, but because he has a context into which he can easily fit any new learning he acquires. The student who knows enough history to have some idea of the way people lived and thought at the time of the Civil War will have no trouble understanding and learning from Bruce Catton's remarks about Grant and Lee. A student who does not know anything about the Civil War except that it had something to do with slavery will be terribly confused by the same essay.

10   How can this problem of ignorance be solved? By starting at the source. As I have said, the roots of the problem lie much earlier than college—they lie in the first 10 to 15 years of a child's life, while his tastes and interests are being formed. It is up to the individual parent to influence these tastes and interests as positively as possible. For example, buy the kid a few books instead of a video game. Put a globe in his room and look at it with him

every now and then. Take him to a symphony concert so that he will be able to appreciate Mozart as well as Meatloaf when he grows up (*and* recognize the name). Walk him through the local museum on a Saturday afternoon. Keep an atlas, a dictionary, a history book, and a set of encyclopedias around the house, and make conspicuous use of them. Ration the TV. A little imagination on the part of a parent can go a long way toward helping a child learn: after pointing out Seurat's dots and Van Gogh's globs, for example, make a game of who-painted-this.

11   It is not the most systematic method of education, but it is, at present, the only way to keep the most advanced civilization on earth from producing the most inexcusably ignorant generation of college graduates in its history.

D.   Comprehension check

Directions: Answer the following questions. If you cannot answer a question, refer to the article to find the answer.

1. What is the essay about? _____

   _____

   _____

2. What is the main point or idea the author is making? _____

   _____

   _____

3. The author believes that some of his students are innocent of the fact that people in former times did not always think and live as they do today.

   a. True _____

   b. False, because _____

4. According to the author, most of his students these days are not simpletons, just "slow."

   a. True _____

   b. False, because _____

5. His students are

    a. college students.

    b. high school students.

    c. junior high school students.

    d. elementary school students.

    e. none of the above.

6. Who does the author accuse of not doing their jobs?

    a. students

    b. parents

    c. private schools

    d. primary and secondary schools

    e. all of the above

7. The author believes that students with a wide range of knowledge learn better.

    a. True, because _____

    b. False, because _____

8. What are the only two things the author can discuss with his students in order to make analogies and illustrations in the classroom? _____

    _____

9. What does the author say should be done to solve what he claims is a problem?

    a. Parents should start in the early years to form a child's tastes.

    b. Parents should buy their child some books instead of a video game.

    c. Parents should look at a globe with their child once in a while.

    d. Parents should take children to symphonies.

    e. All of the above.

10. We can assume the author feels that college graduates today are the most inexcusably ignorant in our history.

   a. True, because _____

   _____

   b. False, because _____

   _____

11. On a separate sheet of paper, (1) write a summary of the main points of the essay, and (2) explain why you agree or disagree with the author.

E.   Vocabulary check

Directions: Write the letter of the correct definition for the italicized words in the blank by the number.

_____   1. a *contemporary* of Mozart   a. preceding

_____   2. a *pronounced* pain   b. wealthy

_____   3. the *former* definition   c. strong; definite

_____   4. *plunging* neckline   d. going far down

_____   5. a *manifest* problem   e. noticeable

_____   6. an *endemic* belief   f. poor; poverty-stricken

_____   7. *impoverished* area   g. person living at the same time

_____   8. *affluent* society   h. excessive; too much

_____   9. *conspicuous* consumer   i. prevalent, widespread with a particular group

_____ 10. running *rampant*   j. evident

Check your answers by using a dictionary. Discuss your answers with your instructor.

R³   *Reading skills check*

A.   Essay organization

The first two chapters have dealt with methods for reading textbooks that deal with such subjects as history, sociology, psychology, and the like. In addition to such reading, many college courses use anthologies containing essays on various subjects. This chapter shows you how to approach such reading.

An *essay* is a short literary composition dealing with a single subject, usually written from a personal viewpoint. Most essays, if they could be drawn, would look something like this:

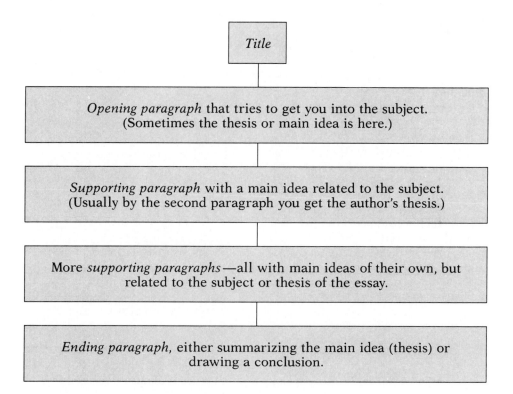

Title

Opening paragraph that tries to get you into the subject. (Sometimes the thesis or main idea is here.)

Supporting paragraph with a main idea related to the subject. (Usually by the second paragraph you get the author's thesis.)

More *supporting paragraphs*—all with main ideas of their own, but related to the subject or thesis of the essay.

Ending paragraph, either summarizing the main idea (thesis) or drawing a conclusion.

Here is a short essay. See if you can determine the subject of the essay and the author's thesis after reading just the title and the opening paragraph. As you read the essay, look at how it is structured as shown in the comments in the marginal boxes.

PASSIVE STUDENTS AND DULL TEACHERS

Title gives clue to subject.

1   Few people would argue that the quality of teaching and learning on college campuses is diminishing. This is not to say that there is no excellence in teaching occurring, but overall there seems to be a lack of concern on the part of many instructors as well as students with the type of education taking place.

1. *Opening paragraph* states thesis: Both students and teachers seem to show a lack of concern with quality in college teaching and learning. *Subject:* quality of education and learning.

2   Recently, a concerned group of educators was asked by the National Institute of Education to report on an agenda that would give directions for improvements in instruction in higher education. Their report, "Involvement in Learning," cites two major problems: passive students and dull instructors.

2. *Supporting paragraph:* Uses an actual study done on the problem to back up the thesis. Two problems cited.

3   Passive students were defined as "those who soak up lecture information and then spit back required bits of it on tests." However, this passivity is often created in students because that is the way many colleges run education.

3. *Supporting paragraph:* Defines passive students and gives one probable cause—the way colleges are run.

4   According to the report, a better way to teach would be to require discussions or even arguments with professors. "This would encourage students to engage more intensely in their own education, learning to feel confident about learning independently."

4. *Supporting paragraph:* Offers suggestion for improvement cited in the report.

5   There are major imperfections in the quality of teaching, according to the report. It is suggested that many scholarly experts may have knowledge of their subjects, but have no idea how to teach. Consequently, their lectures are dull. They are not skilled as teachers. Exposing teachers to methods courses on how to teach would help, but there is great resentment among some college faculty,

5. *Supporting paragraph:* Discusses what's wrong with teachers. Scholarly experts don't always know how to teach their subjects, and many don't want to learn how.

who tend to "look down their collective nose at methodology courses."

6   "The critical issue," says one member of the reporting committee, "is how to increase student involvement in learning. There is enough research around now that tells us that the more time and effort students invest in the learning process and the more intensely they engage in their own education, the greater will be the growth, achievement, and satisfaction with education and persistence in college." It is not enough to just educate oneself for a job; that type of education is too narrow. Students should be required to study some problem in the real world and be forced to bring the many academic disciplines they are learning to solve the problem. In addition, the report suggests that more liberal-arts courses should be required of students.

7   In order for things to change, the report states: "Taking education seriously is the student's responsibility as well as the educator's. We must expect that from our students, and we must expect it from ourselves."

6. *Supporting paragraph:* Discusses what's wrong with students—not enough involvement and the need to engage more intensely in their own education. —Should be required to apply academic disciplines to real problems. —Need for more courses in liberal arts.

7. *Ending paragraph:* Summarizes what is needed to solve the problem mentioned in thesis.

B.   The thesis vs. the subject

The main idea of an essay is called its *thesis*. A thesis is to an essay what a topic sentence is to a paragraph. When the subject of an essay is sports, its *thesis* is what the author says about sports. For instance, notice what the thesis is in this opening paragraph:

Many American universities are known more for the athletic teams they develop than for the level of education they instill in their students. Each year, colleges and universities drop hundreds of thousands of dollars apiece into their athletic programs. The problem is that they measure success by the number of games won and dollars earned in the box office. These standards have nothing to do with the business of education and offer nothing to the majority of students, making sports more important than education.

Notice that the subject of the essay will be college sports, but the author's thesis or main idea of the essay will be that universities are making sports more important than education. The author leads up to this thesis, the last sentence in the paragraph.

When reading an essay or a magazine article, always look for the thesis. Ask yourself, "What is it the author wants to say or prove about this subject?" Once you know the thesis, you can notice what supporting information or facts support the thesis. Often the thesis appears somewhere in the opening paragraph. Occasionally, it is the first sentence, but more often than not, the first paragraph leads up to the thesis and ends with the thesis statement. Sometimes the opening paragraph leads into the thesis, which appears in the second paragraph.

The following opening paragraph introduces us to the subject of the essay, then states the author's thesis in the last sentence.

> Parents, teachers, and other adults across the country have expressed alarm about several aspects of the influence of computers on children. Many are concerned about the violent content of some computer games, especially those in video arcades. Others fear that computing may become an addiction. Still others wonder whether too much computer use encourages withdrawal and an inactive life. But these fears are exaggerated. Children's love affairs with the computer are encouraging.

As we read the opening paragraph, we begin to see that the essay's subject or content will deal with children and computers. The thesis is that we need not fear harm will come to children if they spend time with computers. This is not to say the author is correct, only that this is what the author believes and will attempt to prove in his or her essay.

Here is an example of an opening paragraph with no thesis. It is from an essay entitled "Does Mother Know Best?" The subject of the essay is made clear, but not what the author feels about the subject.

> Children leave home early these days. It used to be that kids remained home until around age 6, when they were dropped at the schoolhouse door for their first day in the classroom. Not any more. By the time to-day's youngsters reach first grade, they have already spent one to three years in a classroom. Psychologists and educators have encouraged this movement, arguing that professionals can do a better job of instructing youngsters at school than amateurs can do at home. Now, however, two British researchers challenge this view. (Paul Chance, "Does Mother Know Best?" *Psychology Today*, August 1985, p. 10.)

Notice how the author describes what has been happening. Children are beginning to spend time in schools at an earlier age than in the past. While this change has been praised by some educators and psychologists, the view is now being challenged. We can assume from the last sentence that the content of the article will discuss the research that presents an opposite view of the ones currently held. We don't know the thesis, that is, how the author of the article feels about the two views. The thesis will probably come near the end of the essay.

Here is an example of an opening paragraph with the thesis stated in the second paragraph:

> Following in father's footsteps (and increasingly in mother's footsteps) is a well-established tradition in many fields, ranging from farming to bullfighting. Despite this, the prevailing view of such action is pessimistic. Sociologists in particular tend to view it as job immobility, and thus a serious social evil.
>
> Our interpretation, based on economic theory, is much more optimistic. Children are not necessarily stuck in their parents' profession, but may choose it freely to benefit from the knowledge and skill passed from one generation to the next. They are motivated by the valuable human capital from their parents. (Adapted from D. N. Laband and B. F. Lentz, "The Natural Choice," *Psychology Today*, August 1985, p. 37.)

In these opening sentences, the authors state in Paragraph 1 that most sociologists tend to view young people following in their parents' footsteps as bad. However, using their own research, the authors state in the first sentence of Paragraph 2 that they disagree—their thesis. We can assume the rest of their essay will show us why they feel as they do; in other words, they will develop their thesis.

Here is an example of a thesis becoming clear by the beginning of the second paragraph. This is the opening of an essay entitled "Turning Success into Failure."

> Vicky—beautiful, talented, very bright, voted "Most Likely to Succeed" in college—got a promising job with a large specialty store after graduation. Then, after two years without promotions, she was fired. She suffered a complete nervous breakdown. "It was panic," she told me later. "Everything has always gone so well for me that I had no experience in coping with rejection. I felt I was a failure."
>
> Vicky's reaction is an extreme example of a common phenomenon. In a society that places so much emphasis on "making it," we fail to recognize that what looks like failure may, in the long run, prove beneficial. When Vicky was able to think coolly about why she was fired, for example, she realized that she was simply not suited to a job dealing with people all the time. In her new position as a copy editor, she works independently, is happy and once again "successful." (Fredelle Maynard, "Turning Success into Failure," *Reader's Digest*, December 1977.)

The first paragraph is about a person named Vicky who felt like a failure. The point of the author is to give us an example of failure so that later, in the second paragraph, she can tell us that the example is part of a common phenomenon: "In a society that places so much emphasis on 'making it,' we fail to recognize that what looks like failure may, in the long run, prove beneficial." This, then, is her thesis, and as alert readers we can expect more examples of "failures" that turned into successes.

Sometimes the thesis appears at the end of an essay. An author generally waits to state the thesis if the readers need many examples and explanations before the main idea becomes clear. Also, special importance is sometimes gained when the thesis is left to be emphasized at the end. Sometimes the thesis is never stated directly, only suggested by the way the subject is treated.

Opening paragraphs

The opening paragraph to an essay is important. Always read the opening paragraph carefully because it leads you into the topic of the essay, sometimes contains the thesis or point of the essay, and gives you a clue to the author's writing style. Here are some opening paragraphs and questions. Check your answers with the comments that follow.

1. Here is an example of an opening paragraph that gets right to the point in the first sentence.

   The most important psychological discovery of this century is the discovery of the "self-image." Whether we realize it or not, each of us carries about with us a mental blueprint or picture of ourselves. It may be vague and ill-defined to our conscious gaze. But it is there, complete down to the last detail. This self-image is our own conception of the "sort of person I am. . . ." (Maxwell Maltz, *Psycho-Cybernetics*, Englewood Cliffs, N.J.: Prentice-Hall, 1960.)

   A. What is the thesis of the essay going to be? _____

   _____

   B. What are your clues? _____

   _____

   ✓ Compare your answers with these:
      A. The thesis is stated in the first sentence.
      B. The author's first sentence comes right to the point: "The most important . . . discovery . . . is the discovery of the 'self-image.'"

The rest of the sentences in the paragraph continue to say more about "self-image" and what it is. The paragraph is the defining type. We can guess that the rest of the essay will continue to discuss self-image.

2. Here is the opening paragraph from an essay entitled "Rx for Depression."

A young college student is constantly discouraged, irritable and unable to sleep. Frequent crying spells have ended, but she's still very unhappy. A middle-aged man has become increasingly indecisive in business affairs. He has strong feelings of worthlessness and guilt, and has lost interest in sex. An elderly woman complains of fatigue and lack of appetite. Her weight has been dropping steadily. Three different problems? Not really. These people—and millions like them—suffer from the most common mental ailment in the book: depression. (Maxine Abram, "Rx for Depression: Accentuate the Positive, Eliminate the Negative," *TWA Ambassador* magazine, January 1977.)

A. What is the essay going to be about? _____

_____

B. Can you tell what the thesis is? _____

_____

✓ Compare your answers with these:
   A. Basically, it will be about depression.
   B. If we connect the thesis with the title—"Rx for Depression"—we can guess the thesis will be that there are remedies (Rx) for depression, or that people do not need to suffer from depression, no matter what type it is. The three examples of depression could lead in to such a thesis. So far, however, we do not really know the thesis.

When reading (or writing) an essay, then, it is important to pay close attention to the opening paragraph or two. By connecting the content with the title, we can often learn what the essay is about and what its thesis is. Then we have our bearings as we read the rest of the essay, looking for the author's support of the thesis.

3. Another way to open an essay is to tell a little story. Here is an example.

> I have a patient, Arlene, who told me she waited anxiously all day to see her husband, Don, to share her exciting news: She had been promoted to senior editor at her publishing firm. When Don came home one hour late she "hit" him with, "Why were you late? Why don't you care? Why didn't you call?" She *thought* she was saying: "I'm so glad you're finally home. I'm relieved. I've been waiting all day to share with you." Instead, she sent out a negative message rather than a positive one. (Dr. Irene Kassorla, *Putting It All Together*, New York: Brut Productions, 1973, p. 53.)

A. What can you guess will be the subject of the essay? _____

_____

B. In what profession is the person writing the essay? _____

How can you tell? _____

_____

✓ Compare your answers with these:
  A. This type of opening paragraph does not get right to the point. However, the story of Arlene and Don is about Arlene's inability to send out a positive message to her husband. It is a good guess that the essay will deal with how we can communicate more positively.
  B. A doctor, because the story begins, "I have a patient," and probably a psychiatrist, because the story deals with emotional problems, not physical ones.

4. See if you can discover the subject and the thesis in these opening paragraphs from an article called "Educational Computing Comes Home."

> Michael Bernstein was not always a morning person. How many twelve-year-olds are? Now he's the early riser in the family, popping out of bed and perching before the computer before breakfast.
> Michael devotes some mornings to his science-fiction writing, or to one of his own fantasy games in progress. Other days, he creates original tunes, using a music-composition package. Depending on the day of the week, he may review his spelling lists, studying words he's not yet mastered as they flash on the computer screen. He polishes his school reports using a word processor. Last spring, he spent several morning hours putting the finishing touches on his Bar Mitzvah speech.

Like kids across the country, from elementary school to high school age, Michael has learned how to make the educational most of his computer. These kids and their families are pioneers, following new paths to learning in the home. (Sally Reed, "Educational Computing Comes Home," *Family Computing*, September 1985, p. 30.)

A. What is the subject of this essay? _____

_____

B. What is the point the author is making by describing what Michael

does? _____

_____

C. What is the author's thesis? _____

_____

✓ Compare your answers with these:
   A. Based on the title and on what Michael is doing on the computer at home, we can guess that the author wants to deal with the benefits of the computer for enhancing learning.
   B. It shows the variety of positive learning experiences that can be gained by using a computer at home.
   C. The computer is providing kids and families with a new way to enhance learning. Michael is used as an example of many family situations where the use of computers is becoming popular in the home for more than just fun.

When reading (or writing) an essay, we should pay close attention to the opening paragraph or the first two. By connecting title with content, we can often learn what the essay is about and what the thesis or author's viewpoint is. Then we have our bearings as we read the rest of the essay, looking for the author's support of the thesis.

C.   Vocabulary tip: key word parts

In Chapter 1 you saw how context clues help you figure out what unfamiliar words mean. Now we want to show you three key word parts—prefixes, roots, and suffixes—that also can help you grasp the meaning of unfamiliar words. *Prefixes* are letters or word elements with meanings of their own that are attached to the beginning of the base part of the word (root). *Suffixes* are letters or word elements that are attached to the end of a root word. By learning some key word parts, you can figure out what many unfamiliar words mean. For instance, if you ran across the word *anthropophobic*, you might panic. But look at the word again. You have heard of anthropology courses. Knowing that the prefix *anthropo-* signals that the word has something to do with "human" (anthropology is the study of human beings), and knowing that *phobia* means "fear," and knowing that the suffix *-ic* on the end of a word signals "of the nature of" (*angelic,* for example), you can figure out that an anthropophobic is "someone or something that fears people."

You already know many words that contain key word parts. Here are a few you probably know.

phonograph	(phono- = sound; -graph = record; write)
photograph	(photo- = light; -graph = record; write)
telegraph	(tele- = far; -graph = record; write)
biography	(bio- = life; -graphy = record; write)
bibliography	(biblio- = book; -graphy = record; write)

Once you learn some very basic key parts, you can begin to understand many unfamiliar words without having to look them up.

Below are some words ("Example" column) with key parts identified and defined (first prefixes, then roots, then suffixes). Look them over carefully. You cannot learn all of them now, but some you will know and some you will want to take time to learn over the next few weeks. In the column "Your Example," write in another word containing the word part. The first one has been done for you. After each list of key parts is a "Practice" section.

1.   Prefixes (key word parts at the beginning of words that change or modify their meaning)

Prefix	Meaning	Example	Your Example
anti-	against	antisocial	*antimissile*
bi-	two or twice	bimonthly	_____
circum-	around	circumference	_____
com-, con-	together or with	combine, connect	_____
contra-	against	contradict	_____
de-	down from	descend	_____

Prefix	Meaning	Example	Your Example
dis-	not	disapprove	_____
ex-	out of	extract	_____
il-	not	illegal	_____
im-	not	immovable	_____
in-	not	inactive	_____
in-	in or into	insert	_____
inter-	between	interrupt	_____
ir-	not	irregular	_____
mono-	one	monopoly	_____
post-	after	postpone	_____
pre-	before	prearranged	_____
pro-	for, in favor of	promote	_____
re-	back, again	return	_____
semi-	half	semicircle	_____
sub-	under	submerge	_____
super-	above	superwoman	_____
trans-	across	transport	_____
un-	not	unpopular	_____

PRACTICE 1

Directions: In the following sentences some words need the correct prefix for the words to make sense. Write the correct prefix from the list in the blanks.

1. The newspaper is published _____ weekly on Tuesdays and Thursdays.

2. Since she was caught cheating, she has become _____ popular with the coach.

3. It is _____ legal to park your car in front of a fire hydrant.

4. She leads a rather _____ active life and seldom goes anywhere.

5. The rock was _____ movable or required more strength than we had.

6. His _____ social behavior turned people away from him.

7. You should _____ pone your wedding plans until you are more certain of your feelings.

8. _____ arranged marriages are not as common today as they used to be; people want to choose their partners.

9. Do not be afraid to _____ dict someone if you are sure your information is more correct.

10. How many minutes can you hold your breath while your head is _____ merged in water?

   2.   Roots (base word parts that appear anywhere in a word to which prefixes and suffixes are added)

Root	Meaning	Example	Your Example
aqua	water	aquarium	_____
aud	hearing	audible	_____
auto	self	automatic	_____
bene	well, good	beneficial	_____
bio	life	autobiography	_____
chrono	time	chronology	_____
cred	belief	incredible	_____

Root	Meaning	Example	Your Example
dict	say	predict	_____
ego	self	egocentric	_____
frater	brother	fraternity	_____
geo	earth	geography	_____
graph, gram	write	autograph	_____
micro	small	microscope	_____
mort	death	immortal	_____
phob	fear	claustrophobia	_____
phon	sound	symphony	_____
poly	many	polygon	_____
port	carry	portable	_____
pot	strength or ability	potential	_____
pseud	false	pseudonym	_____
psych	soul or mind	psychology	_____
script, scribe	write	subscription	_____
sol	alone	solitude	_____
soror	sister	sorority	_____
tele	far	telephone	_____
vert	turn	convertible	_____

PRACTICE 2

Directions: In the following sentences some word roots have been left out. Fill in the blanks with roots from the list above so that the words make sense in context.

1. The music was so low it was in_____ible, and only a few people could hear it.

2. She has studied _____ graphy for years and knows much about earth formations.

3. She can take _____ ation as fast as you can speak.

4. The government could not trans _____ all the ammunition in just one shipment.

5. It has been proven that exercise is _____ ficial to your health.

6. _____ centric people often ignore the needs of others.

7. I wanted my mother to buy a _____ able TV set.

8. She's just a beginner, but the experts say she has great _____ ential to become a tennis pro.

9. Some writers choose not to use their real names; they use _____ onyms.

10. _____ ologists have many different theories to explain why we behave the way we do.

3. Suffixes (key word parts that appear at the end of words that serve to form new words or correct word form)

Most English suffixes add little meaning to words. Their main function is to show that a word belongs to a certain word class, such as nouns, verbs, or adjectives. By adding or changing a suffix, we use a word differently and change its position in a sentence. For example:

This class may be *different* from that one. (adjective)
There may be a *difference* between this class and that one. (noun)
This class may *differ* from that one. (verb)
This class may be taught *differently* from that one. (adverb)

A child *depends* on parents for security. (verb)
Growing older, the child becomes less *dependent* on them. (adjective)
After childhood too much *dependence* on parents is not healthy. (noun)

Usually a suffix is associated with just one word class, but there are exceptions. For example, -ent is an adjective suffix (he is a dependent person) and a noun suffix (he is my dependent).

Study the following noun, verb, adjective, and adverb suffixes.

Noun Suffix	Meaning	Example	Your Example
-al		renewal	_____
-ance, -ence		importance	_____
-cy		infancy	_____
-ness	state of	happiness	_____
-tion, -ion, sion		tension	_____
-ment		government	_____
-ty		certainty	_____
-ology	study of	psychology	_____
-ism	doctrine of	patriotism	_____
-er, -ar, -or	one who	employer	_____
-ist		artist	_____

Verb Suffix	Meaning	Example	Your Example
-ate		create	_____
-en	make or cause to happen	lengthen	_____
-ify		purify	_____
-ize		organize	_____

Adjective Suffix	Meaning	Example	Your Example
-able, -ible	capable of	enjoyable	_____
-ant, -ent		pleasant	_____
-ish	having nature of	childish	_____
-ive		responsive	_____

Adjective Suffix	**Meaning**	**Example**	**Your Example**
-ly	⎫	lively	_____
-ous	⎬ having nature of	ridiculous	_____
-y	⎭	dusty	_____
-ful	full of	thankful	_____
-less	without	weightless	_____

Adverb Suffix	**Meaning**	**Example**	**Your Example**
-ly	in a certain manner	slowly	_____

PRACTICE 3

Directions: Checking the list of noun suffixes, change each word below to a noun.

1. acquaint _____

2. dark _____

3. frequent _____
   (drop *t*)

4. broil _____

5. skeptic _____

Directions: Checking the list of verb suffixes, change each word or word part below to a verb.

6. elev _____

7. magnet _____

8. threat _____

9. solid _____

10. elimin _____

Directions: Checking the list of adjective suffixes, change each word or word part below to an adjective.

11. outland _____

12. pore _____
(drop *e*)

13. persist _____

14. wind _____

15. assert _____

Directions: Change the words in parentheses to adverbs.

16. (Quiet) _____ the burglar removed the jewelry from the

dresser and then (quick) _____ he jumped out the window.

17. "Don't speak to me so (angry) _____," he frowned (sad)

_____.

R⁴   *Reading applications*

Application 1.   Practicing what you learned: "The Lure of Learning," by William J. Bennett

Directions: Read the following essay by the former U.S. Secretary of Education. As you read, make a distinction between the subject and the thesis of the essay by understanding what Bennett means by "the lure of learning."

WILLIAM J. BENNETT

THE LURE OF LEARNING

1   When I arrived at college as a freshman some time ago, I had definite ideas about how I wanted to use my four years of higher education. I wanted to major in English because I wanted to become sophisticated. I wanted to become sophisticated because I wanted to land a good job and make big money. But because of my college's course requirements, I found myself in an introductory philosophy class, confronted by Plato's *Republic* and a remarkable professor who knew how to make the text come alive. It seemed to me and many of my fellow classmates as if we had come face to face with a reincarnation of Socrates himself. Before we knew it, we were ensnared by the power of a 2,000-year-old dialogue. In our posture of youthful cynicism and arrogance, we at first resisted the idea that the question of justice should really occupy our time. But something happened to us that semester as we fought our way through the *Republic*, arguing about notions of right and wrong. Along the way, our insides were shaken up a little bit. Without quite knowing it, we had committed ourselves to the serious enterprise of raising and wrestling with questions. And once caught up in that enterprise, there was no turning back. We had met up with a great text and a great teacher; they had taken us, and we were theirs.

2   Every student is entitled to that kind of experience at college. And if I could make one request of future undergraduates, it would be that they open the door to that possibility. College should shake you up a little, get you breathing, quicken your senses and animate a conscious examination of life's enduring questions. Know thyself, Socrates said. Higher education worthy of the name aspires to nothing less than the wisdom of that dictum.

3   A college is many things. It is a collection of dormitories, libraries, social clubs, incorrigibly terrible cafeterias. But above all, it is a faculty. It used to be said, when this country was much younger, that a log lying on the side of the road with a student sitting on one end and a professor on the other was a university.

4   That essence has not changed. It is the relationship between teachers and their students that gives a campus its own special genius. "Like a contagious disease, almost," William James wrote, "spiritual life passes from man to man by contact." Above all, a student should look for—and expect to find—professors who can bring to life the subject at hand.

5   What else should students find at college? They should discover great works that tell us how men and women of our own and other civilizations have grappled with life's relentless questions: What should be loved? What deserves to be defended? What is noble and what is base? As Montaigne wrote, a student should have the chance to learn "what valor, temperance, and justice are; the difference between ambition and greed, loyalty and servitude, liberty and license; and the marks of true and solid contentment."

This means, first of all, that students should find wide exposure to all the major disciplines—history, science, literature, mathematics and foreign language. And it means that they should be introduced to the best that has been thought and written in every discipline.

6   College is, for many, a once-in-a-lifetime chance to discover our civilization's greatest achievements and lasting visions. There are many great books, discoveries and deeds that record those achievements in unequaled fashion. There are many more that do not. A good college will sort the great texts and important ideas from the run-of-the-mill and offer the best to its students. And that offering will be the institution's vision of a truly educated person.

7   All students have different notions about where they want a college degree to take them. For some, it is law school or journalism. For others, it's public service. That's fine. College *should* be a road to your ambitions. But every student should take the time to tread the ground outside his or her major, and to spend some time in the company of the great travelers who have come before.

8   Why? Put simply, because they can help you lead a better and perhaps happier life. If we give time to studying how men and women of the past have dealt with life's enduring problems, then we will be better prepared when those same problems come our way. We may be a little less surprised to find treachery at work in the world about us, a little less startled by unselfish devotion, a little readier to believe in the capacity of the human mind.

9   And what does that do for a future career? As Hamlet said, "readiness is all." In the end, the problems we face during the course of a career are the same kind that we face in the general course of life. If you want to be a corporate executive, how can you learn about not missing the right opportunities? One way is to read "Hamlet." Do you want to learn about the dangers of overweening ambition? Read "Macbeth." Want to know the pitfalls of playing around on the job? Read "Antony and Cleopatra." The importance of fulfilling the responsibilities entrusted to leadership? Read "King Lear."

10   Even in the modern world, it is still that peculiar mix of literature, science, history, math, philosophy and language that can help mature minds come to grips with the age-old issues, the problems that transverse every plane of life. Students who bring to college the willingness to seek out those issues, to enliven the spirit and broaden the mind, will be more likely to profit in any endeavor.

Now answer these questions:

1. Which of the following best states the *subject* of the essay?

    a. types of learning in college

    b. college learning and theory

    c. teacher-student relationships

    d. getting the most from college

    e. all of the above

2. What is the *thesis* of the essay?

_____

_____

3. In what paragraph is the thesis best stated? _____

4. Do you agree with the author's thesis? _____ Why? _____

_____

_____

5. Why are you in college? _____

_____

_____

Application 2.   Applying what you learned

Directions: In the diagram below, fill in the blanks with a one-sentence statement of the main idea from each paragraph of "The Lure of Learning."

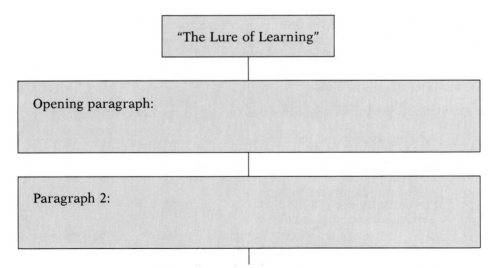

"The Lure of Learning"

Opening paragraph:

Paragraph 2:

Paragraph 3:

Paragraph 4:

Paragraph 5:

Paragraph 6:

Paragraph 7:

Paragraph 8:

Paragraph 9:

Last Paragraph:

Application 3.   Reacting to what you read

Part A

Directions: The following essay, written by a 10th grade high-school student, appeared in the *Los Angeles Times*. Read it carefully, separating the subject from the thesis.

STANLEY THOMPSON, JR.

WHEN WE VALUE INTELLECTUAL PURSUITS, WE'LL BE RICHER

1   The education system in the United States is failing. Most well-informed people know this. Some say that government is at fault for not providing more funds to education programs. This is true; the government does not place a high enough priority on education. Others blame teachers for the schools' failure. Teachers may be partly to blame, but their fault is the least. The responsibility for learning lies with the student. So the real problem is in student attitude, and in American attitude in general.

2   Consider this: Who is most likely to win a popularity contest—a star athlete or a straight-A student? The answer is obvious—the star athlete. But why? There are countries in the world where education is treasured. I'm not saying that the straight-A student would necessarily win the contest in those countries, but he would run a close second.

3   The difference between the United States and those other countries is that American students lack a love of learning. They generally feel that being sent to school is done to them, not for them. It is this lack of love for education that impedes the progress of education. No matter how gifted the teacher, a student will not learn if he or she does not want to. There is not one student who is enthusiastic about learning who will do poorly in school. The reason is that an eager student will work with, not against, a teacher.

4   There is an attitude among students that teachers are supposed to make classes easy so that the student can pass them with a minimum of effort. If a test seems too hard, cheating is acceptable, they say, because they

shouldn't be expected to learn all that "unimportant stuff," like dates in history, or the codes for chemical elements.

5   Why are there very few students who treasure learning? Partly because American society projects the idea to young people that it is fine to be mediocre. Too many people are satisfied with being average; they feel that average is enough. There is no motivation to strive for excellence.

6   Even worse, there is a feeling that being in the pursuit of excellence is not normal, and those who engage in that pursuit are not normal. This attitude tells young people that they will not be socially accepted if they seek knowledge.

7   The United States is slipping as a political and economic power because every year there are fewer graduates from high school who have the drive to achieve excellence. Most, it seems, are content to find a quiet niche in life and stay there in silence and apathy. Those are the citizens who won't vote or take an interest in social issues. They are the ones who don't care to make a difference.

8   Another reason for our national deficit of sharp, determined minds is that many never took it into their hearts as children that the pursuit of excellence is the most worthwhile venture. It is easier to settle for C's than strive for A's. To give up rather than persevere. To flicker out instead of shining brightly.

9   How can the problem be solved? The answer is not simple. The only way to remedy our educational problems is to change the way people think about learning. That is a Herculean task indeed, for trying to reverse the negative course that we are on as a result of a collective lack of internal fire is like trying to reverse the spin of the Earth. The great inertia of the problem is overwhelming the forces trying to counteract it, and the problem keeps increasing. Each time a student chooses an easy class over a challenging one, or decides that a diploma is not worth the effort of staying in school, or settles for being ordinary in order to be accepted, the immensity of this problem grows greater. The need to confront it is urgent. Like an unrestrained object hurtling through space, the problem of mediocrity in education will be unstoppable, driving our nation down the path of self-destruction or other disastrous end.

10   I have painted a picture of an educational depression, a depression from which we might not return. I see a light, however, a beacon: It is shining from all the teachers who are determined to keep the darkness from engulfing us, from all the students who thirst for knowledge and dare to aim high, from all the little children only just starting their education, and from all those who envision a society where the extraordinary person, by today's standards, is unremarkable.

11   It is to these precious few that I plead: Make strong your light and dispel the great darkness. Fuel your mental fire with love of learning and use this fire to prove intellectual illumination and warmth to your neighbors. Make it your goal to defeat this ignorance that threatens a life we love. Dare to make a difference. Can we afford not to?

Now answer these questions:

1. Which of the following best states the *subject* of the essay?

    a. education in the United States

    b. the difference between education in the United States and other countries

    c. student attitudes

    d. student learning

    e. American society's attitudes toward learning

2. What is the *thesis* of the essay?

    _____

    _____

3. In what paragraph is the thesis best stated? _____

4. Do you agree with the author's thesis? _____ Why? _____

    _____

    _____

5. How would you describe your attitude toward learning? _____

    _____

    _____

Part B

Directions: Following are portions of two letters that were written to the editors of the *Los Angeles Times* in response to the student essay in Part A. Read them and answer the questions that follow.

Reaction 1
    As a retired teacher, I know that at my high school most students could get as good an education as they chose to. Too many of them just wanted to slide through—with the consent or indifference of their

parents. I hear our leaders pay lip service to the values of academic studies, but they often fail to put their money—or their trophies—where their mouths are.

   Sports and extracurricular stars get far more popularity, trophies, media coverage, and public recognition than academic achievers.—Thomas Riche, Torrance

Reaction 2

   The lovely lesson depressingly learned from the style and context of Thompson's piece is that the educational system produces dare-to-make-a-difference high school students who communicate with clunky cliches and grandiose terminology written in a classroom lacking an adequate lighting system. This student obviously made challenging educational choices and has tried not to settle for the ordinary. Yet, the medium chosen for his richness is an unconvincing tirade that communicates a concern for adult-approved babble rather than conveying meaningful experience in his own words.

   Perhaps *The Times* editors will dare to require the customary journalism standard of excellence in the next choice for contributions from clever 10th graders rather than accept the kiddy crap of a self-styled elitist.—Don R. Reynolds, Los Angeles

[Reactions to student essay appeared in *Los Angeles Times*, 26 Jan 1989, Section 2, p. 5.]

1. Do both reactions agree with the student Stanley Thompson, Jr.'s thesis?

   _____

   Explain. _____

   _____

   _____

2. What point is Response 1 making? _____

   _____

   _____

3. What point is Response 2 making? _____

   _____

   _____

Part C

Directions: On a separate sheet of paper, write your own letter to the editor in reaction to either the student essay or one of the letters the editors received.

Application 4.   Summarizing what you learned

Directions: On a separate sheet of paper, summarize what you have learned from reading this chapter (a) about yourself, (b) about skills you can apply to your reading of essays, and (c) any questions you still have that need answering. Turn this in to your instructor when finished.

Reading for main ideas

4

R¹   *Reading beyond words*

Here are some quotations for you to practice reading beyond words. Explain what you think each one means. Then on a separate sheet of paper, pick one statement and explain why you agree or disagree with it.

A. "You cannot teach a man anything. You can only help him discover it

within himself."—Galileo _____

_____

_____

_____

_____

B. "What concerns me is not the way things are, but rather the way people

think things are."—Epictetus _____

_____

_____

_____

_____

C. "Knowledge rests not upon truth alone, but on error also."—Carl Jung

_____

_____

_____

_____

D. "Seeing is believing. I wouldn't have seen it if I hadn't believed it."—Ashley

Brilliant _____

_____

_____

_____

_____

R²   *Reading actively*

A.   Vocabulary preview

Directions: Define the italicized words in the following statements. They will appear in the selection you are about to read.

Part A: Defining words in context

1. Many people are willing to accept being *mediocre* because they can't seem to muster the internal sense of pride and purpose which would allow them to be great.

   _____

2. His attitude *detracts* him from having a sense of purpose.

   _____

3. Successful people are those who have *transcended* their own egos, their need to "fit in."

   _____

4. Don't *opt* for the more secure road of just making a living.

   _____

Part B: Using the dictionary to define

5. They can't seem to *muster* the courage to be themselves.

   _____

   _____

   mus·ter (mus′tər) *v.* **1.** To summon or assemble (troops). **2.** To gather up: *muster up courage.* —**phrasal verbs. muster in.** To enlist (someone) in military service. **muster out.** To discharge (someone) from military service.—*n.* A gathering, esp. of troops, as for inspection or roll call.

6. Who is going to eliminate injustice and contribute to the *resolution* of our multitudinous social evils, if not you?

   _____

   _____

   res·o·lu·tion (rĕz′ə-lōo′shən) *n.* **1.** The quality of being resolute. **2. a.** Something that has been resolved. **b.** A formal statement of a decision voted, as by a legislature. **3.** A solving, as of a problem.

7. They opted for doing rather than *carping.*

   _____

   _____

   carp¹ (karp) *n.* an edible freshwater fish [<Med. Lat *carpa*, of Gmc. orig.]
   carp² (karp) *v.* To find fault and complain constantly. [<ON *karpa*, boast.]—**carp′er** *n.*

8. Conduct your life from a *perspective* of self-importance rather than indifference and routine.

   _____

   _____

   per·spec·tive (pər-spek′tiv) *n.* **1.** Any of various techniques for representing three-dimensional objects and depth relationships on a two-dimensional surface. **2.** The relationships of aspects of a subject to each other and to the whole: *a perspective of history.* **3.** Point of view. [<Lat. *perspicere*, to inspect.]

B. Thought provokers

Directions: Before reading the following essay, answer the following questions as honestly as you can.

1. Explain why you are, or will in the future be involved in ridding society of some of its problems, such as the homeless, political reforms, environ-

mental issues and the like? _____

_____

_____

_____

2. Do you believe you have the potential for greatness? _____

3. The title of the reading selection you are about to read is "Who? Me?"

What do you guess is the essay's subject? _____

_____

C. Reading practice

Directions: Carefully read the essay looking for the subject and the author's thesis or main idea about the subject.

WAYNE W. DYER

WHO? ME?

1   Many people fear their own potentiality and consequently settle for much less than what is satisfying and meaningful for them. They are willing to accept being mediocre because they can't seem to muster the internal

From The Sky's the Limit, *copyright by Wayne E. Dyer. Reprinted by permission of Simon & Schuster, Inc.*

sense of pride and purpose which would allow them to be great. Abraham Maslow called this the "Who? Me?" syndrome.

2   If you ask a child if he is going to be a great human being, he will often respond, "Who? Me?" When I talk to young people who are going into medicine, or law, or architecture, or any profession, I ask them about how great they are going to become. Will you be the doctor who comes up with the breakthrough for the cure of cancer? Will you become the attorney who fights for equal justice before the Supreme Court? Will you design the most important new building in the world? Will you end hunger on this planet? Will you be the greatest you which you can become in a certain chosen area? Almost always the answer is, "I just want to make a living; I don't want to change the world."

3   This very attitude is the thing which detracts from having a sense of purpose. If you are only making a living at what you do, going in to work because it is a job, it won't take very long before you'll feel empty inside and lack purpose in your life. If you are not going to solve the energy crisis, cure cancer, rid the world of hunger, eliminate injustice and generally contribute toward the resolution of our multitudinous social evils, then who is going to do it? I'll tell you who. It will be those people who have a sense of purpose in their lives. It will be the people who have transcended their own egos, their own need to be "fitting in," and have gone beyond what most people ever think about in their lives. Those people who are dedicated to making a difference, to making their own lives as well as those around them work at their highest levels, will be the doers with a sense of meaning in their lives. They will be busy, involved, excited and dedicated in what they are doing. Furthermore, they will operate on their inner signals, trusting themselves and conducting their lives from a perspective of importance rather than indifference and routine.

4   You can choose to be a part of the social problem or a resolver of the issues. It is up to you. You can lower your vision, keep yourself from having a self-image of greatness and opt for the more "secure" road of just making a living—and I guarantee you that you will never experience that sense of purpose which you want so desperately. You do not have to be a social reformer in order to feel fulfilled; you have to have an inner sense of doing things which really matter. And the words "really matter" translate to your own sense of fulfillment in making this world a better place for at least one other if not large numbers of others as well.

5   All of us have a potential for greatness within ourselves. Most of us never allow ourselves to think about it. It becomes threatening to be reminded of the need to take risks and become a doer rather than a talker. Consequently, you see people running away from their own greatness. You see a lot of defenses, and you see a whole lot of just plain "settling for less." The more you are inclined to "settle for less," the more you allow yourself to evade that sense of purpose.

6   People look at other human beings who have achieved greatness, and they marvel at their superiority. They view a Leonardo da Vinci, a Copernicus, an Alexander the Great, a Joan of Arc, a Socrates, a Lincoln, a Jonas Salk or a Madame Curie as a person who is superhuman. What we tend to forget is that Socrates and Leonardo had to wrestle with the very same thoughts,

doubts, anxieties and fears as you do. They were not superior people, they were human just like you, except that they were doers. They transcended their own "Who? Me?" attitudes and, instead, opted for being activists—for doing rather than carping. And eventually they became idolized.

7   It is useful for you to imagine yourself as Socrates, contemplating his philosophy as a human being and being willing to take the risks that went with going against the establishment. The times are different, but your humanity is the same as that of Socrates or any other human being who accomplished anything before you. The solution to your own lack of purpose is to allow yourself to feel and think in terms of your own personal greatness.

8   How do you feel around people whom you regard as superior? Do you choose to feel less than adequate around them? Do you quake at the thought of interacting with a great thinker? These kinds of attitudes are not uncommon when "average" people react to superachievers. But once again it gets back to your self-image, to how you elect to view yourself. If you compare yourself to a genius and see yourself as inferior, never allowing yourself to think in transcendent terms, then you will always stay inadequate in your own eyes. It's a vicious circle: any feelings of personal inadequacy which keep you immobilized are the ingredients which also keep you from feeling a sense of purpose in your own life.

9   Think big. Imagine yourself as great and fantastic, and you'll be giving yourself permission to achieve a sense of purpose that may have eluded you up until now. If you are running away from your own greatness and opting for routine and feelings of being a deficient person, then you are really fearing your own perfection as a human being. I discussed earlier the dynamic of allowing yourself to feel perfect and still be able to grow. It applies here as well. All of your personal put downs, your feelings of inadequacy, your willingness to "settle" for what you've become—these are the components of your overall feelings of a lack of real purpose in your life. In order to rid yourself of these feelings and to surpass your own dreams of greatness, you must look carefully at how you personally view all of life, including your own, on this planet.

D.   Comprehension check

Directions: Answer the following questions.

1. What is the *subject* of the essay?

   a. the potential for greatness

   b. being mediocre

   c. self-improvement

   d. changing the world

   e. fitting in

2. What is the author's *thesis?* _____

_____

_____

3. What does the author mean by "having a sense of purpose in life"? _____

_____

_____

4. How does the author define "doers"? _____

_____

_____

5. According to the author, you have to be a social reformer in order to be fulfilled.

    a. True, because _____

    b. False, because _____

6. The author assumes we all know why the following people achieved greatness. For what is each of the following well known?

    a. Socrates: _____

    b. Leonardo da Vinci: _____

    c. Copernicus: _____

    d. Jonas Salk: _____

    e. Madame Curie: _____

    f. Abraham Lincoln: _____

7. How does your self-image make you feel around people whom you regard as superior? _____

_____

8. Explain why you agree or disagree with what the author says. _____

_____

_____

E.   Vocabulary check

Directions: After each word or phrase below is the number of the paragraph where the word appears in the essay. Find each of the words below and define it as used in the essay.

1. mediocre (1) _____

2. muster (1) _____

3. syndrome (1) _____

4. detracts (3) _____

5. multitudinous (3) _____

6. inner signals (3) _____

7. opt (4) _____

8. evade (5) _____

9. carping (6) _____

10. against the establishment (7) _____

R³   *Reading skills check*

Before we can read beyond the words, we must make certain that we understand the main ideas in what we read. It does us little good to be critical or analytical if we don't understand the literal or basic level of comprehension. This section deals with recognizing the main ideas in paragraphs.

A.   Main ideas in topic sentences

As you probably know, a paragraph is a group of related sentences expressing one central idea. Usually, the main idea is expressed in what is called a *topic sentence*. A topic sentence is usually the most general statement in the paragraph. The rest of the sentences are more specific, providing details, descriptions, or explanations that support the main idea. More often than not, the topic sentence is the first one in a paragraph, but a topic sentence can appear anywhere. Some paragraphs have no topic sentence and, as readers, we have to infer or judge what the main idea is by examining the details presented in the paragraph.

Let's look at some paragraphs that have directly stated main ideas. Read the following example:

Topic sentence	Many of us impose unnecessary limitations upon ourselves. We say, or think, we can't do
Supporting details	something without really checking. We hold ourselves back when we could move ahead. We assume that certain good occupations are closed to us, when they're really not closed at all. We think we're Not OK when we're really just as good as the next person.

The topic sentence is the first. Each of the remaining sentences adds more specific detail to the key phrase, "unnecessary limitations." They explain that we think we are Not OK, we hold ourselves back unnecessarily, we automatically assume we cannot do certain things, and we close ourselves off from many possible careers. All of these are ways in which we limit ourselves.

Here is another paragraph in which the topic sentence is first.

Topic sentence	All [hot dogs] are labeled "All Meat Frankfurters," a deceptive practice which means absolutely nothing. Fat is cheaper to put into hot dogs
Supporting details	than meat. In 1950, 17 percent of the frankfurter was fat; today the fat content is up to 33 percent, and in some cases even 50 percent. In addition, there is 10 percent water and 5 percent cereal filler ("all meat?") and other debris. So "all meat" in reality means that the hog dog contains from 70 to 35 percent meat, and substandard meat at that. (Jeffrey Schrank, *Teaching Human Beings: 101 Subversive Activities in the Classroom*, Boston: Beacon Press, 1972.)

The first sentence is the most general statement. The rest of the paragraph adds statistics and reasons to show how the label "All Meat" is deceptive.

Read the following paragraph. Notice that the writer expresses the main idea in the last sentence.

> Many people find working under pressure or against deadlines highly stimulating, providing the motivation to do their best. And they rarely seem affected by bad stress reactions. To slow such "racehorses" down to the pace of a turtle would be as stressful as trying to make the turtle keep up with the horse. Yet others crumble when the crunch is on or the overload light flashes. Some take life's large and small obstacles in stride, regarding them as a challenge to succeed in spite of everything. Others

Example of the ways people respond to stress

> are upset by every unexpected turn of events, from a traffic delay to a serious illness in the family. Truly, different people act differently under stress.

Concluding topic sentence

In your own words, try writing the main idea of this paragraph in one

sentence. _____

_____

_____

The key, of course, is the word *different*. The paragraph gives examples of people acting differently under stress. Some are unaffected by it, others can't handle it. The main idea is stated most generally in the last sentence.

Read the following paragraph. Here the writer leads up to the topic sentence, which draws a conclusion. Again you may need to read the paragraph more than once to feel comfortable with it.

Details leading up to topic sentence

> (1) Most terminally ill patients say they wish not to be alone when they are approaching death. (2) They want access to people, not to feel cut off. (3) However, in many hospitals because of a lack of understanding of how to work with the dying and how to accept their own dying, nurses and doctors and technicians are often not available in any meaningful way to a dying patient. (4) Studies have shown that, not willfully, but because of our subtle psychological tendencies, the call-light of a terminal patient takes longer to be answered by the nursing staff than that of a patient whom the nurses sense they can "do something to help." (5)

Concluding topic sentence

> Therefore, at the time of our greatest hope for contact with life, we have the least opportunity. . . . (Stephen Levine, *A Gradual Awakening*, p. 152.)

Now that you have read the paragraph carefully, try writing the main

idea in your own words. _____

_____

_____

_____

Your answer should say something similar to "Dying people, who have a great need for company, are ignored more than other patients in hospitals." (You probably expressed this main idea using different words than we did. This difference illustrates a point brought out in this chapter—there are many ways to express the same idea.) The first two sentences explain that dying patients do not want to be alone. Sentences 3 and 4 show that hospital staffs often do not offer meaningful support to terminal patients. Sentence 5 is the most general, relating both ideas brought out in Sentences 1 to 4: At the time when we most need support, it is denied us.

PRACTICE 1

Directions: Put brackets [ ] around the topic sentences in the following paragraphs. Then write the main idea in your own words. Make sure you write a complete sentence. Some of these paragraphs are difficult and require more than one reading.

A.   Television is different from all other media. From cradle to grave it penetrates nearly every home in the land. Unlike newspapers and magazines, television does not require literacy. Unlike the movies, it runs continuously, and once purchased, costs almost nothing. Unlike radio, it can show as well as tell. Unlike the theater or movies, it does not require leaving your home. . . . (George Girbner and Larry Gross, "The Scary World of TV's Heavy Viewer," *Psychology Today*, April 1976.)

_____

_____

B.   We don't yet have a clear formulation of what disgust is, or how it arises. . . . We know it is in large part a product of culture. One culture's delicacies are another culture's disgusts. In the feast scene in *Indiana Jones and the Temple of Doom*, the royal diners are in culinary ecstasy while eating eyeballs, baby eels and monkey brains, while

Indiana Jones and his comrades are trying hard to suppress their gag reflexes. (Paul Rozin, *Psychology Today*, July 1985.)

C.   Our history comforts us while our newspaper headlines frighten. We are inspired by our historic heroes but confused by the murder of three leaders who stood before the world as bearers of American ideals. We are proud of our winning streak in wars but unable to understand the devastation of a tiny country on the other side of the world. We consider ourselves peaceful but are shocked to learn that we have a murder rate forty-eight times higher than comparable countries. We are taught that we are just and yet have continually violated the rights of blacks, chicanos, and Indians. We are the only country ever to drop an atomic bomb on human beings, and we now stockpile twenty tons of explosives for every pound of American flesh. We are frightened, confused, and susceptible to violence. (Jeffrey Schrank, *Teaching Human Beings: 101 Subversive Activities in the Classroom*, p. 70.)

D.   The fact that you have two sides to your brain is significant to your mind's growth; each side shows a peculiar preference for facilitating the ways you learn and think. *The left side (LH) tends to favor logical, rational, and analytical mind activity.* It moves step by step as it reasons to a conclusion. It can analyze a problem, take apart a machine, collect a grocery list, count change, match cloth textures and colors, spell words properly, call things by their names, and so on. *The right side (RH) tends to favor feeling, imagination, intuition, and other nonrational nonlogical mind activities.* With the right side, people discover their likes and dislikes, slip into daydreams, flow with music and art, dance, laugh, and experience a whole gamut of feelings. (Louis M. Savary and Margaret Ehlen Miller, *Mindways*, New York: Harper & Row, 1979, p. 2.)

E.   These two learning modes can also *cooperate and act together.* For instance, we tend to keep a more accurate count of checks written this month when we experienced the discomfort of an overdraft last month. We remember names better when we love the persons or places. The artist in all of us has probably enjoyed the right-mode sensation of working materials with our hands—clay, flowers, the words of a poem, the bits and pieces of life—and then afterward, using the left mode, putting a name to our handiwork or understanding its meaning. (Louis M. Savary and Margaret Ehlen Miller, *Mindways*, p. 4.)

_____

_____

Check your answers with your instructor.

B.   Implied main ideas

Now let us examine paragraphs that have implied main ideas. In such paragraphs the writer does not include a topic sentence, but by reading the details carefully, we should be able to *infer* or guess the main point.

Read the following paragraph.

During the course of this year, if you are anything like that nonexistent average American, you have consumed 100 pounds of utterly nonnutritional refined sugar, a pound of emulsifiers such as polysorbates and mono- and diglycerides, a half pound of gum arabic, sodium carboxymethylcellulose, and gelatin, and other additives that stabilize and thicken food, a dozen chemical colorings, large quantities of sodium benzoate, sorbic acid, ethyl formate, propylene oxide; ever-increasing amounts of butylated hydroxyanisole and butylated hydroxytoluene (check labels for BHA and BHT); nearly a pound of acidulants (60 percent of it is artificially produced citric acid); and pounds of flour lacking enough food value to sustain even a rat for three months. (Jeffrey Schrank, *Teaching Human Beings: 101 Subversive Activities in the Classroom*, p. 103.)

You can see that there is no one general statement that covers all of the details. Each sentence adds specific information that suggests the main idea. Even if you have never heard of these chemicals (let alone pronounced them), you should be able to guess the main idea of this paragraph. Try it:

_____

_____

If you wrote something like "The average American has a terrible diet," you were right. Clues in the paragraph are expressions such as "utterly nonnutritional" and "lacking enough food value to sustain even a rat. . . ."

PRACTICE 2

Directions: Read the following paragraphs and write what you infer is the main idea of each. You may need to read some paragraphs more than once. Do not give up if the main idea is not immediately apparent.

A.   To the orthodox Muslim our use of pork is revolting, and to the orthodox Hindu, the thought of eating beef is almost as horrifying as the thought of eating human flesh is to us. . . . East Africans find eggs nauseating, and Chinese students have sometimes become ill at seeing people drink milk. (Ina Corrinne Brown, *Understanding Other Cultures*, Englewood Cliffs, N.J.: Prentice-Hall, 1963.)

B.   More expensive than yachts, more clamorous than street parades, naturally grubbier than your average hobo, they rise at ungodly hours for the sole purpose of providing their parents a long day. In addition to encouraging dogs in the home and playing baseball, they keep far too many bad marriages going. They are permitted excessive holidays from school and spend perfectly good whiskey money on such fluff as dental work and bicycles. Even the Internal Revenue Service values the best of them at no more than $1000. The outraged reader is reminded that Howard Cosell, Spiro Agnew, and Jack the Ripper began as little kids: The obvious moral lesson is "Stomp 'em before they grow." (Larry L. King, "Un-American Peeves," in *Comprehension and Composition*, New York: Macmillan Publishing Co., 1980.)

C.   If the obese person eats bread it should be toasted. If it is toasted, only one slice at a time should be prepared, with the remainder of the loaf being returned to its storage place before eating, and the person should be sitting at the table when that slice of toast is eaten. Therefore in order to eat a second slice he would have to get up from the table, take the bread from its storage place, prepare a slice of toast, return the bread to its storage area, return to the table, sit, and eat the toast.

(Richard B. Stuart and Barbara Davis, quoted in Louis M. Savary and Margaret Ehlen Miller, *Mindways*, p. 75.)

_____

_____

_____

D.   There are societies in which love is regarded as a rare form of insanity. There are other societies which have no word for love except as a euphemism for sexual desire. There are still other societies which speak simply of sexual desire, and have no word for love in their language. (Snell Putney and Gail Putney, *The Adjusted American*, New York: Harper & Row, 1964.)

_____

_____

_____

PRACTICE 3

Directions: Some of the following paragraphs have topic sentences; the others have implied main ideas. After reading each paragraph, write in a complete sentence what the main idea is. If you find a topic sentence, bracket it.

A.   Dazzled by the magic of television, we tend to forget what we might have been doing without television. We might have read more, thought more, written more. We might have filled the hours with games like bridge or Scrabble. We might have played more musical instruments, spent more time outdoors, embroidered, knitted, whittled. We might also have consumed more spirits and drugs, to relieve boredom. What is certain is that we would have spent more time relating and learning to relate to other people. Without the instant smile at the touch of our dial, we would have felt more urgency about creating a more sociable environment for ourselves, and we would have worked harder to achieve it. (Carll Tucker, "Sociable Pong," *Saturday Review*, Nov. 26, 1977, p. 56.)

_____

_____

_____

B.   A major part of our self-image is shaped by the work we do. Consider how we describe ourselves: "I'm just a janitor." "I've just become a senior vice-president." "I'm only a housewife." "I'm not your everyday lawyer; I'm a public interest lawyer." "I don't have a job just now, but. . . ." Our friends and fellow workers, too, describe us in terms of our status in the labor market (realtor, compositor, wife of composer); it is what we do that draws their attention, not our roles as parents, lovers, joggers, or Yankee fans.

_____

_____

_____

C.   The quality that dominated Einstein's personality was a great and genuine modesty. When anyone contradicted him he thought it over, and if he found he was wrong he was delighted, because he felt that he had escaped from an error and that now he knew better. For the same reason he never hesitated to change his opinion when he found that he had made a mistake, and to say so.

_____

_____

_____

D.   Friends are the ones with whom we most naturally share our self-discoveries and experiences. With friends as partners in curiosity we need not be embarrassed if we don't know all the answers. In their presence, we can admit we've never heard of Prime Minister Urhu, or film producer Filanetti, or the Ballet Impromptu. In tight situations we can whisper a word into a friend's ear and get back the answer we need, or a supportive word to go ahead and ask the lecturer a question, tell a salesperson we don't want to buy anything, say to a teacher, "You're going too fast," and so forth. (Louis M. Savary and Margaret Ehlen Miller, *Mindways,* p. 48.)

_____

_____

_____

E.   You consider yourself odd at times; you accuse yourself of taking a road different from most people. You have to unlearn that. Gaze into the fire, into the clouds, and as soon as the inner voices begin to speak, surrender to them, don't ask first whether it's permitted or would please your teachers or father, or some god. You will ruin yourself if you do that. (Hermann Hesse, *Demian*, New York: Harper & Row, 1965.)

_____

_____

_____

F.   An Eskimo baby who was brought up by American parents would speak English, hate castor oil, and act like any other American child; and an American baby who was brought up by an Eskimo family would grow up to be a seal hunter, to like eating blubber, and to speak Eskimo. (Margaret Mead, *People and Places,* Cleveland: World Publishing, 1959.)

_____

_____

_____

G.   For people whose ideal of beauty is a bronze complexion in February, tanning parlors are sprouting faster than dandelions in May. Though no precise figures are available, tanning salons are raking in an estimated $300 million a year. At one of the trendiest, Hollywood's Uvasun, such celebrities as Liza Minnelli, Rod Stewart, Mariel Hemingway and even Mr. Tan himself, George Hamilton, spend upwards of $30 an hour to maintain their sunbaked looks. Less exclusive salons charge between $3 and $15 for half an hour in the synthetic sunlight. UVA Tan, located in an upscale Atlanta suburb, expanded two months ago from four tanning machines to eight, serves a free Continental breakfast in the mornings, and had customers lining up outside at 7 A.M. during January's sub-zero cold. ("Going for the Bronze," *Time,* Feb. 25, 1985, p. 34.)

_____

_____

_____

PRACTICE 4

Directions: Read the following essay and answer the questions as they appear.

ROGER VON OECHS

THE TOILET PAPER SHORTAGE

1   Several years ago, Johnny Carson made a joke on his television show that there was a toilet paper shortage in this country. He then went on to describe what some of the more dire consequences of this shortage might be. The implication of this joke was that the viewers had better go out and stock up on toilet paper right away or else they would have to face these consequences. The subject made for a good laugh, but there was in fact no toilet paper shortage at all. Within several days, however, a real shortage did develop. Because people thought there was a shortage, they went out and bought up all of the toilet paper they could find, and, as a result, they disrupted the normal flow of toilet paper distribution.

The best main idea of the paragraph is that
a. Johnny Carson joked about toilet paper on his show.
b. Johnny Carson caused a toilet paper shortage.
c. there was no toilet paper shortage.
d. people actually created a toilet paper shortage by believing one existed.

2   This serves as a good example of the self-fulfilling prophecy. This is the phenomenon whereby a person believes something to be true which is not, acts on that belief, and by his action causes the belief to become true. As you can see, the self-fulfilling prophecy is a case where the world of thought overlaps with the world of action. And it happens in all avenues of life.

The purpose of this paragraph is to
a. explain the example used in the previous paragraph.
b. define the term "self-fulfilling prophecy."
c. show that self-fulfilling prophecies occur in all walks of life.
d. all of the above.

3   Businessmen are quite familiar with self-fulfilling prophecies. In fact, the whole notion of business confidence is based on them. If a businessman thinks that the market is healthy (even though it may not be), he will invest money in it. This raises other people's confidence, and pretty soon the market will be healthy.

The main idea of this paragraph is that
a. businessmen use self-fulfilling prophecies for business gains.
b. businessmen are familiar with self-fulfilling prophecies.
c. self-fulfilling prophecies are healthy in the business world.
d. all of the above.

4   Educators are also aware of self-fulfilling prophecies. Several years ago, a teacher in New York was told that she had a class of gifted children, when in fact she had an ordinary class. As a result, she went out of her way to develop her students. She spent more time preparing her lessons and staying after class to give them ideas. The class, in turn, responded in a positive way, and scored higher than average on the same tests which had previously classified them as average. Because they were treated as gifted children, they performed as gifted children.

The main point of this paragraph is to
a. show how educators are aware of self-fulfilling prophecies.
b. give an example of a self-fulfilling prophecy at work in education.
c. give another example of self-fulfilling prophecies.
d. all of the above.

5   The same phenomenon is found in athletics. I've noticed that one of the chief differences between winners and losers in athletic competition is that the winners see themselves as winning and losers generally give themselves a reason or an excuse to lose. A person who exemplifies this is Bob Hopper, a college swimming teammate of mine at Ohio State in the mid-1960's. Bob was an NCAA champion who rarely lost a race. One day at the pool, I asked him why he won all of his races. He responded:

There are several reasons. First of all, my strokes are all well developed. Second, I work out hard. I always put in all of my yards. Third, I take good care of myself and eat right. But my top competitors generally do these three things as well. So the key difference between just "being good" and "winning" is my mental preparation before each meet.
Starting each day before the meet, I run the following movie through my mind. I see myself coming into the Natatorium, with three thousand cheering fans sitting in the stands and the lights reflecting off of the water. I see myself going up to the starting block, and my competitors on each side. I hear the gun go off, and can see myself diving into the pool and taking the first stroke of butterfly. I can feel myself pulling through, taking another stroke, and then another. I see myself coming to the wall, turning, and pushing off into the backstroke with a small lead. The lead gets bigger with my underwater pull. Then I push off into the breast stroke. That's my best stroke and that's where I really open it up. And then I bring it home in the freestyle. I see myself winning! I run this movie through my mind thirty-five or forty times before each meet. When it finally comes time to swim, I just get in and win.

Bob seems to be telling us that just thinking a particular thought can have an enormous impact on the world of action.

The main point of this paragraph is to
a. show how athletes are aware of self-fulfilling prophecies.
b. give an example of a self-fulfilling prophecy at work in athletics.
c. give another example of self-fulfilling prophecies.
d. all of the above.

C.   Vocabulary tip: signal words

As an aid to the reader, good writers use *signal words*. Signal words give readers a clue to whether they should speed up their reading, slow down, or pause to make certain they understand. These signal words actually give readers a thought signal. Because "reading beyond words" requires thinking as you read, signal words become important.

Knowing signal words is also helpful for listening to lectures. They can signal what is coming: a change, more of the same, or a concluding point. Listening for signal words helps keep your mind on the speaker and the direction the lecture is taking.

There are basically five groups of signal words. You probably know all of them as words, but perhaps you've never realized their important function in reading and listening. The five groups are (1) words that signal more of the same, (2) words that change direction of thought, (3) words that signal a summary is about to be made, (4) words that signal an order or sequence of events, and (5) words that signal cause and effect.

1.   *Words that signal more of the same*

When you see a word from the first group, you can continue reading rapidly without worrying about a completely new idea or thought coming. For instance, notice how the word *likewise* signals that more of the same is coming up.

> Shirley decided she would study her history tonight.
> Likewise, her friend Janet decided she would study history.

When you see the word *likewise,* you get a signal that whatever idea came before the word is going to be used again. There is no need to slow down your reading-thinking process. You can safely move on quickly. Here is another example:

> I think the movie ratings of G, PG, R, and X are silly; furthermore, I don't think they really prevent people from seeing the movies they choose.

In this sentence the word *furthermore* signals that the same general idea is going to continue; it also signals that more support will be given the original idea. We do not need to slow down.

Words that signal more of the same is coming:

and	furthermore	more than that
also	more	likewise
further	moreover	in addition
for instance	for example	

2. *Words that change the direction of thought*

When you see a word from the second group, you need to slow down. The author is signaling that a change is about to be made. Notice in the example below how the word *but* means "Slow down, a contrast in thought is coming."

I should have studied last night, but I went to the movies instead.

Two different thoughts are presented: first, what should have been done; and second, what actually was done. That small word *but* becomes a valuable reading signal. Here's another example:

Despite the fact that I didn't study, I passed the test.

Again notice that the word *despite* indicates that two thoughts are to be contrasted: first, what was not done; and second, that things turned out all right anyway. Words that change the direction of thought are:

although	however	on the contrary
but	in spite of	otherwise
despite	nevertheless	yet

3. *Words that signal a summary*

A third group of words signals that a conclusion or summary is about to be made.

Thus, I decided I was going to need to put in more time studying.

The word *thus* signals that what will follow is a "wrap-up," that a main point is about to be made. Here's another example:

Therefore, she should not report to work until we can identify what is causing her rash.

When we see the signal word *therefore*, we should be alert to the fact that the main point of whatever has been said before is about to be summarized. Words that signal a summary or conclusion is about to be made are:

as a result	finally	therefore
accordingly	last	thus
consequently	in conclusion	so
as a consequence	for these reasons	

4.   *Words that signal an order*

Some signal words help you keep ideas or points separated. Numbers such as *first, second,* and so on signal an order or sequence to help you keep the author's ideas ordered. Those signals are obvious, but there are others, as in this example of directions.

> *First,* open the book to the index. *Then,* find the listings for the letter *u.* *Next,* look for "utopia." *After this,* check for the page number listing.

Notice how the author uses signal words to give a step-by-step set of directions. Here are some signal words that help you keep order to ideas or steps:

first, second, third, and so on	then	after
and so forth	last	afterward
next	finally	before

5.   *Words that signal cause and effect*

One last set of signal words points to a cause-effect relationship.

> Because I felt good today, I swam a mile.

Feeling good was the cause, and swimming a mile was the effect. The order of thoughts can change:

> I swam a mile today because I felt good.

It doesn't matter where the word goes in the sentence. The point is that it often signals a cause-effect situation.

Sometimes some of the summary signal words listed in Group 3 are also signaling cause and effect. For example:

> As a result of calling the doctor on time, her leg was saved.
> As a result of his contact with many types of people, Gustavas Vassa became a forceful, self-educated man.

Here are some cause-effect signal words that can help you make sense of a sentence or paragraph:

as a result	for	thus
because	for this reason	so
consequently	therefore	

Notice that the last two words in Group 5 also appear in Group 3. Many signal words can give more than one kind of signal, but usually the context makes it immediately clear which signal is intended.

The *definitions* of the signal words in all five groups are not important, really. What is important is the signal they send to you as you read. If you react to them quickly, as you do a red, yellow, or green traffic light, your mind will automatically begin to see the organization of ideas behind the author's words.

EXERCISE 1

Directions: Using the five groups of signal words as a guide, circle any signal words in the following sentences.

1. It is really simple. First, make a list of what you want to do. Then, do it.

2. She wanted to prove her point. Consequently, she spent hours of research getting the information she needed.

3. Time ran out before I finished; however, I think I passed the test.

4. The critics wrote bad reviews of Jane's play. As a result, few people went to see it, and it folded in a month.

5. I need to study more. Furthermore, I think I'm going to need a tutor.

6. Because of the rain, we won't be able to have a picnic.

EXERCISE 2

Directions: Read the sentence and identify the kinds of signals.

1. He *then* took a small brush and painted the gaps the big brush had left.
   Then is used to signal:
   a. cause and effect   c. summary
   b. order   d. more of the same is coming

2. Kip wanted to resign; *however,* he still had four years to go. *However* is used to signal:
   a. more of the same   c. summary
   b. cause and effect   d. change in thought

3. *In conclusion,* no more absences will be tolerated. *In conclusion* signals:
   a. summary   c. order
   b. new thoughts   d. cause and effect

4. *For* without the money, you won't have enough for your ticket. *For* here signals:
   a. cause and effect   c. more of the same
   b. summary   d. order

EXERCISE 3

Directions: Circle the signal words in the following paragraph.

In summary, Commager states that there are at least six common characteristics of the American. First is his carelessness regarding manners, dress, food, education, and politics. Second, his generousness or openhandedness in giving to churches, schools, hospitals, and the like. Third is the American's self-indulgence regarding comfort and luxury. Still another characteristic is his sentimentality toward his children, his alma mater, his history. Fifth is his friendliness. And last is his quest for materialism.

A. Is this probably an opening, supporting, or concluding paragraph?

_____ How do you know? _____

_____

_____

_____

B. How many characteristics of the American are listed? _____

How does the author help separate each characteristic for you?

_____

_____

_____

_____

D.   Overlearning new words: a reminder

In Chapter 1 you learned how to make vocabulary flash cards for words and textbook terms you want to overlearn—words that are hard for you to remember but that would be valuable additions to your daily vocabulary or studying. This section is a reminder that it's a good idea. To make it work, you need to practice with your cards every day. Don't try to learn too many words at once. Start with one or two cards a day and make more if you can handle them. The main thing is that your vocabulary will not get much better unless you do something to help it along. We recommend the flash-card approach.

Take some time now to search through this chapter for words you feel you need to overlearn. Make flash cards for them and add them to your collection for further study.

R⁴   *Reading applications*

Application 1.   Practicing what you learned: "Winners, Losers, or Just (Crazy, Mixed-Up) Kids?" by Dan Wightman

Part A.   *Warming up*

Directions: The title of the essay you are about to read is "Winners, Losers, or Just (Crazy, Mixed-Up) Kids?" As a warm-up for reading, guess what you think the title means. What do you predict the author will tell you?

_____

_____

Part B.   *Reading practice*

Directions: Read the following essay applying the skills you've learned.

DAN WIGHTMAN

WINNERS, LOSERS, OR JUST (CRAZY, MIXED-UP) KIDS?

1   If I envied anyone in high school, it was the winners. You know who I mean. The ones who earned straight A's and scored high on their Scholastic Aptitude Tests. The attractive ones who smiled coyly, drove their own sport cars and flaunted those hard, smooth bodies that they kept tan the year round.

2   By contrast, my high-school friends were mostly losers. We spent a lot of time tuning cars and drinking beer. Our girlfriends were pale and frumpy, and we had more D's than B's on our report cards. After graduation, many of us went into the Army instead of to a university; two of us came back from Vietnam in coffins, three more on stretchers. On weekends, when we drank Colt 45 together in my father's battered Ford, we'd laughingly refer to ourselves as the "out crowd." But, unless we were thoroughly blotto, we never laughed hard when we said it. And I, for one, rarely got blotto when I was 16.

3   The reason I mention this is that last month 183 winners and losers from my Northern California high-school graduating class got together at a swank country club for a revealing 15-year reunion.

4   Predictably, only happy and successful people attended. Not there . . . was the former football player, turned policeman, who bilked his partner's widow out of a $3,000 insurance check. Or the squirrely kid from my art appreciation class who, at 17, shot and killed his father during an argument over whether the family dog should be fed inside or outside the house.

5   The strange thing, though, was that the people I once pegged as losers outnumbered the winners at this reunion by a visible margin. And, during a long session at the bar with my informative friend Paula, I got an earful about the messy lives of people I'd once envied, and the remarkable metamorphoses of people I'd once pitied.

6   Paula reported that Len, a former class officer, was now a lost soul in Colorado, hopelessly estranged from his charming wife. Tim, one of the sorriest students I'd ever known, was a successful sportswriter, at ease with himself.

7   Estelle, who was modestly attractive in her teens, was now a part-time stripper in the Midwest, working to support her young son. Connie, a former car-club "kitten," had become a sophisticated international flight attendant.

8   Paula told me that Gary, a college scholarship winner, was overweight, underemployed and morose. Ron, who had shown little flair for music, had become a symphony violinist.

9   Sipping a Piña Colada, I thought to myself how terribly mistaken my senior counselor had been when she told me that high-school performance indicates how one will fare later.

10   I looked at Paula, a high-school troublemaker with a naughty smile, whose outgoing personality and rebellious spirit had endeared her to

Dan Wightman, "Winners, Losers, or Just (Crazy, Mixed-Up) Kids." Appeared in the Los Angeles Times, *July 25, 1979. Reprinted by permission of the* Los Angeles Times.

me so long ago. Together, we once stole a teacher's grade book, changed some of our low marks, then dropped the book in the lost-and-found box. The savvy teacher never said a word about the incident, but at the end of the year, when report cards were issued, gave us the D's we deserved.

11   Now Paula was a housewife, a volunteer worker and the mother of two sons. She wore a marriage-encounter pin on her modest dress, and sat at the bar tippling Perrier on ice.

12   She shook her head when I reminded her of the grade-book escapade, and the sheepish look on her face reminded me how presumptuous it is to anticipate the lives of others.

13   It also got me thinking about my own life since high school—how I'd gradually shaken my loser's image, gotten through college, found a decent job, married wisely, and finally realized a speck of my potential.

14   I thought about numerous situations where I could have despaired, regressed, given up—and how I hadn't, though others had—and I wondered why I was different, and had more luck, less guilt.

"The past is fiction," wrote William Burroughs. And, although I don't subscribe to that philosophy entirely, the people I admire most today are those who overcome their mistakes, seize second chances and fight to pull themselves together, day after day.

16   Often they're the sort of people who leave high school with blotchy complexions, crummy work habits, fingernails bitten down to the quick. And of course they're bitterly unsure of themselves, and slow to make friends.

17   But they're also the ones who show up transformed at 15-year reunions, and the inference I draw is that the distinction between winners and losers is often slight and seldom crucial—and frequently overrated.

18   In high school, especially, many people are slow getting started. But, finding their stride, they quickly catch up, and in their prime often return to surprise and delight us—their lives so much richer than we'd ever imagined.

Part C.   Comprehension check

1. What is the thesis or main idea of the essay?

   _____

   _____

2. How does the author's definition of "winners" change during the course of the essay?

   _____

   _____

3. What do paragraphs 6, 7, and 8 have in common? What is their function in the essay?

_____

_____

4. In paragraph 15, William Burroughs is quoted as saying, "The past is fiction." What does this mean? Do you agree?

_____

_____

_____

_____

5. How do you see yourself, as a winner or a loser? Explain.

_____

_____

Application 2.   Applying what you learned

Directions: Read the following essay applying all the skills you have learned. Then answer the questions that follow.

MARTY TEITEL

ACTIVISM IN EVERYDAY LIFE

1   The latter half of the 20th century is a time of considerable strain and worry. We are continually exposed to information about possible wars, poisons in our air and food, the alarming decline of species diversity, the loss

Copyright by Marty Teitel. Reprinted by permission of the author.

of individual freedoms around the world, and any number of other modern terrors. Each of us must deal with all of this complex and unpleasant information in the midst of busy lives. But it is all so overwhelming, it is often difficult to know what to do.

2   Most of us do nothing.

3   Citizen activism declined through the 1970s and into the early '80s, due in part to the bewildering assault of social and environmental problems we must try to sort out, and in part to the high cost of admission: I believe a great many people are *concerned* about various problems but do not feel inclined to take major action by sitting down on railroad tracks, attending city council meetings, or inflicting an entirely new lifestyle on themselves and their families. So the question arises, how can we change things about our society without making radical alterations in our lifestyles? How can we integrate modest, low-key activism into our daily lives?

4   A story from the past may illustrate this point. In 1970 my family joined a food co-op. Named the Ecology Food Co-op, it was housed in a church basement, downstairs from our co-op day-care center. The families who made up the membership were required to work a certain number of hours each week to sustain the enterprise.

5   On our first "work day," we arrived with our toddler late in the day to join another couple with a young child in sweeping and scrubbing the co-op. Coming after our regular work day, the extra hours of labor in the damp basement seemed to be a kind of punishment.

6   After we were done, instead of driving home to an organic and nutritious supper, we decided to haul our cranky toddler to a local fast-food joint for hamburgers and fries: Our work for the Ecology Food Co-op had made us too tired, too late, and too discouraged to go home and soak our black beans. Instead we went out and bought greasy but supremely convenient dinners.

7   As we sat down, we discovered the other couple from our work crew wolfing down their own junk food. Everyone ate the meal in silence, staring at our plastic trays, humiliated at being discovered *en flagrante delicto* in mutual ecological sin.

8   For there to be significant changes made in democratic society, there usually needs to be a fairly large number of people who are working for that change. The higher the barriers are to becoming active, the fewer people there will be to get involved.

9   We soon dropped out of the Ecology Food Co-op, largely due to my stubborn refusal to work all day and chug home on the crowded commuter train in order to perform menial tasks in a damp church basement for the privilege of purchasing large sacks of odd-tasting grains and wrinkled organic tomatoes.

10   For political and social action to become broad-based rather than just the territory of "professional activists," the price of admission should be low enough to include as many of us as possible. We should each be able to do small things in our daily lives we know will work toward changing the world.

11   With the new era of activism that is finally beginning to well up, we should learn from our experiences in the past. Those people who will

dedicate their entire lives to making changes in society deserve our respect and our thanks. But we can also pay attention to those who care, but whose family responsibilities, economic conditions, or other factors make them unable to single-mindedly devote their lives to activism.

12   Nature achieves phenomenal changes not by a small number of drastic changes but by a great number of tiny changes applied over time. Eventually, nature patiently builds a person from the genes of a plankton, a soft beach from quartz boulders, a star from grains of dust. This is a good model for us to remember as we rush to find "the answer" that will change the world overnight.

13   For example, one issue I have been very concerned about recently is the dramatic decline in the number of species on our planet—the reduction in the size of our gene pool. Diversity in nature is a prerequisite to survival. One example of this problem is that while there are scores and perhaps hundreds of species of chickens, 95 percent of the people in the United States get their eggs from one kind of chicken. If a disease appeared to which that particular strain of bird had no resistance, we would be out of eggs overnight. And those egg-laying chickens are raised by just nine huge chicken producers, so the chances of such a catastrophe are real: All our eggs are literally in one (genetic) basket.

14   I've been thinking of things that people could do about this problem of declining genetic diversity without quitting their jobs to hold 24-hour-a-day vigils outside chicken farms. Because every one of us eats, we all come into immediate contact with the problem. Consequently each of us can do something about it in the normal, natural course of our daily lives. This is true as well for many other issues on which we can make a difference in small ways, including obvious things like lessening air pollution by walking to work or combatting pesticide pollution by growing your own vegetables.

15   The problem of a declining egg gene pool, for instance, can be addressed simply by buying brown eggs. Inside the shell white and brown eggs are the same—the only difference is in packaging. If a fair number of people make that small adjustment in their lives, buying brown eggs, they will drastically alter the gene pool since the White Leghorn hens that produce most of our eggs just cannot lay anything but white eggs; we will have created a new market that justifies farmers keeping another breed to produce brown eggs. Then at least we'll have two major breeds of chickens producing eggs in this country instead of one. That's not a huge change in the gene pool or in the world, but would you rather sail on a ship with one lifeboat or two? This is just one small example that illustrates how significant acts can be done simply and easily by any person.

16   The few brave activists who risk everything to point the way, whether the Berrigans in the '60s or Brian Wilson in the '80s, deserve our attention and our respect. But there is much that ordinary people, in the natural course of their everyday lives, can do to have an effect on the world's problems. What is needed is some creativity and some recognition of the power of modest action. What will result, as greater and greater numbers of people begin to take gentle action, is the deep and lasting change in our world that we activists of the '60s hoped for but have not yet achieved.

1. What does the author mean by the title? "Activism in Everyday Life"?

   _____

   _____

2. What point is made by the author's use of the story about joining the co-op then dropping out?

   _____

   _____

3. How does the analogy in paragraph 12 about the way nature works fit in with the thesis of the essay?

   _____

   _____

4. Based on its contextual use in paragraph 7, what does *en flagrante delicto* mean?

   _____

   _____

5. Explain why this essay has or has not convinced you to buy brown eggs.

   _____

   _____

   _____

   _____

6. Give your own example of one thing we might all do that would help what the author calls "our assault on social and environmental problems."

   _____

   _____

   _____

   _____

Application 3.   Suggestions for writing and discussion

1. What common theme or subject do the three essays in this chapter have? ["Who? Me?", "Winners, Losers, or Just (Crazy, Mixed-Up) Kids?", "Activism in Everyday Life"]

2. Were you a winner or a loser in high school? Why do you think so?

3. Imagine yourself at a high school reunion in 15 years. How might you be surprised? How might you surprise others?

4. What difference or change would you like to make in the world? Why? Is your desire possible?

Application 4.   Summarizing what you learned

Directions: On a separate sheet of paper, summarize what you have learned from reading this chapter (a) about yourself, (b) about skills you can apply to your reading, and (c) any questions you still have that need answering. Turn this in to your instructor when finished.

Using Writing Patterns to Find Main Ideas

5

R¹   *Reading beyond words*

Try reading beyond words by explaining the following quotations and cartoon:

1. "To be nobody-but-yourself in a world which is doing its best, night and day, to make you everybody else means to fight the hardest battle which any human being can fight; and never stop fighting."
—e.e. cummings

_____

_____

_____

_____

2. "Home—the place where, when you have to go there, they have to let you in."—Robert Frost

_____

_____

_____

_____

3. "The family you come from isn't as important as the family you're going to have."—Ring Lardner

_____

_____

_____

_____

4. "A society which promotes the ownership of firearms, women, and children; which makes homes men's castles; and which sanctions societal and interpersonal violence in the forms of wars, athletic contests, and

mass media fiction (and news) should not be surprised to find violence in its homes."—Norman Denzin

_____

_____

_____

_____

5.

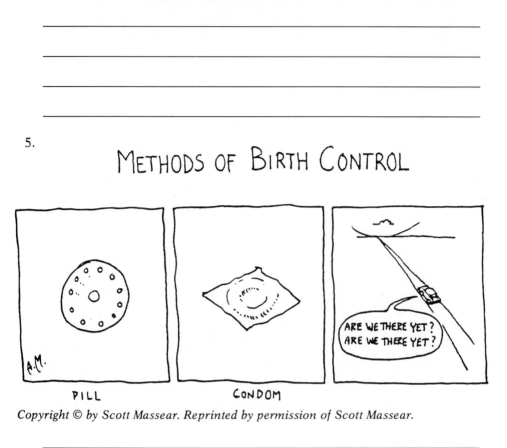

Copyright © by Scott Massear. Reprinted by permission of Scott Massear.

_____

_____

_____

_____

R² *Reading actively*

Before reading the following selection from a textbook for a class on marriage and family, do the following vocabulary preview and thought provokers as a warm-up.

A. Vocabulary preview

Directions: The following words will appear in the chapter you are about to read. Explain the meaning of the italicized words as they are used in the sentences below. If any words are unfamiliar to you, add them to your vocabulary.

Using context clues:

1. It is part of the natural *backdrop* of our lives. _____

   _____

2. The family dates back to prehistoric times when our *hominid* ancestors

   developed the original family unit. _____

   _____

3. We tend to think in terms of the *nuclear family*—the two-parent family

   with children. _____

   _____

4. Some women prefer to defer childbearing or choose not to have children,

   giving themselves greater *autonomy.* _____

   _____

Using the dictionary:

5. Some family characteristics have endured for *millenia.*

   mil·len·ni·um (mi·len′e-əm) *n.,pl.* **·ums** or **ni·a** (-e-). **1.** A period of 1,000 years. **2.** In the New Testament, the thousand-year reign of Christ on earth. **3.** A hoped-for period of joy, prosperity, and peace. [<Lat. *mille*, thousand + Lat. *annus*, year.] **·mil·len′ni·al** (-len′e-əl) *adj.*

   _____

   _____

6. One of a variety of family forms that are emerging is the *egalitarian* marriage.

   e·gal·i·tar·i·an (i·gal′i·tar·e·ən) *adj.* Advocating political, economic, and legal equality for all. [<Lat. *aequalis*, equal.] ·**e·gal′i·tar′i·an** *n.* ·**e·gal′i·tar′i·an·ism** *n.*

   _____

   _____

7. It has to follow the normal course of *gestation*.

   ges·ta·tion (je·sta′shun) *n.* The period of carrying developing offspring in the uterus after conception; pregnancy. [<Lat. *gestare*, to bear.] ·**ges′tate** *v.* ·**ges·ta·′tion·al** *adj.*

   _____

   _____

8. Some procedures are driving a wedge into the previously *inviolate* connection between sex and reproduction.

   in·vi·o·late (in·vi′ə·lit) *adj.* Not violated or profaned; intact. ·**in·vi′o·late·ly** *adv.* ·**in·vi′o·late·ness** *n.*

   _____

   _____

B. Thought provokers

1. What do you think are the most important ingredients of a good marriage?

   _____

   _____

   _____

   _____

2. How would you define *family?*

_____

_____

_____

3. Do you take your family for granted? Explain.

_____

_____

_____

C.   Reading practice

Directions: The following selection is taken from the textbook *Marriage and the Family Experience.* Study-read it applying SQ3R and everything else you have learned so far.

BRYAN STRONG and CHRISTINE DEVAULT

THE MEANING OF MARRIAGE AND THE FAMILY

1   We generally take the family in which we grow up for granted. It is part of the natural backdrop of our lives. At various times, we may like or dislike our parents or siblings, fight with them, love them, ignore them; but the roles they play in our lives are generally invisible. We are usually not aware of them. This taken-for-granted quality of families is important. It exists when a family is more or less performing its functions. Only during a crisis—a severe illness, a sudden conflict, unemployment, divorce, or some other incapacitating event—do we notice the roles each person plays and recognize how vital our family and its members are to us.

2   The family dates back to prehistoric times when our hominid ancestors developed the original family unit. Although the family has evolved, it has maintained many of its original functions. It produces and socializes

children, acts as a unit of economic cooperation, gives us significant roles as children, husbands, wives, and parents, and provides a source of intimacy. Modern society, however, is altering many of these functions, taking over some of them from the family and making others more difficult to perform. Many of the most recent changes in marriage and the family—divorce, single-parent families, working mothers—are adjustments to our contemporary society. However, our culture tends to idealize the nuclear family—the two-parent family with children. Any variation on it is seen as a decline, instead of as an alternative family form. Furthermore, because we think in terms of the nuclear family, we fail to appreciate the rich network of kin—aunts, uncles, cousins, grandparents—that most of us have. It is within the complex web of family life that we gain our identities. Whatever our feelings about them, our families are responsible for much of who we are and who we will be.

3   The main characteristics of the family were developed in prehistoric times. The males hunted and defended territories while the women remained near home. Males and females bonded in love relationships and shared the same hearth. This pattern seems very familiar. Some males still like to think of themselves as hunters as they set forth to "bring home the bacon" in the form of a paycheck. These characteristics have endured for millennia.

4   Now, however, the family unit is undergoing fundamental alterations. The traditional nuclear family has become a minority family in contemporary America. Women no longer remain at home; they too go out to bring home the bacon, blurring the sexual division of labor and creating the dual-worker marriage. Similarly, women defer childbearing or choose

not to have children, creating the childless marriage and giving themselves greater autonomy. Divorce rates are high. The single-parent family, usually headed by a woman, is common. Yet these changes do not signify the end of the family. Rather, they are signs of its resiliency in the face of sweeping changes in American society. Families continue to carry out their functions.

The functions of the family

5   Marriage is a union between a man and a woman: they perform a public ritual (which means that their union is socially recognized), they are united sexually, and they cooperate in economic matters. The union is assumed to be more or less permanent. If they have children, their children will have certain legal rights. *Cohabitation* ("living together") may be similar to marriage in many of its functions and roles, but it does not have equivalent legal sanctions or rights.

6   A family has traditionally been defined as a married couple or group of adult kin who cooperate and divide labor along sex lines, rear children, and share a common dwelling place. A variety of family forms are emerging to challenge this definition: the single-parent family, egalitarian marriage, dual-worker marriage, and childless marriage, for example.

7   The family performs four important functions. First, it produces and socializes children. Second, it acts as a unit of economic cooperation. Third, it assigns status and social roles to individuals. Fourth, it provides a source of intimate relationships. Technology, industrialization, mobility, and other factors are altering the way the family performs its functions. While these are the basic functions that families are "supposed" to fulfill, families do

not necessarily fulfill them all nor always fulfill them well.

Reproduction and socialization

8   The family makes society possible by producing and rearing children to replace the older members of society as they die off. In the past reproduction resulted only through sexual intercourse between a man and a woman. Through marriage it became an essential function of the family. But even this domain has not remained immune to technological change. The development of techniques for artificial insemination has separated reproduction from sexual intercourse. In addition to permitting infertile couples to give birth, such techniques have also made it possible for homosexuals to become parents. In 1978, the first "test-tube" baby was born after an ovum was fertilized by sperm in a glass dish and then implanted in the mother's uterus to follow the normal course of gestation. Although such procedures are relatively rare, they may nevertheless become more widespread, driving a wedge into the previously inviolate connection between sex and reproduction.

9   Children are helpless and dependent for years following birth. They must learn how to walk and talk, how to take care of themselves, how to act, how to love, how to touch and be touched. Teaching the child how to be human and how to fit into his or her particular culture is one of the family's most important tasks. It is socialization, or what Virginia Satir (1972) calls "peoplemaking."

10   Traditionally, the family has been responsible for socialization. This role, however, is dramatically shifting away from the family. One researcher (Guidubaldi, 1980) believes that the increasing lack of commitment to childrearing may be one of the most significant societal changes in our lifetime. With the rise of compulsory education, the state has become responsible for a large share of socialization after a child reaches the age of five. The increase in working mothers has placed many infants, toddlers, and small children in day-care centers, reducing the family's role in socialization. As many as half of the children between the ages of three and five may be in nursery school, day care, or kindergarten. Even while children are at home, television rather than their family may be mainly rearing them. Watching television is the most important activity for most children up to age fourteen. So strong is the role of television in young children's lives that, according to one study of four- to six-year-olds, 44 percent said they preferred television to "daddy" (Federal Trade Commission, 1978).

D.   Comprehension check

Directions: Try not to look back for answers to the following questions.

1. According to the authors, it is a healthy sign when we take our families for granted.

a. True, because _____

_____

b. False, because _____

_____

2. The main characteristics of the family were developed in prehistoric times.

a. True, because _____

_____

b. False, because _____

_____

3. State three changes in the concept of family that are occurring in our

contemporary society. _____

_____

_____

4. What has happened to the idealized concept of the nuclear family? _____

_____

_____

5. In the "Thought provokers" section on page 165 you wrote a definition of family. How does it differ from the definition given in the reading selection?

_____

_____

6. How does the family make society possible? _____

_____

_____

7. Which of the following, according to the text, is the *most* important teaching function of the family?

   a. teaching children how to walk, talk, etc.

   b. teaching children how to be human and fit in to the culture

   c. teaching responsibility

   d. teaching sex education

   e. all of the above.

8. What problems are arising because of the change in family structure?

   _____

   _____

9. What, if any, information presented did you find useful or informative?

   _____

   _____

10. Do you believe there is a place in a college curriculum for courses on

    marriage and family? _____ Why? _____

    _____

    _____

E. Vocabulary check

Directions: After each word below is a number which refers to the paragraph in the reading selection where the word appears. In the blanks provided, write a definition of the words as they are used in context.

1. granted (1) _____

2. incapacitating (1) _____

3. network (2) _____

4. defer (5) _____

5. autonomy (5) _____

6. cohabitation (6) _____

7. egalitarian (7) _____

8. inviolate (9) _____

9. peoplemaking (10) _____

10. rearing (11) _____

R³ *Reading skills check*

A.   Finding main ideas through writing patterns

In Chapter 4, you learned about finding main ideas in paragraphs by looking for topic sentences or implied statements. This section discusses the more common types of writing patterns used by writers of textbooks and essays.

Many, though not all, writing passages fall into types or patterns. By examining the way a writer develops a passage, you can usually find the main idea in it. When you are having difficulty understanding what a writer is saying, it can be helpful to look for one of the following writing patterns:

1. passages that use examples, statistics, or anecdotes
2. passages that compare and/or contrast two or more ideas or subjects
3. passages that define terms
4. passages that show the effect of some cause or action
5. passages that combine two or more patterns

These patterns do not apply just to writing. We use these patterns unknowingly when we think and speak. For instance, if you are not being clear when speaking to someone, that person might say, "Can you be more specific?" Your reply might be to provide an example that would make what you are saying more clear. Or, that person might respond to what you are saying with, "So what?" Your response then might be to show the effect of an action or cause. If you use a word or phrase your listener doesn't know, you might have to provide a definition. If the person says, "Is it like. . . ," then you have to provide a comparison or show the contrast.

The point is that these writing patterns are not really new to you. Writers use these patterns because it is the way we think and organize our thoughts. Here are some examples of these patterns.

The use of examples

Writers often use statistics, anecdotes, research, or quotations of others as examples of the main idea they are trying to make. Usually, though not always, the writer will make a statement and then say, "For instance," "As an example," "To illustrate my point," or something similar. Such words are clues that the main idea has been made and that what is coming up is support of that point.

Notice how examples are used in this passage:

Topic sentence {

Supporting examples {

> Many family-like relationships exist that do not begin with a legal marriage ceremony. For example, some couples cohabit without legally marrying. They live together in an intimate relationship and share resources. A division of labor with rights and responsibilities is established and some bear and raise children. Recent court cases in the United States illustrate how cohabitation is becoming a social and legal relationship much like marriage.

Here the words "for example," and "illustrate" let you know that these are supporting the main idea stated in the first sentence: many family-like relationships exist without marriage.

Can you find the example used to support the main idea in the following passage?

> One of the major functions of the family is economic cooperation. Legally and socially, marriage is an economic partnership. Married couples are expected to pool their resources, share a household, and divide their labor. Much economic consumption occurs by family units. For example, houses and food are usually purchased by families and jointly shared. Money and property acquired during marriage are generally considered to be jointly owned and must be equitably distributed if divorce occurs. Unwillingness to contribute to the economic support of one's spouse is grounds for divorce in many jurisdictions. In divorce actions one spouse is often ordered by the court to give the other spouse money and property, which shows that marriage is defined by law as an economic partnership. [Stephen Bahr, *Family Interaction*]

As you can see, the main point the author is making is that marriage is an economic example to support this point.

The use of comparison and contrast

To compare means to show likenesses; to contrast means to show differences. Writers frequently compare and contrast two or more people, ideas, or actions. In such cases, you have to be able to sort out the likenesses and the differences being shown. Read the following paragraph and look for what is being compared and contrasted.

> A comparison of child rearing in Japan and the United States was recently done by Durrett *et al.* (1986). They compared thirty Caucasians and fifty-two Japanese mothers who had healthy firstborn infants who were three to four months old. Through interviews and observation they obtained an assessment of mother-child interaction and of mother's perception of emotional support received from her husband. Husbands were perceived to be more supportive, sensitive, cooperative, accepting, and respectful in America than in Japan. Among both Japanese and American mothers, the perception of support from their husbands influenced interaction with the infants. In both cultures, the more the mother perceived support from her husband, the more she was involved with her infant. Compared to the American mothers, the Japanese mothers emphasized responsibility more and were more likely to use personal appeals to teach principles to their children.

As you can see, the first sentence lets us know a comparison was made between child rearing in Japan and the United States in a study by Durrett, *et al.* in 1986. The second sentence provides us with the numbers of people involved and the age of the infants involved in the study. The third sentence narrows the study down to the "assessment of mother-child interaction and of mother's perception of emotional support received from her husband." From that point on, each sentence shows the similarities or differences in the perceptions of the mothers of the two cultures.

What is being compared or contrasted in the following passage?

> Some cultural groups are peaceful; others are warlike. In some cultures, violent solutions of conflicts are common; in others, they are rare. For some groups, killing is a sin; for others, it is a virtue. The enormous variations in the level of violence between societies underline the importance of social influences on human aggression. Biological factors exert a significant influence on aggressive behavior. But the influence of biological factors is very much dependent on the social context and the organism's past experiences. (Seymour Fleshback and Bernard Weiner, *Personality*, 2d ed. Heath, 1986, 484)

Careful reading is necessary here because two things are being compared and contrasted. The most obvious is the contrast between violent and peaceful cultural groups. Less obvious is the comparison of the influence of biological and social context on such behavior.

The use of definition

Sometimes writers will provide the definition of terms they are using, especially when a contextual understanding of the term is necessary. Sometimes a one-sentence statement is all that is needed, at other times an extended definition is necessary. Notice the way definition is used in the following passage:

> A **nuclear family** is a kinship group of two or more persons who live in the same household and are related by marriage, blood, or adoption. A childless couple, a couple with two children, and a mother and her child are all different types of families. A couple with children is probably the most popular conception of the family, although other family types are common. The number of single-parent families in America has increased substantially in recent years.
>
> Most individuals belong to at least two different family systems during their lives. The **family of orientation** is the family in which one was born and raised. The **family of procreation** is the system created by a couple who marry.
>
> The **extended family** is a combination of two or more nuclear families across generations. For example, a grandmother living with her married son, his wife, and their children would be described as an extended family. (Stephen Bahr, *Family Interaction*)

Here the author provides a series of definitions related to family so that later in the discussion he can use these terms knowing that the reader will be aware of what the terms mean. In addition, he boldfaces (darkens) the type on the terms used to help the reader distinguish the terminology from the definitions.

What is being defined in this passage?

> A type of maturity is needed before a person enters marriage. This type of maturity is not necessarily a fixed state, but an ongoing process that may last throughout the person's life. The question of maturity contains a number of subparts: physical maturity (the ability to reproduce), moral maturity (a code of life that gives guidance and direction to one's life), emotional maturity (the ability to control one's emotions), social maturity (the ability to play a part within the society), and vocational maturity (the ability to support one's family). Without these elements of maturity, it is doubtful that a solid marriage can be built, although there are always exceptions.

In this passage, the author defines the type of maturity necessary for marriage by breaking it down into subparts and defining each subpart in parentheses. This writing pattern is fairly easy to spot.

The use of cause and effect

A cause-and-effect pattern answers the question, "Why did it happen?" Key words often used by writers are "For this reason," "because of this," "results in," "causes," "and the effect is." This type of passage either could begin with a cause and give its effect or give the effect first and go back to the cause. Sometimes the cause-and-effect pattern is one sentence, as in:

cause ⟶   Individuals in unhappy marriages will not feel intimacy and
             support, and
effect ⟶   the result is that they are no different from single people in
             rates of mental illness.

But more often such passages are more complicated, as in the following:

cause
{
      After the revolution in 1917, the new Soviet government
      radically changed marriage and divorce laws in an attempt to
      alter the power of existing groups. As a result, the church lost
      its power to solemnize marriages and men and women were
      declared equal. Abortion was legalized and laws against adultery, bigamy and incest were eliminated. Divorce became easy
      to obtain and the legal obligations between parent and child
      were minimized. The traditional family was seen as an institution that enslaved women and perpetuated the power of existing religious and political groups. The new laws were not

effects
      designed to eliminate the family but rather to remove the inequities associated with it. The decreased legal responsibility
      for children and spouses added to the social crisis that occurred
      after the revolution. In the years that followed, abortion, divorce, and delinquency increased dramatically while birthrates
      declined. To counteract these problems, a new code of family
      law was enacted between 1934 and 1936. [Bahr, 40]

Notice that the main idea is to show what happened (effect) when the marriage and divorce laws (cause) in Russia changed after the revolution of 1917. The phrase "As a result" in the second sentence begins a series of sentences which show the effects of the change in the laws.

Here's another example of cause and effect:

Topic sentence states effect ⎰   Sometimes we bury or hide our
                              ⎱ undesirable emotions. We do this
                                because (1) we have been "program-
                                med" to do this. By the time we are
                                five years old, our parents have
                                influenced us to be affectionate,
                                tender, angry, or hateful. (2) We
                                "moralize" our emotions. We tell
                                ourselves it is good to feel grateful,
Rest of paragraph details causes ⎰ but bad to feel angry or jealous. So
                                   ⎱ we repress emotions we should
                                release. (3) We get into "value con-
                                flicts." Boys and men are not sup-
                                posed to cry or show fear. So some
                                men attempt to bury these conflicts
                                and also bury their true feelings
                                and create a false self-image.

The main idea here is that sometimes we hide our undesirable emotions
(the effect). The rest of the paragraph gives at least three reasons (or causes)
why we hide them: (1) we are programmed to do so by age 5; (2) we moral-
ize our "good" and "bad" emotions; and (3) we get into value conflicts—our
values as opposed to what society says we should like. Thus, the main idea is
divided into three parts, so that we can understand the cause, or *why* we
sometimes hide or bury our own true emotions or values. The last sentence
restates the effect.

The use of combined patterns

Sometimes a passage is of no one type but rather a combination of
patterns. What patterns are being used in the following passage?

One of the recent responses to the problem of marital violence has
been the establishment of shelters for battered women. Berk, Newton,
and Berk (1986) have studied how use of a shelter may impact on future
violence. They found that the effects depend on the attitudes of the victim. Women who have started taking control of their lives seem to benefit from shelter use. Going to the shelter may be an important step
toward establishing a new independent lifestyle. On the other hand, for
some women going to the shelter may encourage retaliation. This in
turn could create more problems. The solution to this problem may be
better support from the legal system.

Can you see how the cause-and-effect pattern as well as comparison-
contrast is being used? In the first sentence a cause (recent responses to
marital violence) states an effect (the establishment of shelters for battered

women). The passage also deals with the positive effects of battered women's attitudes and shelter use. With the phrase "On the other hand," the passage contrasts the positive effects with possible negative effects. So the passage uses a combination of cause and effect along with contrast to support the main idea.

Here is one more example of a passage using a combination of writing patterns. What are they?

> Women in Japan tend to favor egalitarian gender roles. For example, 86 percent of Japanese mothers feel that husbands should share in the housework when wives are employed (Bankart and Bankart 1985). However, American women agree more consistently with egalitarian ideals than Japanese women (Campbell and Brody 1985), and most Japanese women still adhere to a rather traditional division of labor by gender (Kumagai 1984).

No doubt you can see that the passage uses both example and comparison-contrast.

One last word on writing patterns. Identifying the writing pattern is not really what is important; understanding the main idea *is*. However, when you have trouble finding the main idea, look at the writing pattern being used. It can usually help you separate the details from the main point being made.

PRACTICES

Directions: Read the following passages looking for the main idea. Notice how the supporting details are organized. After each paragraph, write the main idea in a sentence of your own. Then circle the letter or letters of the writing pattern(s) used.

A.   White, Booth, and Edwards (1986) interviewed a national sample of individuals and found that the presence of children was associated modestly with reduced marital interaction, increased dissatisfaction with finances, and increased dissatisfaction with household division of labor. These three changes tended to reduce the level of marital satisfaction. However, according to some recent research the effect of children on marital quality may be small. Although Abbott and Brody (1985) found that childless wives reported higher marital satisfaction than mothers with children, planned comparisons revealed that the differences were due primarily to mothers with two children and mothers with male children. The marital quality of mothers with female children was no different than the marital quality of childless wives.

   1. What is the main idea? _____

   _____

   _____

   2. Which writing pattern(s) does the writer use? Circle the letter(s) of the correct response:

     a. example   c. definition

     b. cause and effect   d. comparison and contrast

B.   The most common form of marriage is monogamy, which is one female married to one male. However, polygamous marriages have existed throughout history. **Polygamy** is the practice of having two or more mates at the same time. There are three types of polygamy: (1) **Polygyny** is the marriage of one male to two or more females. (2) **Polyandry** is the marriage of one female to two or more males. (3) **Group marriage** is the marriage of two or more males to two or more females. Societies that practice polyandry or group marriage are rare. Throughout American history monogamy has been the accepted form of marriage, although polygamy has been tried by several different groups. (Stephen Bahr, *Family Interaction*)

   1. What is the main idea? _____

   _____

   _____

   2. Which writing pattern(s) does the writer use? Circle the letter(s) of the correct response:

     a. example   c. definition

     b. cause and effect   d. comparison and contrast

C.   When children have problems, too often the response of parents is to attempt to assert control to straighten the child out. The child often needs direction, but needs love and support much more. A friend of mine was counseling some families with delinquent boys recently. One of his major goals was to get the parents to give their boy one or two sincere compliments each day. The interaction between the boys and their parents had deteriorated to the point that there were never compliments, praise, or positive interactions. The boys felt unloved and criticized. Any good things they did were not recognized. Before control or direction would be accepted, the boys had to perceive some support from their parents. When my friend was able to get the parents to exhibit some supportive behaviors toward the boys, they would sometimes reciprocate. Over time, mutually supportive behaviors increased and some of the boys felt that their parents did care. When this occurred some of them were able to decrease their antisocial behavior and increase their social competence.

One of the ways parents may develop a more supportive environment for the children is to spend time with them in leisure and recreational activities. Time spent in family leisure activities tends to increase feelings of support and well-being in children. Bonds are often developed in leisure activities that cannot be built in other ways.

1. What is the main idea? _____

   _____

2. Which writing pattern(s) does the writer use? Circle the letter(s) of the correct response:

   a. example   c. definition

   b. cause and effect   d. comparison and contrast

D.   Some researchers have suggested that being married is more stressful for women than men, and causes married women to have poorer mental health than married men (Bernard 1972; Cove 1972). They have argued that for women marital roles are confining, stressful, and limit their opportunities. In short, they maintain that marriage may be beneficial for men but performing traditional marital roles makes women sick.

There are three ways in which marriage might create stress for women. First, the career development of women is often restricted when they marry. Their primary role is wife and mother and career development is subordinated to family demands. This often results in delaying or terminating educational and occupational desires while the husband pursues his occupational goals. Second, women are assigned the child care and housekeeping roles that do not provide intellectual stimulation, prestige, power or money. Third, married women who work still perform most of the household chores (Coverman and Sheley 1986). Thus, women are in a double bind. If they don't work they sacrifice career development; if they do work they have the dual burden of employment and household chores.

Although marriage may create stress for women, all available data show that married women have better mental and physical health than single women. Either married women have less stress than single women, or the intimacy of marriage insulates married women from the effects of the stresses. The research of Pearlin and Johnson (1977) and Kessler and Essex (1982) suggests that the intimacy of marriage reduces the negative effects of stresses among married women, particularly under conditions of high stress. Having a good marriage was associated with good mental health among women and men according to Cove *et al.* (1983).

1. What is the main idea? _____

   _____

   _____

2. Which writing pattern(s) does the writer use? Circle the letter(s) of the correct response:

   a. example   c. definition

   b. cause and effect   d. comparison and contrast

E.   Even though married women have better mental health than single women, marriage still may be more stressful for women than men. Cleary and Mechanic (1983) studied this issue among a sample of one thousand people in a midwestern community. They found little difference between men and women in role satisfaction, support, or amount of stress. Nevertheless, women had more depression than men when faced with similar strains. They concluded that it is important to distinguish between the presence and the impact of the strain.

1. What is the main idea? _____

   _____

   _____

2. Which writing pattern(s) does the writer use? Circle the letter(s) of the correct response:

   a. example   c. definition

   b. cause and effect   d. comparison and contrast

F.   It is noteworthy that the United States was consistently among those countries with the highest homicide rates. When the United States is compared with other English-speaking nations, it can be seen to have had about ten times the homicide rate of Ireland or England, and four to six times that of Australia, Canada, or Scotland. Very little change has occurred in this pattern since 1975. Of this English-language group, only Northern Ireland, beset by civil war, has a higher rate of killings than the United States. It has been argued by some theorists that the amount of violence in any culture is a constant, so that if violence is not expressed outwardly, as in homicides, then it will be expressed inwardly in the form of suicides. From this perspective, the amount of violence is largely biologically determined, while the role of culture is to shape the form or direction in which the violence is expressed. However, homicide and suicide are not inversely related; one can find every combination of high, middle, and low homicide and suicide rates among these nations. The amount as well as the form of violence varies with the culture. (Seymour Fleshback and Bernard Weiner, *Personality*, 2d ed. Heath, 1986, p. 484.)

1. What is the main idea? _____

   _____

   _____

   _____

2. Which writing pattern(s) does the writer use? Circle the letter(s) of the correct response:

   a. example   c. definition

   b. cause and effect   d. comparison and contrast

G.   Some researchers have found that parenthood has a negative impact on marital satisfaction. For example, Belsky, Lan, and Rovine (1985) studied how marriages changed over the transition to parenthood. They used interviews, questionnaires, and observation to assess marital quality during the last trimester of pregnancy, three months after the birth, and nine months after the birth. They found that there was a moderate decline in marital satisfaction over this period. The marriages became somewhat less romantic and expressive and somewhat more instrumental. Other researchers have found similar declines in marital satisfaction following the birth of a child, and that the decreases are greater for women than men (Cowan et al. 1985; Waldron and Routh 1981). Using six national surveys, Glenn and McLanahan (1982) found that marital satisfaction was higher among the childless, even after controlling for sex, race, education, religion, employment status, and desired number of children. Similarly Houseknecht (1979), Polonko, Scanzoni, and Teachman (1982), and Feldman (1981) all observed higher marital quality among the childless.

1. What is the main idea? _____

   _____

   _____

   _____

2. Which writing pattern(s) does the writer use? Circle the letter(s) of the correct response.

    a. example   c. definition

    b. cause and effect   d. comparison and contrast

H.   Another important factor affecting adjustment to parenthood is support from spouse. Because women tend to be responsible for a large majority of baby care tasks, support from their husbands is particularly important. Involvement of the father with the baby is associated with better marital and parental adjustment. If the wife expected the husband to be involved with child care and he helps very little, marital satisfaction decreases significantly. Some of the other variables that have been associated with good adjustment to parenthood are preparation for parenthood, wanting the child, and the significance of the parental role in the lives of the couple. In addition, a difficult pregnancy, health problems for the mother after the birth, a baby that cries a great deal, and health problems in the baby all increase the stresses associated with parenthood.

1. What is the main idea? _____

_____

_____

2. Which writing pattern(s) does the writer use? Circle the letter(s) of the correct response:

    a. example   c. definition

    b. cause and effect   d. comparison and contrast

B.   Vocabulary tip: using glossaries

Because many students never survey their textbooks, they tend to overlook an important resource for dealing with new words in a course. A glossary appears near the end of many subject matter textbooks for such courses as history, psychology, sociology, economics, marriage and family, and the like. They are especially helpful because they alphabetically list and define words and terms as they are used in the textbook. Even though we may find that most terms are defined as we read along in a chapter, we may forget some definitions as new ones are introduced. When we encounter a forgotten definition of a word or phrase in later chapters, we can quickly turn to the glossary and usually find the definition.

Once you have finished reading a chapter, it's a good idea to look up any new words in the glossary and compare them with their use in the text itself. As we have already suggested, the smart thing would be to select the words or phrases you find difficult to remember and make vocabulary cards for them.

R⁴ *Reading applications*

Application 1.   Practicing what you learned

Directions: Notice the title of the essay you are about to read. In the space below, write down at least four things you think make a good family.

_____

_____

_____

_____

Now read the essay and see how many, if any, of your points are mentioned in the essay.

JANE HOWARD

WHAT MAKES A GOOD FAMILY

1   Call it a clan, call it a network, call it a tribe, call it a family. Whatever you call it, whoever you are, you need one. You need one because you are human. You didn't come from nowhere. Before you, around you, and presumably after you, too, there are others. Some of these others must matter. They must matter a lot to you and, if you are very lucky, to one another.

Their welfare must be nearly as important to you as your own. Even if you live alone, even if your solitude is elected and ebullient, you still cannot do without a clan or a tribe.

2   Families, as all who read newspaper headlines know, are embattled and confused and irksome—so irksome that their members plot and scheme to leave them behind, dwelling at length on their shortcomings. The United States, as Rebecca West somewhere said, is a nation of middle-aged men running around complaining about their mothers. What folly. What misspent energy. However frail and perforated our families may have become, however they may annoy and retard us, they remain the first of the givens of our lives. The more we try to deny or elude them, the likelier we are to repeat their same mistakes. The first thing we have to do is to stop such efforts. Instead we must come to terms with our families, laughing with them peaceably on occasion if we can manage to, accepting them as the flawed mortals they are, or were, if we cannot.

3   If you long to improve your family, consider these earmarks common to good families:

- Good families have a chief or a heroine or a founder—someone around whom others cluster, whose achievements, as the Yiddish word has it, let them *kvell*, and whose example spurs them on to like feats.
- Good families have a switchboard operator—someone who plays Mission Control to everyone else's Apollo. This role, like the first one, is assumed rather than assigned. Someone always volunteers for it. That person often also has the instincts of an archivist and feels driven to keep scrapbooks and photograph albums up-to-date, so that the clan can see proof of its own continuity.
- Good families are fortresses with many windows and doors to the outer world. The families I feel most drawn to were founded by parents who are nearly as devoted to whatever it is they do outside as they are to each other and their children. Their curiosity and passion are contagious. Everyone in their home is busy. Paint is spattered on eye-glasses. Mud lurks under fingernails. Person-to-person calls come in the middle of the night from Tokyo and Brussels. Catchers' mitts, ballet slippers, overdue library books, and other signs of extrafamilial concerns are everywhere.
- Good families are hospitable. Knowing that hosts need guests as much as guests need hosts, they are generous with honorary memberships for friends, whom they urge to come early and often and to stay late. Such clans include surrounding rings of relatives, neighbors, teachers, students, and godparents, any of whom might at any time break or slide into the inner circle.
- Good families prize their rituals. Nothing welds a family more than these. Rituals are vital, especially for clans without histories, because they evoke a past, imply a future, and hint at continuity. No line in the Seder service at Passover reassures more than the last: "Next year in Jerusalem!" A clan becomes more of a clan each time it gathers to observe a fixed ritual (Christmas, birthdays, Thanksgiving, and so on), grieves at a funeral (anyone may come to most funerals; those who do declare their tribalness), or devises a new rite of its own.

- Good families are affectionate. This, of course, is a matter of style. I know clans whose members greet each other with tentative handshakes or, in what pass for kisses, with hurried brushes of side jawbones, as if the object were to touch not the lips but the ears. I don't see how such people manage. "The tribe that does not hug," as someone who has been part of many *ad hoc* families recently wrote to me, "is no tribe at all."
- Good families have a sense of place, which these days is not achieved easily. Once I asked a roomful of supper guests who, if anyone, felt any strong pull to any certain spot on the face of the earth. Everyone was silent, except for a visitor from Bavaria.

4   So what are we to do, when soaring real estate taxes and splintering families have made the family home all but obsolete? For a start, think in terms of movable feasts. Live here, wherever here may be, as if we were going to belong here for the rest of our lives. Learn to hallow whatever ground we happen to stand on or land on. Good families find some way to connect with posterity. "To forge a link in the humble chain of being, encircling heirs to ancestors," as Michael Novak has written, "is to walk within a circle of magic as primitive as humans knew in caves."

5   It is a sadly impoverished tribe that does not make much of children. Not too much, of course: It has truly been said that never in history have so many educated people devoted so much attention to so few children. Attention, in excess, can turn to fawning, which isn't much better than neglect. Still, if we don't regularly see and talk to and laugh with people who can expect to outlive us by 20 years or so, we had better get busy and find some.

6   Good families honor their elders. The wider the age range, the stronger the tribe. Jean-Paul Sartre and Margaret Mead both remarked on the central importance of grandparents in their own early lives. Grandparents now are in much more abundant supply than they were a generation or two ago when old age was more rare. If actual grandparents are not at hand, no family should have too hard a time finding substitute ones to whom to give unfeigned homage.

1. The numbers following the words and phrases below refer to the paragraph where they appear in the essay. Use context clues to define them in your own words.

   a. ebullient (1) ⎯⎯⎯⎯⎯⎯⎯⎯⎯⎯⎯⎯⎯⎯⎯⎯⎯⎯⎯⎯⎯

   b. frail and perforated (2) ⎯⎯⎯⎯⎯⎯⎯⎯⎯⎯⎯⎯⎯⎯

   c. earmarks (3) ⎯⎯⎯⎯⎯⎯⎯⎯⎯⎯⎯⎯⎯⎯⎯⎯⎯⎯⎯

   d. archivist (3) ⎯⎯⎯⎯⎯⎯⎯⎯⎯⎯⎯⎯⎯⎯⎯⎯⎯⎯⎯

   e. learn to hallow (4) ⎯⎯⎯⎯⎯⎯⎯⎯⎯⎯⎯⎯⎯⎯⎯⎯

2. What is the main idea of paragraph 1? _____

_____

_____

3. a. Paragraph 3 is very long. What writing pattern is being used? _____

_____

b. What is the point of paragraph 3? _____

_____

4. a. What would you say is the main writing pattern used throughout the

   essay? _____

_____

b. Why? _____

_____

_____

5. Before you read the essay you were asked to write down at least four
   things that you believe make up a good family. Which, if any, items that

   you listed are also mentioned in the essay? _____

_____

_____

6. a. What, in your own words, is the main idea of the essay? _____

_____

_____

b. Why do you agree or disagree with the author? _____

_____

_____

Application 2.   Applying what you know

Directions: Read the following essay and answer the questions that follow.

STEVEN O'BRIEN

ONE SON, THREE FATHERS

1   The first time I met him, he fell asleep in his spaghetti. It didn't matter. I was in love. Not with him, but with his mother. She had kept Sebastian from napping so that we wouldn't be interrupted after dinner. He was only 18 months old, a tiny little body topped off by a big head covered with blond hair.

2   His divorced mother and I, both 25, dated for a month, lived together nine more, and then married. It was Karen I wanted, not Sebastian, but they were a package deal. Ironically, he turned out to be the best part of the bargain.

3   Because my teaching schedule matched Sebastian's preschool schedule, I spent more time with him than his mother did. On the way home after school in the afternoon, he loved to sit on his ScoobyDoo lunch box in the back seat of my car and sing hit pop tunes like "Fly, Robin, Fly" and "SOS."

4   His biological father wasn't as available as I was to deal with the un-scheduled traumas of childhood. I slowly began to fill his role. Seb turned to me for comfort the night before he had to face a bully who had promised to hurt him. At age 4, he didn't understand, and I couldn't explain, why the world needed bullies. I could only repeat what my father had said: fight back as best you can and don't let anyone know that he can push you around, or it will never end. He cried at breakfast, regained his composure before school, stood up for his rights and got thoroughly trounced. When he couldn't fall asleep that night, he asked to borrow my wool knit sailor cap. "Tomorrow," he said, "with this on, I won't be afraid. I'll be 100 times stronger." The bully ignored him the next day, in order to torment someone else.

5   Brian, Sebastian's father, and I had been trained as teachers. Perhaps this was why both of us wanted to help the boy. Then, too, I had been raised with a stepsister and had seen the psychological damage that loss of contact with a parent could cause. In any case, Seb continued to spend time with me and with his father even after Brian remarried. Seb never had any prob-lem distinguishing between the two of us, although other people were often confused because he referred to us as Daddy Steve and Daddy Brian. We all

benefited from the arrangement. Sebastian shared things with Brian that I couldn't give him. For instance, I never followed sports, but Brian had studied to be a sports announcer.

6   After eight years of marriage, my wife and I separated. At first, Seb stayed with me and visited his mother, but after her remarriage, she missed him too much. He was moved to her new home nearby. Legally, of course, I had no rights. A child counselor I consulted suggested that I fade out of the picture as soon as possible. Instead, I maintained my home, with a bedroom for Seb, within walking distance of his. With his mother's consent, he started spending one night a week at my place. He loved to show off his second home to his friends by bringing them around, unannounced, for snacks.

7   Seb's grandparents had died years before. My place in his life gradually changed to resemble the role my favorite uncle and grandparents played in mine. It was hard at first, relinquishing my old relationship with him, but I grew to like the new one. I had the fun of seeing him without the frustration of trying to live with and discipline him.

8   Although we talked about it, and he understood after the divorce that we were no longer legally connected, Seb insisted on continuing to call me dad and using my last name as his own. I asked, "What's in a name, anyway?" He responded, "It says whose son I am." I told him that wasn't the issue. That I didn't have any choice. Neither biology nor law gave me the right to claim such a role; but he shattered my logic in a quavering voice with the question, "Don't you want to be my father anymore?" We hugged; I said: "Of course I want to. As long as you want me to be your father, I will be." That was five years ago.

9   Because Sebastian and I live in the same community, I often learn details about him I would otherwise miss. My neighbor, Sebastian's eighth-grade social-studies teacher, told me that he was going up and down the aisles asking each student at the end of the year if they had any brothers or sisters who would be going to the junior high the next fall. When he got to Seb, he said, "Oh, that's O.K. Seb, I used to live next door to you, and I know that you are an only child." Sebastian answered with a smile, "That's right, Mr. Tulley, there are so many parents in my family that there isn't room for any more kids."

10   After the laughter died down, several fellow students asked Seb how many parents he had. He said three fathers and two mothers. Another said, "Wow, Christmas must be great." Seb hesitated and then explained, "Christmas is about a 7, but birthdays are a definite 10."

11   Still, I wonder how he and his generation will view marriage. One night, we were talking about girls, the next-most-important issue on his mind, after driving. I said, "Well, someday, you'll find the right young woman and you won't be satisfied until you marry her." I wasn't prepared for his reply: "No, dad, I don't think so. It never works for long, and divorce hurts too much." Taken aback, I assured him that marriage did work, and that just because his parents' marriages hadn't, it was no reason to give up on the institution. He looked at me patiently and said: "Dad, none of my friends' parents are still together. Everybody gets divorced sooner or later. Don't worry, I'm all right. I can take care of myself. Love 'em and leave 'em. Right?"

12   I don't think I had realized until that moment that, since my divorce from Sebastian's mother, "love 'em and leave 'em" exactly described the way I had been living and handling my own relationships with women. What could I say to Seb?

1. How does O'Brien's family life fit the family life described in the essay in Application 1? Does it contain any of the elements of a "good family"?

    _____

    _____

    _____

2. O'Brien is told by a counselor to "fade out of the picture as soon as possible," but he doesn't. Do you think he did the right thing? _____

    Why? _____

    _____

    _____

3. If you were Seb's actual mother and father, how would you feel about O'Brien's relationship with Seb? Explain. _____

    _____

    _____

Application 3.   Suggestions for writing and discussion

1. Based on what Seb says in the last paragraph of the essay in Application 2, what are his chances of having a "good family" as described in Application 1?

2. Which of the reading selections in this chapter did you like best? Why?

3. Based on what you have read in this chapter and what you have observed of the world on your own, how would you describe the "normal" family of today?

Application 4. Summarizing what you have learned

Directions: On a separate sheet of paper, summarize what you have learned from reading this chapter (a) about yourself, (b) about skills you can apply to your reading, and (c) questions you still have that need answering. Turn this in to your instructor when finished.

Distinguishing fact from opinion, drawing inferences, and detecting propaganda techniques

6

R¹   *Reading beyond words*

A. Explain the following sayings in your own words:

1. "The chief function of your body is to carry your brain around."—
    Thomas Alva Edison

    _____

    _____

    _____

2. "There are three sides to every story; your side, my side, and the right
    side."—Source unknown

    _____

    _____

    _____

3. "Common sense is the collection of prejudices acquired by age eight-
    een."—Albert Einstein

    _____

    _____

    _____

4. "The contrary is also true."—Groucho Marx

    _____

    _____

    _____

B. Look at the picture below. What connection can you make with what you
    see and the following quote by Winston Churchill: "No idea is so out-
    landish that it should not be considered with a searching but at the same
    time with a steady eye"? Write your thoughts below.

_____

_____

_____

_____

_____

_____

R² *Reading actively*

A.   Vocabulary preview

Directions: The italicized words in the following sentences appear in the selection you are about to read. If they are unfamiliar, see whether you can use the context clues provided to guess their meanings. Use the dictionary to learn the meanings of the ones you don't know. Knowing the meanings of these words will make it easier to read the selection.

1. You need *analytical* skills, those skills that enable you to understand and evaluate ideas.

   analysis: _____

   _____

2. Most people use analysis only *sporadically*, unconsciously, and inefficiently rather than continually.

   sporadic: _____

   _____

3. Try to avoid lumping all considerations together *indiscriminately;* try to make distinctions.

   indiscriminate: _____

   _____

4. You will judge arguments on whether the speaker is of your race, religion, or political *affiliation.*

   affiliation: _____

   _____

5. A fact is something known with certainty, something either objectively *verified* or proven true by evidence.

   verify: _____

   _____

6. How could you make a *plea* on behalf of the rich?

   plea: _____

   _____

7. Closer inspection will show he made a *mockery* of that plea; you just thought he was serious.

   mockery: _____

   _____

8. The clues are *subtle*, yet undeniably there.

   subtle: _____

   _____

9. Most philosophers would enthusiastically *endorse* the idea of loving your family.

   endorse: _____

   _____

10. Not everything writers say is intended *literally;* sometimes they say the opposite of what is meant.

   literal: _____

   _____

B. Thought provokers

1. The selection you are about to read is from a textbook entitled *The Art of Thinking.* Do you consider thinking an art? Explain. _____

   _____

   _____

2. How much thought have you given to your opinions on such issues as abortion, prayer in schools, mercy killing, and other controversial issues? Have you truly examined the various arguments for such issues, or have you developed opinions without investigating their merits? Explain.

   _____

   _____

   _____

3. Do you consider yourself an analytical thinker? Explain. _____

   _____ _____

_____

_____

4. List what you consider to be the qualities of a good thinker. _____

_____

_____

C.   Reading practice

Directions: The following selection is from a college textbook, *The Art of Thinking: A Guide to Critical and Creative Thought.* Use it not only to learn more about thinking skills, but to practice study reading. Do the following:

1. Survey the selection the way you were taught in Chapter 1.

2. Read from heading to heading, stopping to take notes or mark passages to help you remember what you read.

3. Look for (a) a definition of reading and (b) how to make important distinctions between people and ideas, taste and judgment, fact and interpretation, and literal and ironic statements.

VINCENT RYAN RUGGIERO

SHARPEN YOUR ANALYTICAL SKILLS

1   A lively curiosity . . . can help you become a better thinker by revealing the challenges and opportunities around you. To be successful in meeting those challenges, however, you need more than curiosity. You need analytical skills. These skills enable you to understand and evaluate any ideas you encounter. Undoubtedly you have some of them already. (If you did not have at least rudimentary analytical skill, your education would not

have proceeded this far.) But since analysis is not usually taught systematically in American education, you probably learned it haphazardly and use it sporadically, unconsciously, and inefficiently. This chapter will help you use your analytical skills more effectively.

Improving your reading

2   The term *reading* is used here in the broad sense, covering not only printed material, but all received ideas, including those you get from listening. Almost 400 years ago, Francis Bacon warned about the danger of reading the wrong way. He advised people as they read not to dispute the author's view, nor to accept it uncritically, but to "weigh and consider" it. In the nineteenth century, British statesman Edmund Burke expressed the same view in more dramatic terms. "To read without reflection," he said, "is like eating without digesting."

3   The definition of reading these men had in mind is best explained as follows:

> There is one key idea which contains, in itself, the very essence of effective reading, and on which the improvement of reading depends: *Reading is reasoning.* When you read properly, you are not merely assimilating. You are not automatically transferring into your head what your eyes pick up on the page. What you see on the page sets your mind at work, collating, criticizing, interpreting, questioning, comprehending, comparing. When this process goes on well, you read well. When it goes on ill, you read badly.

4   Reading with the mind, and not just with the eyes, is not equally intense during every reading occasion. A bus schedule or a menu, for example, can be read well with little or no reasoning. But even the smallest reading challenges involve considerably more reasoning than we realize at the time. Consider the following sentences:

He who hesitates is lost. (Proverb)

We never step into the same river twice. (Heraclitus)

The girl who can't dance says the band can't play. (Yiddish proverb)

5   The first one, of course, is familiar enough that you may be unaware you are reasoning when you read it. But consider the first time you encountered it (probably as a small child). You undoubtedly wondered, "Just who does 'he' refer to in this sentence? And what does 'lost' mean here?" In time, when you considered and tested some possible meanings, you reasoned out the meaning.

6   The other two sentences are even more challenging. The key to the Heraclitus line is the relationship between *same* and *river*. Only when you perceive that, and grasp the idea that the river is constantly changing, can you be said to have read the line. And you can understand the Yiddish proverb only when you see that the message is not just about girls and bands, but about anyone who can't do something and resorts to face saving.

7   The kind of reading Bacon and Burke had in mind, and which concerns us here, is not a passive process, but an active, dynamic one. It

consists of examining ideas and deciding what they mean and whether they make sense, rather than merely receiving and accepting them. Unfortunately, most of the reading done in grade school and high school consists of getting the facts—and remembering them for the examination. Not only do the teachers expect that—the textbooks offer no real alternative to it. They are filled with facts to be accepted, rather than ideas to weigh and consider. If your school experience has been similar, you are bound to be a little uncomfortable with critical reading. More specifically, you are apt to be confused by long or complex passages, and nervous about reaching conclusions.

8   Such reactions are completely understandable. But it is important to realize that any difficulty you experience while mastering this chapter's approaches is a result of the material's newness, not of your lack of capacity. Thinking, remember, is largely a matter of acquiring the right skills and the habit of using them.

Making important distinctions

9   One of the best ways to overcome confusion about ideas is to make important distinctions—that is, to avoid lumping all considerations together indiscriminately. Here are the distinctions that are most often overlooked. Keep them in mind whenever you are reading (or listening):

Distinctions between the person and the idea

10   Your reaction to a sentence beginning "Adolf Hitler said . . ." would likely be very different from your reaction to one beginning "Winston Churchill said. . . ." In the first instance you might not even continue reading. At the very least you would read with great suspicion—you'd be ready to reject what was said.

11   There's nothing strange about that. You've learned things about Hitler and Churchill, and it's difficult to set them aside. In one sense, you *shouldn't* set them aside. Yet in another sense, you *must* set them aside to be a good thinker. After all, even a lunatic can have a good idea, and even a genius will, on occasion, be wrong.

12   If you do not check your tendency to accept or reject ideas on the basis of who expresses them, your analysis of everything you read and hear is certain to be distorted. You will judge arguments on whether the speaker is of your race, religion, or political affiliation, or whether you like her hair style. And so you might embrace nonsense and reject wisdom. Aristotle's contemporaries tell us he had very thin legs and small eyes, favored conspicuous dress and jewelry, and was fastidious in the way he combed his hair. It's not hard to imagine some Athenian ignoramus muttering to his fellows the ancient Greek equivalent of "Don't pay any attention to what Aristotle says—he's a wimp."

13   To guard against confusing the person and the idea, be aware of your reactions to people and try compensating for them. That is, listen very carefully to those you are inclined to dislike and very critically to those you are inclined to like. Judge the arguments as harshly as you wish, but only on their merits *as* arguments.

Distinctions between matters of taste and matters of judgment

14   . . . There are two broad types of opinion: taste and judgment. They differ significantly. In matters of taste we may express our personal preferences without defending them. In matters of judgment, however, we have an obligation to provide evidence.

15   Many people confuse taste and judgment. They believe their right to hold an opinion is a guarantee of the opinion's rightness. This confusion often causes people to offer inadequate support (or no support at all) for views that demand support. For example, they express judgments on such controversial issues as abortion, capital punishment, the teaching of evolution in the schools, mercy killing, hiring discrimination, and laws concerning rape as if they were matters of taste rather than matters of judgment.

16   Keep in mind that whenever someone presents an opinion about the truth of an issue or the wisdom of an action—that is, whenever someone presents a judgment—you not only have a right to judge his view by the evidence. You have an *obligation* to do so.

Distinctions between fact and interpretation

17   A fact is something known with certainty, something either objectively verified or demonstrable. An interpretation is an explanation of meaning or significance. In much writing, facts and interpretations are intertwined. It is not always obvious where one leaves off and the other begins. Here is an example of such intertwining:

The Writer's Interpretation (Note that merely calling interpretation *fact* does not make it so.)	People don't seem to care much about family life any more. A recent study has made that unfortunate fact very clear. The study, in which 1596 Americans were surveyed, was conducted for *Psychology Today* magazine in March, 1982, by Potomac Associates. It revealed that Americans are more concerned about the standard of living, personal health, economic stability, and employment than about family concerns. William Watts, President of Potomac Associates, commented as follows: "Traditionally, when asked to talk about their most important hopes and fears, Americans have ranked family concerns near the top of the list . . . Americans now talk less in interviews about the happiness and health of their families." The cause of this
The Writer's Interpretation (Both the classification of the trend as a "moral decline" and the assertion about its cause are interpretive.)	moral decline is without question the emphasis on the self that has dominated our culture for the past two decades.

Fact

18   The danger in failing to distinguish between fact and interpretation is that you will regard assumptions that ought to be questioned and contrasted with other views as unquestionable. If the habit of confusing the two is strong enough, it can paralyze your critical sense.

Distinctions between literal and ironic statements

19   Not everything a writer says is intended literally. Sometimes a writer makes his point by saying the exact opposite of what he means—that is, by using irony or satire. Suppose, for example, you encountered this passage in your reading:

> The present administration is right in reducing the taxes of the wealthy more than those of the working classes. After all, wealthy people not only pay more into the treasury, but they also have a higher standard of living to maintain. If the cost of soybeans has risen, so also has the cost of caviar; if the subway fare has increased, so has the maintenance cost of a Rolls-Royce and a Learjet. If the government listens to the minor grumbling and whining of the unemployed, it surely should be responsive to the plight of the affluent.

20   On the surface, this certainly looks like a plea on behalf of the rich. But on closer inspection it will be seen as a *mockery* of that plea. The clues are subtle, to be sure—the reference to the higher standard of living, the comparison of travel by Rolls-Royce or jet with travel by subway, the reference to the "plight" of the rich. Yet the clues are undeniable.

21   Such tongue-in-cheek writing can be more biting and therefore more effective than a direct attack. Yet you must be alert to the subtlety and not misread it, or the message you receive will be very different from the writer's intention.

Distinctions between an idea's validity and the quality of its expression

22   A thought's expression can deceive us about its validity. This is why a mad leader like Hitler won a large popular following even among intelligent and responsible people, and why Jim Jones' followers killed their children and committed suicide in Guyana. Impassioned, eloquent expression tends to excite a favorable response, just as lifeless, inarticulate, error-filled expression prompts a negative response. Compare these two passages:

> A man's gotta love his Momma and Daddy more than he love a stranger. If he don't do right by his kin, he can't never be a righteous man.

> To achieve success in a competitive world, you must honor the first principle of success—treat well those people who can benefit you and ignore the others.

23   The first passage is less appealing than the second. And yet it contains an idea most philosophers would enthusiastically endorse, while the second contains an idea most find reprehensible. The careful thinker is able to appraise them correctly because she is aware that expression can deceive. Careful thinkers make a special effort to separate form from content before judging. (The careful writer strives for clarity and correctness of form for exactly the same reason.) Thus he is able to say "This idea is poorly expressed, but profound" and "This idea is well expressed, but shallow."

D.   Comprehension check

Directions: Answer the following questions as carefully as you can. Use any notes you took if you need to.

OBJECTIVE QUESTIONS

1. Reading is defined as

   a. reasoning.

   b. assimilating what you read.

   c. criticizing what you read.

   d. analytical.

   e. none of the above.

2. Most of the reading done in grade school and high school consists of

   a. reading critically.

   b. memorizing and accepting facts.

   c. remembering facts for tests.

   d. all of the above.

   e. both b and c.

3. Circle the letter of any of the following important distinctions we should make when we read or listen that are mentioned in the chapter:

   a. between the person and the idea

   b. between matters of taste and judgment

   c. between literal and ironic statements

   d. between an idea's validity and the quality of its expression

   e. between fact and interpretation

4. There are two broad types of opinion: taste and judgment.

   a. True

   b. False

5. How is a fact defined in this chapter?

   _____

   _____

6. What writing pattern(s) is/are used in paragraph 17 to support the main idea?

   _____

SUBJECTIVE QUESTIONS

7. Choose one of the proverbs in Paragraph 4 and, by "actively reading," explain its meaning.

   _____

   _____

   _____

8. Do you agree with Ruggiero that most of the instruction in schools deals with getting facts and not reading critically? _____ Explain.

   _____

   _____

   _____

9. Is the statement "People don't seem to care much for family life" a fact or an opinion? _____ How do you know?

   _____

   _____

   _____

E.   Vocabulary check

Directions: Define the following words.

1. analysis ————————————————————————————

2. sporadic ————————————————————————————

3. indiscriminately ——————————————————————

4. affiliation ——————————————————————————

5. verify ——————————————————————————————

6. plea ————————————————————————————————

7. mockery ——————————————————————————————

8. subtle ——————————————————————————————

9. endorse ——————————————————————————————

10. literal ——————————————————————————————

Check your answers with your instructor.

R³   *Reading skills check*

A.   Recognizing fact and opinion

Too many readers, unfortunately, read only at a literal level. They can recognize main ideas and distinguish supporting details, but they often stop there and never question what they read. They tend to accept everything they read as fact. "If it's in print, it must be true," they say. The trouble with this point of view is first that it is not correct that whatever is in print must be true. Second, they misread what is factual because they do not distinguish fact from opinion, make inferences, or see the author's bias or tone. To read critically means to be aware of those things as we read.

You probably have a fair idea of what fact and opinion are, but try this quiz. Put an F in front of the statements of fact and an O in front of the statements of opinion.

_____   1. The metric system is better than using inches and feet.

_____   2. There are 12 inches in a foot.

_____   3. Portsmouth, Virginia, has a navy base.

_____   4. Portsmouth is the best place for a navy base.

_____   5. Rosebushes need water.

_____   6. A rose is the most beautiful flower.

_____   7. Television commercials are boring.

_____   8. Cigarettes can't be advertised on television.

_____   9. The school cafeteria has great food.

_____ 10. Our cafeteria serves pizza.

Statements 1, 4, 6, 7, and 9 are all opinions. Notice that opinion statements usually have "qualifier words"—words such as *better* in Number 1, *best* in Number 4, *most beautiful* in Number 6, *boring* in Number 7, and *great* in Number 9. These words give opinions and reflect our values and feelings.

Separating fact from opinion is not always easy. Usually, a fact is defined as something that can be proved, that actually exists, or that everyone agrees is true. However, facts can be slippery. They can change in time. At one time in the past, it was a "fact" that the earth was flat. It was also once a "fact" that the sun moved around the earth. And at one time, flights to the moon or outer space were considered ridiculous. Thus, facts today might not be facts tomorrow.

An opinion is usually defined as someone's feeling, belief, or judgment about someone or something. For instance, some people believe that McDonald's hamburgers are better than Jack-in-the-Box's hamburgers; other people believe the opposite. If a vote were taken and 80 percent of the people said that one company's hamburgers were better than the other's, they would be stating their opinions, not stating a fact. The only fact would be that 80 percent of the people said that one company's hamburgers were better than the other's. That could be proved.

Notice also that there is a difference between a true statement of fact and a false statement of fact. The statement in item 10 above, "Our cafeteria serves pizza," is a statement of fact. However, we might go to that cafeteria and discover that it never has served and never will serve pizza. It then becomes a false statement of fact. Here are examples of true and false statements of fact.

> False statement of fact: Cleveland is the capital of Ohio.

> True statement of fact: Columbus is the capital of Ohio.

Unlike opinions, statements of fact can be checked to see if they are correct.

Read the statements below and place TF for "true statement of fact," FF for "false statement of fact," or O for "opinion" in each of the blanks. Mark NI for "no information" if you do not have enough background knowledge to answer.

_____ 1. The most wonderful thing about the New York public school system is that it offers sex education.

_____ 2. A Volkswagen is more economical than a Mercedes.

_____ 3. The new movie playing at the Granada is not worth the price of admission.

_____ 4. The Shopwell has more checkout counters than the A&P.

_____ 5. "Datsun Saves."

_____ 6. Vienna is a large city in Germany.

_____ 7. Your October issue on the Western hero was perfect.

_____ 8. Every year during the fall semester, an American Studies course is offered on our campus.

The first one is opinion because of the qualifier word *wonderful.* On first thought, item 2 might seem a fact, but who can tell over a long period of time? It could be that sometimes this claim proves true and sometimes not; so it is just an opinion. The third one is opinion because it uses qualifier words. Number 4 is TF; it can be verified, whereas number 5 is opinion. Item 6 is FF because Vienna is in Austria, not Germany. Item 7 is opinion; *perfect* is a qualifier. And the last one is TF, if it can be proved; otherwise, it is false information.

Do the following practices to help develop your ability to separate fact from opinion.

PRACTICE 1

Directions: Read the following statements and answer the questions that follow them.

1.   Although 47% of Los Angeles' felony arrestees tested positive for co-caine, the percentage was even higher in New York City, Chicago, Detroit and Washington, while in San Diego and New York an even higher per-centage than Los Angeles' 16% tested positive for opiates (mostly heroin) on arrest. When we factor in the contributions to the arrest rate by those using amphetamines and PCP, it turns out that for all these cities about 70% of those arrested for robbery, weapons offenses and larceny test pos-itive for at least one illegal drug other than marijuana.

What we must do is fairly clear. We must institutionalize routine urinaly-sis of those who are arrested for any of the typical crimes arising out of drug use, and then we must act on the information. Urinalysis is an accu-rate, although not foolproof, method that costs only $5 per person. It should be a requirement of all who are released on bail or, after convic-tion, placed on probation or released parole. A positive urine sample must mean a return to jail for a relative short period so that the effects of the drug dependence can, for the most part, wear off. (John Kaplan, "A Posi-tive Check on Crime," *Los Angeles Times*, March 16, 1988, Section 2, p. 7)

a. Is the statement mostly a true statement of fact, a false statement of

   fact, or opinion? _____

b. What is the main point? _____

   _____

   _____

2.   The atom is an indivisible unit of matter. The atomic number of an atom is simply the number of neutrons in its nucleus. The atomic weight of an atom is given in most cases by the mass number of the atom, equal to the total number of protons and neutrons combined. An atom is conveniently symbolized by its chemical symbol with the atomic number and mass number written as subscript and superscript. For example, uranium is U, and its weight is 95; hence, U^{95}.

a. Is the statement mostly statement of fact, a false statement of fact, or

   opinion? _____

b. Explain your answer. _____

_____

_____

c. What knowledge is necessary to answer Item 2a above?

_____

_____

3.   There is a reason for our decline in foreign-affairs spending. It is not, again, that we lack concern about the rest of the world. But our concerns are unfocused; we are uninformed. To be blunt, the problem in good part is ignorance, which begins in the failure of our elementary schools to teach world geography. It continues in high schools that neglect not just foreign languages but world history. Colleges and universities compound the problem, offering students the chance to study business administration or pre-law or pre-something else without learning what any good citizen needs to know about the world—or even about our own society, as a recent study sponsored by the Carnegie Foundation for the Advancement of Teaching made clear. (Peter Bridges, "America's Hazy View of the World at Large," *Los Angeles Times*, March 29, 1987, Section 5)

a. Is the statement mostly fact or opinion? _____

b. Explain your answer. _____

_____

_____

4.   Before there were people on the earth, the Chief of the Sky Spirits grew tired of his home in the Above World, because the air was always brittle with an icy cold. So he carved a hole in the sky with a stone and pushed all the snow and ice below until he made a great mound that reached from the earth almost to the sky. Today it is known as Mount Shasta.

Then the Sky Spirit took his walking stick, stepped from a cloud to the peak, and walked down to the mountain. When he was about halfway to the valley below, he began to put his finger to the ground here and there, here and there. Wherever his finger touched, a tree grew. The snow melted in his footsteps, and the water ran down in rivers. . . . Pleased with what he'd done, the Chief of the Sky Spirits decided to bring his family down and live on the earth himself.

(Erdoes/Ortiz, *American Indian Myth and Legends,* New York: Random House, 1981, p. 85)

a. Is the statement most fact or opinion? _____

b. Explain your answer. _____

_____

_____

5.   When the Lord God made earth and heaven, there was neither shrub nor plant growing wild upon the earth, because the Lord God had sent no rain on the earth; nor was there any man to till the ground. A flood used to rise out of the earth and water all the surface of the ground. Then the Lord God formed a man from the dust of the ground and breathed into his nostrils the breath of life. Thus the man became a living creature. Then the Lord God planted a garden in Eden away to the east, and there he put the man whom he had formed. The Lord God made trees spring from the ground, all trees pleasant to look at and good for food; and in the middle of the garden he set the tree of life and the tree of knowledge of good and evil. ("Genesis," *The New English Bible*)

a. Is the statement mostly fact or opinion? _____

b. Explain your answer. _____

_____

_____

c. What do items 4 and 5 have in common? _____

_____

_____

6.   The coral crab is considered one of the prettiest creatures in the Caribbean. Its bright red and yellow coloring catches the diver's eye, because it offers such a contrast to the surrounding blues, purples, and greens. The delight of underwater photographers, it is an ideal model for close-up work and a highly desirable subject for anyone's marine photo collection. (Geri Murphy, "The Coral Crab," *Skin Diver,* November 1981, p. 25.)

a. What is fact in this statement? _____

_____

b. What is opinion? _____

_____

7.   The coral crab is commonly found in Caribbean waters, but also ranges from the Bahamas to as far south as Brazil. It is six inches in body size and has a larger, heavier right claw that is used to crush small shelled animals for food. The upper surface is red-brown with varying splotches of white and yellow. Its underside is bright yellow. A purplish color is found along the outer edges of the crab's shell, and around the eyes and the joints of the legs. (Geri Murphy, "The Coral Crab," *Skin Diver*, November 1981, p. 25.)

a. Is this statement mostly fact or opinion? _____

Explain: _____

_____

b. How does this statement differ from Statement 6? _____

_____

_____

8.   Science is much more than a body of knowledge. It is a way of think-ing. This is central to its success. Science invites us to let the facts in, even when they don't conform to our preconceptions. It counsels us to carry alternative hypotheses in our heads and see which best matches the facts. It urges on us a fine balance between no-holds-barred open-ness to new ideas, however heretical, and the most rigorous skeptical scrutiny of everything—new ideas and established wisdom. We need wide appreciation of this kind of thinking. It works. It's an essential tool for a democracy in an age of change. Our task is not just to train more scientists but also to deepen public understanding of science. (Carl Sagan, "Why We Need to Understand Science," *Parade*, September 10, 1989, p. 6)

a. Is the statement mostly statement of fact, a false statement of fact or

opinion? _____

b. Explain your answer. _____
_____
_____

9.   Scientists around the globe offered chilling visions of a world condemned to "nuclear winter," the end of life as a result of fallout. It was a grudging recognition of this protest, coupled with Congressional reluctance to continue to vote billions on the controversial but unproven MX missile and similar programs, which persuaded President Reagan to embrace as a substitute for the arms race the so-called "Star Wars" defense program: an anti-nuclear system based on exotic technologies and designed to search out and destroy all incoming offensive weapons. In a televised address to the nation in 1983, Reagan proposed this "Strategic Defense Initiative," which, he implied, would make all existing nuclear missiles "impotent and obsolete." Though critics charged that the system would never be feasible, Congress endorsed a five-year research program which was expected to cost some $30 billion. The long-range program called for trillions. (Allan Nevins and Henry Steele Commager, *A Pocket History of the United States.* Washington Square Press, 1986, p. 630)

a. Is the statement mostly statement of fact, a false statement of fact, or

opinion? _____

b. Explain your answer. _____
_____
_____

c. What knowledge is necessary to answer Item a above?
_____
_____

✓ Compare your answers with these:
1a. the first paragraph is mostly fact, the second, mostly opinion;
1b. The main point being made is that urinalysis should be given to those arrested for robbery, weapons offenses and larceny;
2a. incorrect information since the atom is divisible and is actually U^{92};

3. Opinion, even though the information is based on a study cited, and even though what he says may be true in many cases;

4 and 5 are both opinion, having in common the story of earth's creation and existence of man;

6a. the coral crab's color; 6b. "considered one of the prettiest," "delight of underwater photographer," "ideal model";

7a. fact; 7b. it contains more facts that can be verified;

8a. opinion;

9a. mostly fact; 9b. it can be verified in other history books; 9c. a knowledge of that period of history.

B.   Drawing inferences

If you were invited to someone's home for the first time, someone you did not know well, and noticed that there were seven albums by Bruce Springsteen, what would you guess or infer about that person? Chances are you would infer that the person likes "the Boss's" music. You could not be positive, but you could guess or draw this conclusion. To be certain, you would have to ask the person. Maybe the albums do not even belong to that person, but to a visiting friend. In that case, your inference would be wrong. Yet, we draw inferences everyday, often without knowing it.

An inference has been defined as "a statement about the unknown made on the basis of the known." In other words, an inference is an educated guess. For instance, if a woman smiles when you congratulate her on her speech, you can infer she is pleased. If she frowns, you can infer that she is not pleased. Because smiles generally mean happiness or pleasure, and frowns generally mean concern or displeasure, we can make inferences or guesses about people's moods from their expressions.

We also draw inferences from things we hear as well as from what we read. Read the following examples of drawing inferences.

Example 1.   *A student–instructor conversation:*

INSTRUCTOR: "Here's your test, Gary. I'd like to suggest you come in during my office hours and talk about it."

GARY: "I blew it again? Maybe I'd better drop this course."

INSTRUCTOR: "Now, don't panic. It's only the second test."

GARY: "I never was good in history."

Circle the items below that can be inferred from the conversation.

A. Gary failed his test.

B. It's not the first time Gary has failed in the class.

C. The instructor feels the fault in Gary's failure is that he doesn't study enough.

D. Gary feels like a failure in his history class.

E. Gary doesn't like his history instructor.

You should have circled Item A; we can infer he failed the test when he says, "I blew it again?" and the instructor says not to panic. Item B should be circled, because Gary says "again," and the instructor says it's only the second test. Item C should not be circled; there's nothing in the conversation that suggests the instructor feels Gary hasn't studied. Item D should be circled, because Gary wants to drop the course and claims he was never good in history. Item E should not be circled. We don't know from the conversation how he feels about the instructor.

Example 2. *An opening paragraph from an essay:*

Grocery shopping is like trying to solve math problems while riding carnival bumper cars. You make a list and then leave it on the kitchen table. You dodge abandoned and child-driven carts, scanning 5000 labels and searching for the unit-pricing sticker (Aha! It fell on the floor.) to see which brand gives you the most for your money. The nutrition labels make you feel like you're drowning in alphabet soup. Conquered, you just hope the basket will yield balanced meals, and you pray for enough money to cover it all. (Susan Seliger, "The Eat-the-Best-for-the-Least Computer Diet," *National Observer,* May 23, 1987.)

Circle the items below that you can infer from the statement.

A. The author probably likes grocery shopping.

B. The author's thesis or main idea of the essay will probably deal with the need to make shopping easier.

C. The author wants to buy nutritional food for the least amount of money.

You should have circled Items B and C. It is a good guess the author does not like shopping from the hassled feeling she portrays: "math problems," "bumper cars," "dodge," and so on.

Example 3. *A closing paragraph from an essay:*

You might say that the sex-hygiene classes bring into the open many of the stereotyping attitudes toward women shown in the rest of the school curriculum. It is the high school's last chance to indoctrinate girls and put us in our place.

Answer the questions below.

A. Is the author a man or a woman? _____

B. Does the author like the sex-hygiene classes as they are? _____

C. What can you infer are some of the things taught in the sex-hygiene

classes the author is writing about? _____

The author must be a woman because the last line reads "put us in our place." The "us" refers to girls and women. The reference to "stereotyping attitudes toward women" implies the author does not like the hygiene classes as they are. As to the last question, we can infer the things taught are based on stereotyped attitudes of women's roles: homemaker, faithful wife, mother, and so on.

Following are some practices in recognizing inferences in print.

PRACTICE 2

Directions: Read the following statements and answer the questions for each.

A.   It was in the tiny Caribbean island of Grenada, with a population of 113,000, that President Reagan decided to demonstrate that America could still "stand tall." On October 25, 1983 (only two days after the tragic bombing in Beirut), some 4,600 troops landed in Grenada. The intervention followed a coup in which hard-line Marxists overthrew and subsequently murdered the soft-line Marxist Prime Minister, Maurice Bishop, and was prompted by a request from the Organization of Eastern Caribbean States to re-establish law and order in Granada, and the perceived need to "rescue" the nearly 1,000 Americans studying at an American-run medical school. Within three days the U.S. had arrested the leaders of the coup and overcome the resistance of a handful of soldiers and some 700 armed Cuban construction workers. An American public, still remembering the frustrations of the war in Vietnam and the Iranian hostage crisis, rejoiced in a return to the style of the "Rough Riders." (Allan Nevins and Henry Steele Commager, *A Pocket History of the United States*, Washington Square Press, 1986, p. 631)

Circle the items below that you can infer from the statement.

1. The authors don't believe that the invasion of Granada was necessary.

2. The authors don't believe the invasion of Granada was as important an event as the administration made it out to be.

3. The authors believe the invasion was necessary to rescue Americans there.

B.   Consider some of the examples of language and symbols in American history. When schoolchildren learn from their textbooks that the early colonists gained valuable experience in governing themselves, they are not told that the early colonists who were women were denied the privilege of self-government; when they learn that in the eighteenth century the average man had to manufacture many of the things he and his family needed, they are not told that this "average man" was often a woman who manufactured much of what she and her family needed. Young people learn that intrepid [fearless] pioneers crossed the country in covered wagons with their wives, children, and cattle; they do not learn that women themselves were intrepid pioneers. (Casey Miller and Kate Swift, "Is Language Sexist?" *New York Times Magazine*, April 16, 1972.)

Circle the items below that you can infer from the statement.

1. The authors feel that most American history textbooks do not provide enough factual information about women's roles in the development of history.

2. The authors believe history textbooks should make it more clear that women were not allowed to vote during the early years of American history.

3. Because women's roles are downplayed in history texts, children grow up stereotyping the early colonists and pioneers.

4. Most history texts are sexist.

C.   Stereotypes are one way in which we "define" the world in order to see it. They classify the infinite variety of human beings into a convenient handful of "types" toward whom we learn to act in stereotyped fashion. Life would be a wearing process if we had to start from scratch with each and every human contact. Stereotypes economize on our mental efforts by covering up the blooming, buzzing confusion with big recognizable cut-outs. They save us the "trouble" of finding out what the world is like—they give it its accustomed look. (Robert L. Heilbroner, "Don't Let Stereotypes Warp Your Judgment," *Think Magazine*, June 1961.)

Circle all the items below that you can infer from the statement above.

1. The author thinks we need to stereotype.

2. Not to stereotype requires too much effort on our part.

3. Without stereotyping we would not be able to function in our normal, accustomed way.

4. We stereotype because we are lazy.

D.   The first bomb was named Trinity and it was called a "gadget." The "gadget" was hoisted to the top of a tower in Alamagordo Desert in July 1945. On a stormy night with lightning everywhere the "gadget" exploded. One scientist described how he felt when it blew up. He said, "The noise went on, and on, and on, like thunder, never stopping. The desert suddenly became small."

They were not sure before they blew up the bomb that the whole atmosphere would not go critical. They were worried about this probability, so they redid their calculations and the probability remained the same. It was not extremely small. One technician was upset to hear Enrico Fermi taking side bets as the "gadget" was hoisted to the tower, that New Mexico could be incinerated.

After the explosion, the radioactive cloud hovered overhead for some time, worrying the scientists, because if it did not blow away in the direction they had prescribed, it could have killed them or injured them severely. However, it did eventually blow away. That night the scientists had a party.

The next bomb was blown up or tested over a human population on August 6, 1945, at 8:15 in the morning. In fact, the air force had been told to spare two cities in Japan so that we could see the effects of these weapons on human populations. The bomb was dropped from a plane called the *Enola Gay*, which flew over Hiroshima. Men looking up saw one parachute opening and they were pleased because they thought the plane had been shot down. Another parachute opened adjacent to the first. Then there was a blinding flash and tens of thousands of people were vaporized. People, in fact, when they disappeared, left their shadows on concrete sidewalks behind them. Children were seen running along streets shedding skin from their bodies like veils; a man was standing in a state of acute clinical shock holding his eyeball in the palm of his hand; and a woman lay dying in a gutter with her back totally burned with her baby suckling at her breast as she lay dying. (Helen Caldicott, "This Beautiful Planet," *Speak Out*, edited by Herbert Vetter, Beacon Press, 1982, p. 227. Copyright by Helen Caldicott. Reprinted by permission of the author.)

Circle all the items below that you can infer from the statement above.

1. The author is probably against developing more nuclear weapons.

2. The author feels the scientists working on the development of the first nuclear bombs were reckless regarding the possible results.

3. The author admires the scientists for their ingenuity.

4. It was necessary to drop the bomb on a human population.

E.   More than 1,800 demonstrators were arrested last September while trying to blockade the nearly completed Diablo Canyon nuclear power plant on the central California coast. It was dangerous, they argued, to situate the $2.3 billion plant near San Luis Obispo, about 2.5 miles from an offshore earthquake fault. When the Nuclear Regulatory Commission granted a license for low-power testing at Diablo Canyon later that month, the protest seemed a failure, but last week antinuclear forces scored a belated, though perhaps temporary, victory. The NRC, by a 5-0 vote, reversed itself and suspended the operating license for Diablo Canyon. The NRC decision followed discovery of several errors in design and calculation at the plant, raising questions about its safety in event of an earthquake. NRC chairman Nunzio J. Palladino said the suspension was "a strong sign that the commission doesn't like what it's seen." ("Diablo Canyon," *Newsweek*, November 30, 1981, p. 31.)

Circle all the items below that you can infer from the statement above.

1. The demonstrators wasted their time protesting.

2. The demonstrators were happy with the final NRC decision.

3. The author is happy with the decision.

4. There is little question that the plant's safety during an earthquake is in doubt.

F.   There are quite a few similar modern stories in which a child is more able and more intelligent than the parent, not in never-never-land, as in a fairy tale, but in everyday reality. The child enjoys such a story because it is in line with what he would like to believe; but the ultimate consequences are distrust of the parent on whom he still has to rely, and disappointment because, contrary to what the story makes him believe, parents remain superior for quite some time. (Bruno Bettelheim, *The Uses of Enchantment*, New York: Vintage Books, 1977, p. 134.)

Circle all items below that you infer from the statement above.

1. There are many stories for children that show them as superior to adults.

2. Such stories are dangerous for children.

3. The author wants to keep such stories out of the reach of children.

4. It is important to be selective regarding what children read.

G.   The war in Vietnam is over, along with the great national debate about its morality. The only question remaining is whether we learned anything from it. The United States has been involved in dubious, suspicious, military escapades before but never on such a huge scale. It seems certain that future historians will date our decline as a world power from the moment when we began to squander our energy and resources in this futile orgy of destruction. (Philip Slater, *The Pursuit of Loneliness*, Boston: Beacon Press, 1976, p. 38.)

Circle all the items below that you can infer from the statement above.

1. The author is an American.

2. The author was probably opposed to U.S. involvement in Vietnam.

3. The U.S., according to the author, has lost some of its prestige in the world.

4. The author wants the U.S. to learn from its mistakes.

H.   In walks these three girls in nothing but bathing suits. I'm in the third checkout slot, with my back to the door, so I don't see them until they're over by the bread. The one that caught my eye first was the one in the plaid green two-piece. She was a chunky kid, with a good tan and a sweet broad soft-looking can with those two crescents of white just under it, where the sun never seems to hit, at the top of the back of her legs. I stood there with my hand on a box of HiHo crackers trying to remember if I rang it up or not. I ring it up again and the customer starts giving me hell. She's one of those cash-register-watchers, a witch about fifty with rouge on her cheekbones and no eyebrows, and I know that it's made her day to trip me up. (John Updike, "A&P," in *Pigeon Feathers*, New York: Alfred Knopf, 1962.)

Answer these questions by drawing some inferences from the passage above.

1. Where does the story take place? _____

2. What time of year is it? _____

3. What can you infer about the narrator, the "I" telling the story?

_____

_____

4. How does the narrator feel about his mistake? _____

I. My friend, I am going to tell you the story of my life, as you wish; and if it were only the story of my life I think I would not tell it; for what is one man that he should make much of his winters, even when they bend him like a heavy snow? So many other men have lived and shall live that story, to be grass upon the hill.

It is the story of all life that is holy and is good to tell, and of us two-leggeds sharing in it with the four-leggeds and the wings of the air and all green things; for these are children of one mother and their father is one Spirit. (John G. Neihardt, *Black Elk Speaks*, Lincoln, Nebraska: Bison Books, 1961, p. 1.)

Answer the following questions by drawing inferences.

1. For what two reasons is the narrator going to tell his story?

_____

_____

2. What does this reasoning tell us about the narrator?

_____

_____

3. Is the narrator young or old? How do you know?

_____

_____

4. Does the narrator feel that humans are superior to animals?

_____

_____

5. Why can we infer the narrator is an Indian?

_____

_____

C.   Detecting propaganda techniques

Propaganda is used to change or convert people to a particular view. Advertisers use propaganda techniques to convince us to buy a product, or at least to make the product so well known that we buy it without thinking. Propaganda is also used by parents, teachers, newspapers, magazines, the government, the church—by practically everyone and every group. We are hit by propaganda in one form or another every day in all media from radio to billboards.

Not all propaganda is bad or "evil." Propaganda is often used for worthy purposes. It is used to raise money for good causes, such as campaigns to fight cancer, alcoholism, and other diseases. It is used to pass reform bills and bond issues for community causes. It is also used to develop healthy, positive attitudes toward other people's problems and needs. The trouble comes when our own ignorance about the propaganda techniques used causes us to accept false information.

Clever propagandists know that most people are not critical listeners, readers, or thinkers. They use these human weaknesses to get people to react with their emotions rather than with their minds. Reading beyond the words requires an understanding of some common propaganda techniques. Here are some you need to know if you are to critically detect their use on you.

1.   Name calling
This technique uses words that have bad or negative meanings to certain people. Words or phrases such as "sexist," "Commie," "yuppie," "pro-gay," "anti-Christ," "pro-Moral Majority," or "pro-life" can be used to sway people to be for or against a person or a group. By painting someone as "pro-abortion," a propaganda campaign can immediately turn anti-abortionists against that person simply because of the group's bias. No facts may be presented, but if the label is used often enough, that person's name will soon be connected with the label.

2.   Glittering generalities
This technique is the opposite of name calling. It is used to win you over by using words or phrases that are acceptable to most people: "motherhood," "our founding fathers," "America," "honesty," "faith in God,"

"a family man." But words and phrases such as these are often overused. They are sometimes used in vague and meaningless ways, in the hope that the "nice" words will become associated with the person or group being praised. For instance, what does this statement really say?

> And so I say to you, my fellow Americans, that we have right on our side. Our faith in God and the wisdom of our founding fathers will carry us through these troubled times.

The words here "glitter" with nice sounds, but their sparkle is not real because the meaning is empty. Yet, not many people want to challenge "right on our side" (but right about what?), or "faith in God" (whose God?), or "wisdom of our founding fathers" (which ones and what wisdom are meant?). As far as the British were concerned, our founding fathers were rebels!

3.   Guilt by association

This method attempts to get people to think someone or some cause is connected with a group that is disliked or distrusted. During the 1980 presidential campaign, this anti-Carter ad was used to make Carter look bad:

> In 1976 Jimmy Carter said, "Why not the Best?" Let's look at what he gave us. Andrew Young, Carter's U.N. Ambassador who called Iran's Ayatollah Khomeini a saint, was forced to resign after lying to the president. Bert Lance also forced to resign. Dr. Peter Bourne, the Carter drug expert, forced to resign after supplying drugs to a White House staffer. And the list goes on. If you want a president you can trust, then vote for Ronald Reagan for President. (From Kathleen Hall Jamieson, *Packaging the Presidency,* Oxford University Press, 1984, p. 423.)

The object was to make Carter guilty by association. However, note that once the men named were suspected of a wrongdoing, they were forced to resign, which is really in Carter's favor. The ad says, "And the list goes on." What list? If there were more, why not mention them? And what in the ad proves that Reagan is "a president we can trust"?

We must be careful that our biases against a person or a group aren't swayed by such tactics.

4.   Distortion or twisting

This technique uses only half-truths or part-truths. Rather than telling the whole truth, propagandists (and advertisers) sometimes only pick what sounds good or bad and "twist" the facts in a way that best suits the purpose. For example, in 1964, President Lyndon B. Johnson twisted some facts in his campaign against Senator Barry Goldwater. Johnson ran ads that made Goldwater look like a "trigger-happy" person who would start a nuclear war "at the drop of a hat." The truth is that Goldwater had been interviewed with a question asking him to tell the difference between the *reliability* and the *accuracy* of guided missiles. He replied that they were accurate enough "to lob one into the men's room at the Kremlin." In another interview he stated that "it would be *possible* to destroy" the forests of Vietnam by using low-yield atomic weapons. These were theoretical answers. Goldwater did not recommend these actions, but Johnson distorted or twisted his answers to create a campaign that frightened people into thinking Goldwater would start an atomic war. It worked.

5. Slogans

The use of catchy words or phrases is another technique of propagandists. During World War II, the slogan "Remember Pearl Harbor" was used to get people to buy war bonds and to make certain sacrifices needed for the war effort. Phrases such as "In God We Trust" and "United We Stand" are all used to influence our thinking and to make us feel we are together and of one mind. Or, in the Reagan-Mondale presidential campaign, the phrase "Where's the beef?" became a slogan of Mondale's. Reagan's slogan was "Ronald Reagan for President. He'll make American Great Again."

This method can be good or bad. As with all propaganda methods, we need to read or think beyond the words and seek the facts.

EXERCISE

Directions:
A. Find an advertisement or a political propaganda piece that uses one of the methods listed above. Bring it to class to share.
B. Write what you think is a good use of propaganda to promote something you believe in. Share it with the class.

D.   Vocabulary tip: denotation and connotation

When you look up a word's meaning in a dictionary, you are given the *denotative* definition, an agreed-upon meaning. However, many words have *connotative* meanings. For instance, the word "home" *denotes* the place where one lives, but the word also *connotes* family ties and feelings, comfort, privacy, familiarity, or sometimes negative thoughts. In other words, the denotative meaning of a word is its dictionary definition, whereas the connotative meaning is all the things the word suggests to us.

Being aware of connotative definitions of words is especially important when reading propaganda or advertisements. For instance, suppose you agree with a politician's views on how to reduce taxes. You think his or her ideas are clever or astute. However, someone who disagrees with the politician's views says those ideas are sly or calculating. Although the words "clever," "astute," "sly," and "calculating" all have a similar denotative meaning, they have different connotative meanings: "clever" and "astute" connote intelligence and trustworthiness, but "sly" and "calculating" connote trickiness and dishonesty.

Here is a list of words that basically mean the same, yet their connotative meanings may be either complimentary or uncomplimentary. Circle the word you think is uncomplimentary.

unimaginative/practical	phony/imposter
cautious/cowardly	sensitive/touchy
fat/heavy	tight/thrifty
gullible/trusting	come clean/acknowledge
proud/conceited	noise/racket

Basically, each pair of words has a similar denotative meaning. Yet you would probably prefer to be called practical rather than unimaginative, cautious rather than cowardly, and heavy rather than fat. Certain words, as you can see, connote or suggest an attitude that is nicer than that connoted by certain other words.

Connotative meanings can create strong emotions, visual images, and sensory awareness. For instance, words such as "gringo," "nigger," and "honkie" usually trigger negative feelings. Words such as "politician" or "radical" can create visual images in our minds of real politicians and radicals or what we think of as typical examples. Words such as "shrill," "ice-cold," "castor oil," "incense," and "bubbly" provide us with various feelings of sound, taste, or smell.

Obviously, advertisers and propagandists use words with "good" connotation for their product or cause, and words with "bad" connotation for their competitors or opposition. Being aware of these devices is another step in reading beyond the word.

EXERCISE 1

Directions: Look up the following words in the dictionary. First, write in the denotative meaning of the word. Then, write in the connotative meaning the word has for you.

1. wired: _____

_____

2. wasted: _____

_____

3. slick: _____

_____

4. punk: _____

_____

5. burned: _____

_____

6. gross: _____

_____

EXERCISE 2

Directions: In the space below, write in four words that you know have connotative meanings different from their denotative meanings. Write in the different meanings as you did in Exercise 1.

1. _____ : _____

_____

2. _____ : _____

_____

3. _____ : _____

_____

4. _____ : _____

_____

EXERCISE 3

Directions: If you were writing advertisements for the following list of products, you would want to select only words that had positive connotative meanings. Circle the words below that you would use in writing ads for each product. Look up any words you don't know.

1. coffee: mixture, blend, hodge-podge, concoction

2. perfume: odor, fragrance, smell, aroma

3. automobile: peculiar, unmistakable, special, distinctive

4. diet food: fat, obese, paunchy, overweight

5. diamonds: flashy, brilliant, glittering, auspicious

6. jewelry: craftsmanship, genius, skill, artistry

Discuss your answers in class. Note that Question 4 in Exercise 3 is meant to trick you: The words certainly don't have *positive* connotative meanings, but nevertheless you would probably want to use them in your advertisement, because their *negative* connotations would influence the reader or listener to consider going on a diet. If, instead, you used words such as "solid," "substantial," "large," and "imposing," your ad would be weakened.

E.   Overlearning new words: a reminder

Here is a reminder to make vocabulary flash cards for any words you have discovered you need to overlearn. Mix them in with your growing stack of cards and practice flashing the cards and identifying the definitions as quickly as you can. Also make certain you can use the words in a sentence. Are there any words from this chapter you should make cards for?

R⁴   *Reading applications*

Application 1.   Practicing what you learned: "Propositions and Arguments" by W. Edgar Moore, *et al.*

Directions: The following selection is from a textbook entitled *Creative and Critical Thinking.* Read it carefully, applying note taking and marking techniques you learned in Chapter 2. Then answer the questions that follow.

W. EDGAR MOORE, *et al.*

PROPOSITIONS AND ARGUMENTS

1   In order to develop into effective thinkers, we need to learn how to evaluate the procedures of thinking that we and others use in decision making. The principles for evaluating thinking are the same whether our own or someone else's reasoning is at stake. However, decision making can at times be a lengthy and complex process. Thus, in order to evaluate thinking accurately, we have to be able to break down complex thought-processes into constituents that lend themselves to logical analysis.

Propositions

2   Each of us has in his frame of reference and value system innumerable propositions, or statements that are either true or false. These are the elements of thought that carry the information we have gathered and developed in the past. The most obvious examples of propositions are those signified by simple declarative sentences, such as "It is raining" or "There are mice in the attic." Sometimes, though, smaller propositions can be combined into larger ones, as in "Either it is raining or there are mice in the attic." All these statements are either true or false; hence all are propositions. By contrast, commands ("Shut the door!") and questions ("Is it the 29th or the 30th today?") are not propositions, for they are neither true nor false. The position of statements about things that do not exist is less clear. Can it be true or false that Hamlet was Prince of Denmark? Any analysis of Hamlet's actions in the play would assume that he was. Moreover, an instructor who included as a true or false question "Hamlet was Prince of Norway" would expect the answer "False!" and would not settle for a refusal to answer on the ground that since Hamlet did not exist, we cannot talk about whether he was prince of anything. Therefore, such statements are propositions because there are contexts in which they are true or false. It is also clear that while questions and commands are not themselves propositions, they may communicate information and thus imply that certain propositions are true. For example, to say "Shut the door!" is to imply that the door is open. The question "Should a spendthrift Congress be allowed to waste more of your tax money by setting up these useless and inefficient committees?" presupposes a number of assumptions. It assumes that Congress is spendthrift, that the committees are useless and inefficient, and that the money spent in setting them up would be wasted.

Arguments

3   Sentences, of course, usually occur in groups, in which they are combined according to the rules of language so that they elucidate one another in a meaningful way. Such combinations of sentences are called

discourse. And while discourse often involves sentences expressing questions or commands, sentences that express propositions are by far its most numerous components. At times, but not always, discourse is argumentative. Whether this is so depends on how the propositions it includes are related.

4   What exactly is an argument? In ordinary language, we usually use the word argument to refer to any kind of dispute from a debate to a fight. ("They carried on an argument all night about the existence of God, so I didn't get any sleep at all"; "Honestly, Officer, we were just having a little argument about who was supposed to pay for the beer, and. . . ."). In the study of reasoning, however, we use the logician's meaning of the word. In logic, an argument embodies an inference, that is, an implicit or explicit claim that something follows from something else. An example is Descartes's famous inference: "I think; therefore I am." The second proposition, "I am," is supposed to follow from the first proposition, "I think."

5   Most arguments are longer than that of Descartes, for they state more than one proposition as the basis from which the inference is drawn. For example, one might say "Either it is raining or there are mice in the attic, and it is not raining, so there are mice in the attic." Here two propositions are asserted as the basis for the conclusion, and in other cases there are many more. An argument, then, is a set of propositions related in such a way that one of them is claimed to follow from the other or others. A great deal of discourse is argumentative, for arguments are used whenever a person tries to prove something: to show that it is true by supporting it with reasons. For example, much of the discourse in textbooks is composed of arguments because most textbooks, including this one, have a great deal to prove.

6   The first skill you must develop in dealing with arguments is to recognize when an argument occurs. At times this is not hard because, as in the above examples, the person giving the argument will use words such as so and therefore, which make it clear that an argument is intended. At other times, however, arguments are presented in such a way that they are difficult to spot. For instance, one of the following weather reports is an argument while the other is not.

> Tomorrow will be fair and sunny, with a high in the low nineties and a low in the mid-seventies. However, there is a 20 percent chance of thundershowers.

> A cold front is headed our way from the Rockies, bringing with it high winds and thunderstorms. If you were planning to go sailing on the Gulf this weekend, you'd better think about some indoor sports instead.

The first report states facts that are related only in that they are all about the weather. Such discourse as this we call exposition. Exposition is simply a matter of setting forth information in a coherent and unified way. The propositions it contains are claimed to be true, but no effort is made to show that they are true. The first report is expository in that it seeks simply to describe the weather, without trying to prove any of the propositions stated.

7　　　By contrast, the second of the above weather reports contains an argument. This report seeks to establish a conclusion concerning what you should do today, based on facts about the weather. Thus, it implies a logical relationship between propositions—that one is supposed to follow from the others. Moreover, not all of the propositions required for the argument are explicitly stated. One of them, that thunderstorms and high winds make sailing dangerous, is only implied. Formally structured and explicitly stated, the complete argument would read something like this:

Whenever sailing is dangerous, it should be avoided.

High winds and thunderstorms make sailing dangerous.

This weekend will be a time of high winds and thunderstorms.

Therefore this weekend will be a time when sailing should be avoided.

What makes the second report an argument, then, is that rather than simply giving information it uses the information it contains to support a further claim, namely, that sailing should be avoided this weekend. It is the effort to demonstrate the truth of one proposition based on information provided by others that distinguishes argument from strictly expository discourse. Of course, some discourse that is mostly expository will contain a few inferences, and argumentation will contain exposition. With practice, however, you will learn to disentangle the two. The key question is always whether the speaker or writer is trying only to provide information or trying to prove something. The former is exposition; the latter is argument.

1. Define *proposition* as used in the passage.

_____

_____

2. Define *argument* as used in the passage.

_____

_____

3. If your English instructor returned your essay because it was an *exposition* rather than an argument, what would you have to do to change it?

_____

_____

4. What implications can you draw from the statement: "Break down the door!"

   _____

   _____

5. Explain what Descartes meant when he said, "I think; therefore I am."

   _____

   _____

6. The passage you just read is

   a. an argument.

   b. an exposition.

   c. a discourse.

   d. a proposition.

   e. all of the above.

7. Using the example in Paragraph 7, write a structured and explicitly stated argument substituting your argument for or against one of the following:

   a. driving after drinking alcohol

   b. procrastinating on homework

   c. skateboards on campus

   d. cutting classes

   e. your choice

Application 2.   Applying what you learned: "Physics as a Liberal Art" by James S. Trefil

Directions: Read the following preface from a physics textbook. Apply everything you have learned as you read it.

JAMES S. TREFIL

AUTHOR'S PREFACE

1   One of the great joys of a liberal education is the chance that it gives you to study things, just for the fun of it, that will in all likelihood be of no practical use to you in the future. Certainly, when I look back on the courses I took as an undergraduate, the ones that stand out most are not those needed for my profession, as good as they were, but, those courses with names like "Art Appreciation," and "Opera Appreciation." These courses added nothing to my skills as a physicist and never earned me a dollar, but I know that I would be a much poorer person if I hadn't taken them.

2   The idea of the "Appreciation" course is simply to open a new world—a new way of looking at things—to each student. These courses do not teach skills; they teach ideas and concepts. My courses did not turn me into an artist or a musician. What they did was give me some understanding of the art or music of a particular period so that when I encountered it, I had a deeper understanding of it than I would otherwise have had. This is the kind of enrichment of life that is supposed to be the legacy of a liberal education.

3   I began to wonder why courses like this were so seldom found in the offerings of science departments. After some investigation, I discovered that the reason had to do with two rather rigidly held set of prejudices— one set for scientists and another for humanists. Unfortunately, the vast majority of students, holding neither set of prejudices themselves, seemed to be denied the opportunity to learn about science because of them.

4   On the one hand, we have the humanist prejudice. Hasn't it ever struck you as odd that a man who has never read Shakespeare would be considered uneducated, while a man who had never studied Newton or Einstein would not? This sort of attitude is not so uncommon among people who have studied the traditional literary subjects. In some way, science is excluded from "culture," even though the unique contribution of western civilization to human knowledge has been the scientific outlook.

5   On the other side of the coin, when I discussed the ideas for this course with my colleagues, I frequently encountered remarks like "Well, if you teach it that way, you won't really be teaching physics, will you?" In other words there is a strong feeling in the sciences that unless someone is willing to put in the years of study needed to learn a science in its fullest sense, it just isn't worth teaching him anything. The idea of a "Science Appreciation" course with the same goals as an "Art Appreciation" course is incompatible with this way of thinking.

6   In a way, this book is an attempt to find a way between these two conflicting viewpoints, one saying that science isn't worth studying and the other saying that it isn't worth teaching. An attempt is made to see science

in general, and the science of physics in particular, as a part of the development of western civilization. The connection between the cultural background of a scientist and the kind of scientific outlook that emerges is
discussed in several examples, so that when we get to modern science, we
can see it as a part of modern life.

7   The idea of the book is not to teach someone how to work physics problems or to make anyone into a miniature physicist. Instead, I have tried to
explain the central ideas of modern science in simple terms, with an eye
toward giving the student some idea of how science operates and how a
scientist sees the world. If, after going through the book, the student can
pick up the "Science" section of a newsmagazine and have a little deeper
understanding of what he reads than he would ordinarily have had, then I
will consider the experiment in teaching contained herein a success.

1. The author uses the term "liberal education." What does he mean by it?

_____

_____

2. What inferences can you make about his opinion of liberal arts?

_____

_____

3. Circle any of the following that we can infer from the passage.

   a. Some scientists don't think it's possible to teach a science appreciation course.

   b. The book from which the passage is taken is different from most traditional science textbooks.

   c. Studying Newton and Einstein is more important than studying
   Shakespeare.

   d. The author believes that science is human knowledge's best contribution to western civilization.

   e. The author believes most students don't get enough exposure to the
   understanding of science.

4. List some words or phrases that the author uses for their connotative
rather than denotative value.

_____

_____

Application 3.   Looking for propaganda:
                 "America—Casting Light and
                 Shadows" by Mikhail S. Gorbachev

Directions: Since the end of World War II, what's come to be known as the "Cold War" has existed between Russia and the United States. Both literal and verbal wars have been fought because of the differences in the ideologies of the two countries. Propaganda of all types and forms has been used successfully by both countries to further what each believes is right. Read what one Russian has to say about the U.S.

America—Casting Light and Shadows

By MIKHAIL S. GORBACHEV

1   We have too often encountered distorted perceptions about our own country as well as widespread anti-Soviet stereotypes—and therefore we know only too well what evil can be produced by a conscious or unconscious falsehood—to view the United States solely in black and white.

2   I know that American propaganda—yes, propaganda—presents America as a "shining city atop a hill." America has a great history. Who will question the importance of the American Revolution in mankind's social progress, or the scientific-technological genius of America and its achievements in literature, architecture and art? All this America has.

3   But America today also has acute social and other problems, to which not only has American society not yet found an answer, but, even worse, is looking for answers in places and in such a way that may lead to others having to pay.

4   The United States has a huge production potential and an enormous material wealth, but, at the same time, it has millions of unfortunate people.

5   This is something to ponder—an almost missionary passion for preaching about human rights and liberties and a disregard for ensuring those same elementary rights in their own home. This also provokes thought about the endless talk of man's freedom and the attempts to impose a way of life on others.

6   How are we to understand this? Arrogance of power, especially military power, constant growth in arms spending and gaps in the budget, and internal, and now also an external, debt. For what? What motivates the United States? We ask ourselves all these and many other questions, trying to grasp the American reality and to see the mainsprings behind U.S. policy.

7   I admit frankly that what we know does not support the idea of the United States as a "shining city atop a hill."

With equal definiteness I can say that neither do we consider the United States an "evil empire." Like all countries, America in reality casts both light and shadows. We see the United States as it actually is—diverse in its opinions both in and about American society.

8 The Soviet leadership does not perceive the United States in just one dimension, but clearly distinguishes all the facets of American society: the millions of working people going about their daily chores who are generally peacefully disposed; realistically minded politicians; influential conservatives and, alongside them, reactionary groups that have links with the military-industrial complex and profit from arms manufacturing. We see a healthy normal interest in us and also a fairly widespread, blinding anti-Sovietism and anti-communism.

9 We believe the political system and social order of the United States is the business of the American people themselves. They have to decide how to govern their country and how to elect their leadership and their government. We respect this sovereign right.

10 If we began to doubt the choice of the American people, what would come of it? Politics must be built on realities, on an understanding of the fact that each nation has a right to independently choose its way of life and its own system of government.

• *Excerpts from* Perestroika *by Mikhail S. Gorbachev. Copyright © 1984 by Harper & Row, Publishers, Inc. Reprinted by permission of the publisher.*

Questions for writing or class discussion:

1. Because you were told the selection was written by a Russian, did you expect to read what you did? Explain.

2. Is this a propaganda piece? What is its purpose? For whom is it intended?

3. With what do you agree in the essay? With what do you disagree?

4. What, if any, propaganda techniques are used in the essay and how are they used?

Application 4. Examining advertisements

A. *Directions:* Answer the following questions about the advertisement on the next page.

1. What facts are presented in the ad? _____

_____

_____

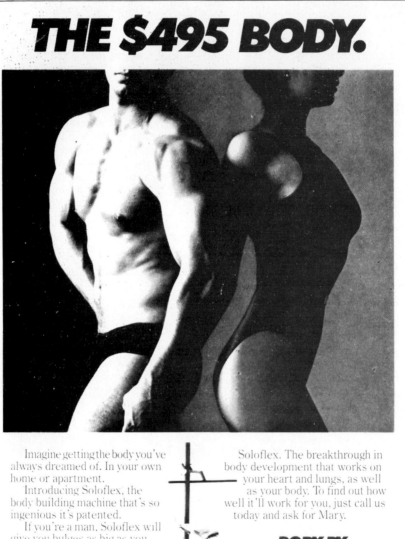

THE $495 BODY.

Imagine getting the body you've always dreamed of. In your own home or apartment.

Introducing Soloflex, the body building machine that's so ingenious it's patented.

If you're a man, Soloflex will give you bulges as big as you want, where you want them. If you're a woman, Soloflex will get rid of bulges, where you don't want them.

Soloflex. The breakthrough in body development that works on your heart and lungs, as well as your body. To find out how well it'll work for you, just call us today and ask for Mary.

BODY BY SOLOFLEX

FOR A FREE BROCHURE,
CALL OUR 24 HR. TOLL-FREE NUMBER
800-453-3301

Soloflex, Hawthorn Farms Industrial Park, Hillsboro, Oregon 97123. All major credit cards accepted.

Jerry L. Wilson, CEO Soloflex, Inc. Soloflex Advertising Department, Hillsboro, Oregon. Reprinted by permission.

2. What words or phrases are aimed at your emotions or values rather than at your powers of reasoning? _____

_____

_____

3. What do you think the people who made up the ad see as being impor-tant to you? What are they using to get your attention? _____

_____

_____

4. What inferences can you draw from the ad? _____

_____

_____

5. What about the ad pleases or displeases you? _____

_____

_____

6. Does the ad persuade you that you need the product? _____

Explain. _____

_____

_____

B.   *Directions:* Answer the following questions about the advertisement on the next page.

1. What facts are presented in the ad? _____

_____

_____

2. What words or phrases are aimed at your emotions or values rather than

at your powers of reasoning? _____

_____

_____

3. What do you think the people who made up the ad see as being important to you? What are they using to get your attention? _____

_____

4. What inferences can you draw from the ad? _____

_____

_____

5. What about the ad pleases or displeases you? _____

_____

_____

6. Does the ad persuade you that you need the product? _____

Explain. _____

_____

_____

_____

C.   *Directions:* Answer the following questions about the advertisement on
the next page.

1. What facts are presented in the ad? _____

_____

_____

2. What words or phrases are aimed at your emotions or values rather than

at your powers of reasoning? _____

_____

_____

3. What do you think the people who made up the ad see as being impor-

   tant to you? What are they using to get your attention? _____

   _____

4. What inferences can you draw from the ad? _____

   _____

   _____

5. What about the ad pleases or displeases you? _____

   _____

   _____

6. Does the ad persuade you that you need the product? _____

   Explain. _____

   _____

Application 5. Summarizing what you have learned

Directions: On a separate sheet of paper, summarize what you have learned from reading this chapter (a) about yourself, (b) about skills you can apply to your reading, and (c) questions you still have that need answering. Turn this in to your instructor when finished.

Recognizing attitude, tone, and bias

7

R¹   *Reading beyond words*

A. Explain in your own words what the following statements mean:

1. "The self-fulfillment search is a more complex, fateful, and irreversible phenomenon than simply the by-product of affluence or a shift in the national character toward narcissism. It is nothing less than the search for a new American philosophy of life."—Daniel Yankelovich

   _____

   _____

   _____

   _____

2. "Business is today the most significant force shaping American life and the strongest influence determining the everyday values of the average citizen."—Otto A. Bremer

   _____

   _____

   _____

   _____

3. "To have a good grasp of your own viewpoint you must understand the arguments of those with whom you disagree. It is said that those who do not completely understand their adversary's point of view do not fully understand their own."—David L. Bender

   _____

   _____

   _____

   _____

B. Explain the values the cartoon below touches upon.

"*Boys, this gentleman would like a show of hands from those who would prefer to watch the public television channel.*"

© 1974 Saturday Review Magazine Co. Reprinted by permission.

_____

_____

_____

R² *Reading actively*

A. Vocabulary preview

Directions: Define the italicized words in the following sentences. Use your dictionary if you need to.

1. If a person *asserts* a statement without having any reason for it, the assertion might be called a matter of opinion.

_____

2. There are several standards by which the *relevance* and the strength of reasons can be evaluated.

   _____

3. They are concerned with what is *prudent,* what is good etiquette, what is good technique.

   _____

4. The social philosopher is concerned with behavior that *entails* either significant harm or benefit for others.

   _____

5. Social philosophy is the study of *communal* conduct.

   _____

6. Ethics and social philosophy are not to be confused with the social or *behavioral sciences.*

   _____

B.   Thought provokers

Directions: Before reading the following selection, answer the following questions.

1. What do people mean when they speak of moral values?

   _____

   _____

2. Name three moral values that you think are among the most important.

   _____

   _____

   _____

3. Who is primarily responsible for teaching moral values?

_____

_____

4. How important are ethics to becoming a successful person? Explain.

_____

_____

C.   Reading practice

Directions: Read the following textbook selection applying all the study-reading and note-making skills you have learned.

PETER A. FACIONE, DONALD SCHERER, and THOMAS ATTIG

THE CONCERNS OF ETHICS AND SOCIAL PHILOSOPHY

1   It is customary to distinguish statements of fact from expressions of opinion. When we distinguish statements of fact from matters of opinion, we have in mind that the statements of fact are known to be true whereas the matters of opinion are statements that nobody is now in a position to know. For example, someone might believe that soccer will have more fans in the year 2000 than football will. Since no one today can know whether this will prove true, this assertion about the future popularity of soccer is a matter of opinion.

2   Normative statements are assertions that express our value judgments which say or imply that something is good or bad, better or worse, ought to be or ought not to be. Whether a given normative statement should be regarded as a matter of opinion is, in the first place, a question of whether any reasons can be given in support of it. If a person asserts a normative statement without having any reasons for it, the assertion might be called a matter of opinion. Normative assertions, however, can be backed by

Facione/Scherer/Attig, Values and Society: An Introduction to Ethics and Social Philosophy. *Copyright © 1978, pp. 8–11. Reprinted by permission of Prentice-Hall, Inc., Englewood Cliffs, New Jersey.*

reasons. Moreover, there are several well-accepted standards by which the relevance and the strength of those reasons can be evaluated. Ethics and social philosophy are in large part attempts to define the relevance and strength clearly. Accordingly, we should not assign all normative statements to the category of matters of opinion. In contrast to normative opinions we should be aware of reasoned, normative assertions.

Concerns of ethics and social philosophy

3   Ethics and social philosophy focus upon concerns expressed in normative statements that have immediate implications for human conduct. Thus, they are concerned with the value judgments appropriate to human behavior. Yet, not all such judgments are correctly understood as having ethical or social philosophical significance. The following normative statements would not ordinarily be understood as having such significance:

Brush your teeth after every meal.

Excuse yourself before leaving the table.

Allow your coffee to cool before drinking it.

Don't use a standard screwdriver in a Phillips screw.

Though these statements have immediate behavior implications, they concern what is prudent, what is good etiquette, or what is good technique. In ordinary circumstances, such matters lack a certain seriousness or weightiness that attaches to the concerns of the ethicist or social philosopher: behavior that either entails significant harm or benefit for others or for oneself, is in accord with or in violation of duties, or involves respect or disrespect for human or moral rights. Examples of statements expressing such concerns are the following:

Murder is wrong.

Self-mutilation is immoral.

You should almost always respond to a cry for help.

Wealth should be distributed equitably.

Promises should be kept.

One must never tell a lie.

The right to live is most fundamental.

The state has no right to tax citizens without representation.

The difference between ethics and social philosophy

4   How, then, are ethics and social philosophy to be distinguished? Ethics is the normative study of individual conduct, and social philosophy is the normative study of communal conduct. If the question of euthanasia is treated as one about the possible behavior of an individual, as in "Would it

be right for me to perform a mercy killing?", then the problem is one of personal ethics. On the other hand, if the normative issue is a possible communal act, as in "Should euthanasia be legalized?", then the problem is one of social philosophy. In terms of content, then, there is a considerable overlap between ethics and social philosophy.

5   Ethics and social philosophy are both disciplined studies. They approach normative problems from a rational, intellectual point of view. Their aim is to arrive at reasonable resolutions of normative issues through the use of rational argumentation and careful consideration of relevant information. In other words, they strive for well-thought-out value judgments.

6   In pursuing these normative questions, ethics and social philosophy bridge the gap between theory and practice. Obviously it is desirable to reach a reasonable resolution to the moral problem presented by a given situation. There are practical concerns such as determining the obligations or responsibilities of people and groups: "What should I do?" and "What should we do?" But there is also the theoretical concern for finding the more general principles or the more universal moral standards that can be relied upon in a variety of situations: theories of moral obligation, theories of praise and blame, and theories about the meaning of individual good and social well-being.

The practical and theoretical sides

7   Ethics and social philosophy have a very practical side, and yet they are not to be confused with other practical human activities that are also concerned with human behavior. Ethics is not advising; it is not counselling. Ethics is not concerned with telling people what is best for them; it is not concerned directly with helping people to deal in a more emotionally stable way with their personal problems. Ethics is not values-clarification. Values clarification techniques can help people find out what they value or prize. The concern of ethics, however, is not with what one *does* value but with what one *should* value. Ethics should not be confused with behavior modification, which aims to alter how a person acts—often through the use of rewards and punishments to reinforce behavior, or even through drug therapy. Ethics does not concern itself with forcing, causing, or encouraging people to act in certain ways. Its immediate goal is knowledge. This knowledge can serve as a guide to one's behavior, but it does not program that behavior.

8   Just as there are similar yet different concerns on the practical side, there are also similar yet different concerns on the theoretical side. Ethics and social philosophy are not to be confused with the social or behavioral sciences. Unlike sociology or anthropology, the concern is not with describing the values, norms, or customs of a given community. Unlike psychology, the concern is not with discovering motivations nor with explaining and predicting human behavior. Unlike history, economics, or political science, the concern is not with understanding the causes or factors that contributed to economic, social, or political phenomena past or present. The primary concern of the scientist is to tell how the world is, why the world is that way, and how it is likely to be in the future. In contrast, the primary

concern of the ethicist or social philosopher is with how the world should be, what will make it *better,* how one *ought* to live.

9   The problems of ethics and social philosophy are problems about "conduct." They are problems about what people should *do, how they ought to behave.* They may be questions about goals, such as "Should legislation be passed to support the maxim of equal pay for equal work?" They may be questions about the means to a goal, such as "Is price fixing for higher prof-its justified in today's market?" Whether they concern goals or means, they remain questions about human behavior and whether or not it is moral, justified, or right.

D.   Comprehension check

Directions: Answer the following questions.

OBJECTIVE QUESTIONS

1. Normative statements are assertions that express our value judgments which say or imply that something is good or bad, right or wrong.

   a. True

   b. False, because _____

   _____

2. Which of the following are normative statements:

   a. Murder is wrong.

   b. Given two equally qualified candidates for a job, one a woman and the other a man, we should hire the woman.

   c. There is nothing more important than human life.

   d. Always obey your parents.

   e. None of the above.

3. In Question 2, items *a* through *d* are opinions.

   a. True

   b. False, because _____

   _____

4. What is the basic function of paragraph 7? What writing pattern is used?

   _____

5. What is the basic function of paragraph 8? What writing pattern is used?

   _____

6. What is the difference between ethics and social philosophy?

   _____

   _____

SUBJECTIVE QUESTIONS

7. Which of the following are moral issues? Place check marks in the space provided.

   _____ a. the use of hard drugs

   _____ b. adultery

   _____ c. pornography

   _____ d. occasional smoking of marijuana

   _____ e. euthanasia

   _____ f. living with someone of the opposite sex before marriage

   _____ g. abortion

   _____ h. getting drunk frequently

   _____ i. shoplifting

8. Pick one of the items you checked above and explain why it is a moral issue.

   _____

   _____

   _____

   _____

9. Using your answer to question 8, write a normative statement about it.

_____

_____

_____

_____

E.   Vocabulary check

Directions: Define the following words or phrases. If you need to, refer to the paragraph whose number follows the word.

1. normative statement (2) _____

2. ethics (2) _____

3. asserts (2) _____

4. relevance (3) _____

5. prudent (3) _____

6. entails (3) _____

7. euthanasia (4) _____

8. communal act (4) _____

9. moral obligation (6) _____

10. behavioral sciences (8) _____

R³ *Reading skills check*

A.   Critically reading for attitude, tone, and bias

When people get angry or excited, they usually raise their voices, move their bodies more, and speak faster. Or they get quiet and say nothing. Their attitudes and feelings are expressed through physical movements or the tone of their voice. But when we read, we cannot see the author's face or hear the tone of voice being used. Still, as critical readers we can learn to recognize an author's attitude, bias, and tone.

By an author's *attitude*, we mean the author's personal feelings toward the subject. When authors write so that it is impossible to tell what they personally feel about the subject, they are being *objective*. When authors let their feelings be known, they are being *subjective*. Writing objectively means that personal feelings and biases are not brought into the writing. Writing subjectively, then, means the author's likes, dislikes, agreements, disagreements, and biases are exposed. Sometimes it is easy to detect the author's attitude and tone; sometimes it's not.

Tone in writing is created by the way the author uses words so that even though we cannot see the author's face or hear a voice, we can tell the writing is meant to be serious, funny, sympathetic, personal, impersonal, honest, or sarcastic. For instance, a good writer can take a serious concept, such as war, and create a tone that is funny or humorous. The novel M*A*S*H deals with the Korean war, a serious topic, but the author's tone makes the war so absurd that we laugh at many of the episodes. This is not to say the author thinks war is funny. Quite the contrary, he makes us laugh at the absurd part of ourselves that allows war to even occur.

An author's attitude and tone toward a topic will reveal whether or not an author is *biased* for or against a subject. As an example, read the following paragraph. The author is writing about moral issues, such as racial prejudice, mercy killing, the death penalty, and abortion, and whether such topics should be debated in public. The paragraph is taken out of context, but see if you can tell what the author's attitude and bias are regarding the subject.

> Nowhere is modern thinking more muddled than over the question of whether it is proper to debate moral issues. Many argue it is not, saying it is wrong. This view is shallow. If it is wrong, then ethics, philosophy, and theology would be unacceptable in a college curriculum—an idea that is obviously silly.

Notice that the subject is whether it is or is not proper to debate moral issues. The author writes subjectively, allowing personal attitude and bias to show. The writer feels moral issues *should* be debated. But more than bias is revealed. By using such words as "muddled," "shallow," and "silly," the author creates a tone, enabling us to see her belief that those who oppose her views are not very deep or clear thinkers.

Here is a sample of a paragraph that is taken from an essay about gun control. The author is reacting to the slogan "Guns Don't Kill; People Do." See if you can recognize his *attitude* and *tone*.

> Despite the popular misconceptions, most Americans' rifles, for example, are used as tomato stakes. Or as curtain rods, or softball bats.

Sometimes as rudders on small rafts. Many rifle owners also stuff bundles of straw up the barrels of their rifles and—presto!—they've got a child's toy broom. (Richard Lipez, "Guns and Batter," *The Progressive*, 1975.)

Notice that the author makes some seemingly rather silly comments: Americans use rifles as tomato stakes, curtain rods, softball bats, rudders, and brooms. But as critical readers we must be aware that his attitude about guns is serious. He does not believe that "guns don't kill; people do." We know because of his *tone*, his exaggeration of what guns are used for. We know he does not really mean what he is saying. His tone is sarcastic, almost angry, and his attitude toward his reader seems to be: "You can't be fool enough to believe that slogan. If you do, you *are* a fool." Thus, attitude and tone are closely connected.

Notice how the author's attitude and tone come out in the following paragraph:

> The supermarket is to modern man what the jungle was to primitive people. It is the source of food that has to be sought out with great skill in order to obtain the best quality. Economic traps and threats camouflaged as harmless goodies lurk in every aisle. Shopping, like hunting, is a game of skill with survival as the prize. (Jeffrey Schrank, *Deception Detection*, Boston: Beacon Press, 1975.)

Here we get the author's attitude about supermarkets through his tone. He compares/contrasts the modern supermarket with the jungle. This is our clue; it shows us that his attitude is that supermarkets are dangerous. His attitude toward the reader is that he wants us to wake up and see those dangers. We know this through his tone, which is brought out by such word choices as "economic *traps*" (as opposed to animal traps), "threats *camouflaged* as harmless goodies" (as opposed to hunters and animals camouflaging themselves), "*lurk*" (dangerous animals lurk in the bush), "*game of skill*" (hunting). But because his analogy of the supermarket with the jungle is so exaggerated, we see a touch of humor, a tone. His attitude and tone reveal he is cynical about supermarkets and our ability to survive in them. Recognizing attitude and tone requires reading beyond the words.

EXERCISE

Directions: Read the following essay looking for the author's subjective or objective attitude toward his subject, any biases that might show, and the tone of the writing. Do you think the author treats the subject fairly?

ARTHUR KROPP

TEEN SUICIDE: A TABOO SUBJECT

1   Teen suicides have become routine front-page news. The recent suicides in New Jersey, New York, and Washington, D.C., are just the latest in a growing national tragedy that takes up to 5,000 young American lives a year. In fact, among teen-agers between 15 and 19 years of age, suicide is the second biggest cause of death.

2   Teen suicide, however, has not produced the research or public concern devoted to, say, teen-age drug abuse or teen pregnancy. Many solutions are being offered, and the fear of AIDS has encouraged a renewed interest in sex education in the schools, as well as scientific research into how to stop the virus. But the growing rate of teen suicide remains one of our society's most taboo subjects.

3   Unfortunately, suicide, like any complicated problem, cannot be prevented by being ignored. Yet as the deadly statistics keep rising, efforts to keep the subject hushed up—especially in the classroom—are also growing.

4   Phyllis Schlafly, a spokeswoman for the far right, rails against even mentioning the subject of stress and confusion in the classroom. "It is not normal for children to have stress," she proclaims, "and it is a lie to teach them it is." Schlafly's Eagle Forum and other self-appointed morality censors are out to rid the schools of books, plays and classroom discussions for "promoting" suicide or being "too depressing." Their logic: if you don't talk about difficult issues or feelings, nothing bad will happen.

5   Last year, for example, this logic led to efforts to keep Shakespeare out of the classroom. The film of "Romeo and Juliet" was attacked in Oklahoma for encouraging "suicide and drug use," and in Nebraska because it "romanticizes teen-age suicide." Another Shakespearean play, "Macbeth," was the target of objections, this time in Colorado, because it focused on "death, suicide, ghosts and Satan." Literature such as Ken Kesey's "One Flew Over the Cuckoo's Nest" and Maya Angelou's "I Know Why the Caged Bird Sings" were also attacked as depressing and thus not suitable for students. One of the authors whose work is most challenged today is Judy Blume, who writes about the difficulties, confusions and joys of growing up.

6   But the Schlaflys of the world do not simply want to keep students from being exposed to the very real problems of drugs, heavy drinking, depression, and even suicide. They are against aspects of school curricula that teach students to deal with conflict, to make difficult choices, to hear different points of view, and to learn about themselves. Questioning and open discussions become taboo.

7   To many who oppose programs, literature, and classroom discussions about difficult subjects, learning about such subjects can only lead to abuse—not responsible choices. Thus, sex education courses, health textbooks, and drug abuse prevention programs are favored targets of censorship campaigns. Last year, far right groups tried to ban drug abuse programs in New York, California, Wisconsin and Washington state. In some instances, they succeeded. And sex education courses came under fire in 10 states, from Maine to Oregon. Most of these courses were criticized for not teaching moral absolutes and for focusing on teaching students how to make choices and decisions.

8   The leaders of the far right suffer from a misguided moralism that, if realized, would hinder, not help, society. They believe the real cause of teen pregnancy is rock and roll music, and that sex education leads to instant promiscuity. Their response to the drug problem is to keep students ignorant of the pitfalls and dangers of such a path. The head-in-the-sand approach also applies to teen-age suicide. Just say no to depression and anxiety, they say.

9   Growing up has always been difficult, in all times and places. But isn't it better to face that universal fact, and try to help teen-agers confront and understand the many conflicting ideas and feelings that they are experiencing, instead of trying to pretend they don't exist? The growing problems of drug abuse, teen-age pregnancy, and suicide have placed the future of our children at risk. While many continue to argue that only parents or the church should be responsible, these problems have an enormous impact on the dropout rate in schools, which is now over 30 percent. They affect the learning atmosphere of every classroom. If effective programs dealing with social problems and books and plays that take on these issues fall victim to the censors' demands, then the only winners are ignorance and further abuse.

Now answer these questions:

1. The essay is mostly written subjectively.

   a. True

   b. False

2. The author seems to be biased toward student exposure to certain Shakespeare plays.

   a. True

   b. False

3. The tone of the essay is mostly (circle those that apply):

   a. serious

   b. impersonal

   c. sad

   d. sarcastic

   e. humorous

   f. concerned

4. Reread Paragraph 4. What attitudes/biases are represented there?

   _____

   _____

5. Is Paragraph 5 mostly subjective or objective? _____

   _____

6. What's the author's attitude toward questioning and open class discussion in Paragraph 7? _____

   _____

7. Reread the first sentence of Paragraph 9. What is your answer to the author's question? _____

   _____

8. Did any of your own biases/attitudes toward the subjects mentioned get triggered as you read this essay? Explain. _____

   _____

   _____

   _____

B.   Reader and author bias

To read critically requires good reasoning on your part, or you are likely to find yourself accepting opinions and biases of others and thinking they are your own ideas. Many of us, without knowing it, are slaves to other people's ideas. Learning to read critically helps us to reason and think for ourselves.

We do not read or think critically when we draw hasty conclusions or poor inferences. We do not read or think critically when we oversimplify an issue, or when we willingly accept what we read and hear without checking the source or thinking about an author's opinion. We do not read or think critically when we resist someone else's ideas only because they are different from ours and for no other reason. Neither do we read critically when we try to place everything into a neat category or stereotype, when we want quick, "pat" answers to everything. Sometimes there are no ready answers.

To read critically, we also need to be aware of our own bias or prejudice as well as the author's. To be biased or prejudiced is to have a closed mind about something or someone. We can be so biased about something that we do not allow ourselves to reason and think for ourselves. For instance, we may grow up hearing our parents and friends say negative things about neighbors, religious groups, politicians, other countries, and the like until we begin to believe those things ourselves. We become biased and prejudiced without even realizing it. All of us have biases, even authors; so as critical readers we must be careful not to let our biases interfere with our comprehension. Similarly, we must be able to recognize an author's bias so that we are not influenced until we have investigated the facts.

EXERCISE

Directions: Read the following passages and answer the questions that follow.

A.   America's leadership role in the world has been lost because of moral decay from within. Many of us can remember when our nation's top officials were shining symbols of what every red-blooded American wanted to emulate. These leaders radiated honesty, integrity and moral strength which in turn provided hope, strength and compassion to the people.

Today, no day goes by without the discovery of more fraud, more deceit and more scum in high places. Most are clever lawyer–politicians who know how to steal from the public—legally. When caught doing illegal acts, they may even have to perform the same kind of public service the rest of us volunteer freely.

When America decides to elect decent citizens to public office again instead of slick, professional politicians, most of our economic and crime problems will disappear. (James Baker, *Los Angeles Times*, September 19, 1989, Section 2, p. 6.)

1. What is the author's attitude toward the subject being discussed?

   _____

2. What words describe the tone? _____

   _____

3. Does your bias agree with the author's? Explain. _____

   _____

   _____

   _____

4. Is the author correct? Explain. _____

   _____

   _____

   _____

B.   A few weeks ago, *The New York Times* reported that McDonald's, Kimberly-Clark and other large corporations canceled advertisements on a Fox network TV series, "Married . . . With Children," after one woman wrote letters denouncing the show as "anti-family." At about the same time, several CBS affiliates pulled the program "TV-101" off the air after protests from anti-abortion groups. . . . The growing number of incidents gives new urgency to a question that was once debated only in ethics classes at business schools—what is the responsibility of corporations with regard to the First Amendment?
     The corporations usually argue that they have little or no special responsibility. Our business, they say, is business, i.e., making money by serving customers, not leading the battle for the First Amendment. They often justify their actions by saying their intent is not to take sides but to avoid controversy. . . . The recent events, however, show how flawed this argument is. Too often, by attempting to avoid controversy, they let themselves become accomplices to extremism. Surely corporations can and should do better than that. (Arthur Kropp, "Business

Should Do Its Part to Fight Censorship," *The Sunday Telegram* (Nashua, NH, April 9, 1989.)

1. What is the author's attitude toward the subject being discussed?

   _____

2. What words describe the tone?

   _____

3. Does your bias agree with the author's? Explain.

   _____

   _____

   _____

4. Is the author correct? Explain.

   _____

   _____

   _____

C.   A recent *TV Guide* cover illustration of Oprah Winfrey, looking sensational in a seductive, leggy pose on a stack of money, was an eye-catcher. It was also a fraud. We all know by now that we were duped, fooled, bamboozled, tricked, deceived. The only thing that was Oprah's was her head. The body, the dress, the pose were Ann-Margret's—and almost 10 years old. The incident is by no means trivial. It should have responsible journalists and the entire reading public steaming mad and genuinely concerned about the media's commitment to truth.

Apparently, *TV Guide* editors, without the permission of either Winfrey or Ann-Margret, decided to make a composite to create an "effect." . . . Nothing in the magazine indicated that the illustration was a composite. The hoax was revealed when the designer of Ann-Margret's dress recognized his creation. (Michael Josephson and Christopher Tyner, "Media's Dirty Little Practices," *Los Angeles Times*, September 19, 1989, Section 2, p. 6.)

1. What attitude toward the subject being discussed do the authors reveal?

   _____

2. What words describe the tone?

_____

3. Does your bias agree with the authors'? Explain.

_____

_____

_____

4. Are the authors correct? Explain.

_____

_____

_____

C. Vocabulary tip: biased and emotional language

As you have seen by now, words not only have various meanings depending on context, but they also can create feelings and imply a sense of values. Some words help us to stereotype people, places, and ideas: American way, un-American, punk, playboy, communist, politician, yuppie, idealist, bum, sexy, handsome, and so forth. Such words give us a kind of visual image or idea we associate with the words; yet they do not really have the same meaning for all of us. What seems to be "the American way" to you is "un-American" to another. What is "beautiful" to you is so-so to another. Yet these words, because of our biases and their emotional appeal, are used as though we all knew what we were talking about.

Good writers and speakers are aware that their choice of words can influence the way we respond and see things. Advertisers, journalists, and politicians, for instance, consider every word they use to sway us to their way of thinking. If we are not careful, we end up following their line of thought without having thought for ourselves.

Notice the following advertisement caption:

Nothing else feels like real gold.
Nothing else makes any moment so precious.
Give her the gleaming, elegant, enduring gift she will treasure all of her
   life.

What is the ad selling? What is so "gleaming, elegant, enduring" that

"she will treasure" it all of her life? _____

The advertisement is for karat gold jewelry and sponsored by the Jewelers of America. Look at the words the ad uses: "Nothing else," "precious," "gleaming," "enduring," "elegant"—all words with positive emotional appeal. Yet why should gold be something "she" will treasure all of her life? The world treasures gold. Some countries' economies are based on the gold standard. People steal and kill for it. Why? What has made gold—and not zinc, say—so "treasured"? Mostly, it is because a few control the world's gold and can force us to think it is "precious." Others have made it a wealth symbol, a standard, that most of us just accept. The advertisement appeals to our need for social status, but is that a real need?

Advertising language is easy to spot. Here is an example taken from a magazine ad, but extra words have been inserted. See if you can figure out which words were used in the ad and why. Circle the ones you pick.

Our women's shoes are (manufactured, fabricated, built, made, bench-

crafted) by (clever, skilled, cunning, nimble) hands. They aren't rolled

off the assembly line. They never will be. No one has been able to (du-

plicate, equal, imitate, match) our (uncommon, atypical, one-of-a kind,

unique) (look, appearance, image, style).

In the space below, explain why you think the words you circled are the ones originally used.

_____

_____

_____

_____

During political campaigns, biased and emotional language flies. Read the following "press release" and circle all the positive words in the parentheses:

Senator Zorch is a man of (firm/stubborn) (prejudices/convictions)

with the (courage/gall) to (speak out/mouth off) about them. He has a

(gentle/weak) disposition and is very (fussy/meticulous) in his habits.

Mrs. Zorch is (notorious/famous) for her (outgoing/interfering) nature and her (articulate speech/glib chatter) as well as her (relaxed/dull) dinner parties. The Senator and Mrs. Zorch (spoil/dote upon) their six-year-old son, an (energetic/hyperactive) (brat/child) with his father's (smirk/grin). (J. MacKillop and D. W. Cross, *Speaking of Words*, New York: Holt, Rinehart and Winston, 1978, p. 64.)

Now go back and read the paragraph ignoring the circled words and see the difference.

Following are some words used frequently in politics. In the space in front of the word, place a P for those that have positive connotations and an N for the negative ones:

_____   1. politician

_____   2. welfare state

_____   3. conservative

_____   4. liberal

_____   5. civil rights

_____   6. federal spending

_____   7. socialized medicine

_____   8. communism

_____   9. socialism

_____ 10. states' rights

Discuss these in class.

Here are some pairs of words. For each pair, circle the word you would rather be called.

original/weird	adventurous/reckless
slender/skinny	relaxed/flaky
arrogant/proud	stubborn/pigheaded
obese/overweight	trusting/gullible

There is a saying, "Sticks and stones may break my bones, but words will never hurt me." Would that statement hold true if you were called any of the words above? Explain.

_____

_____

_____

_____

As you continue to read and listen to what people say, pay attention to the words that are used. They can often tell you about a person's biases as well as your own.

R⁴ *Reading applications*

Application 1. Examining your biases

Directions: Below is a list of incomplete sentences. Complete each one with the first word that comes to mind. If you can't immediately think of a word or phrase, skip it and go on to the next sentence. Don't stop to evaluate what you write in.

1. Teachers are _____

2. Mothers are _____

3. Democrats are _____

4. Babies are _____

5. Communists are _____

6. Welfare recipients are _____

7. Elderly people are _____

8. Protestants are _____

9. My neighbors are _____

10. Vietnamese are _____

11. Republicans are _____

12. Lawyers are _____

13. Girl Scouts are _____

14. Baseball players are _____

15. Catholics are _____

Some of your responses may be flippant or silly, but most of them are probably based on some experience you have had or a bias you have learned from others. On a sheet of paper, pick one item from above and write down where you think your attitude came from. Was it a real experience or one you have heard or read about? What does this tell you about your biases? What did you learn in this chapter that might help you overcome some of your biases?

Application 2. Reading and reacting: "Moral Issues Frustrate Our Bent for Compromise" by Cynthia Harrison

Directions: Read the following essay looking for the author's thesis, attitude, tone and bias. But first, answer these questions:

1. Are you for or against abortion? _____

2. Do you believe the federal or state governments should attempt to legalize moral issues? _____

3. Should individual states have the right to their own separate laws on issues such as abortion? _____

CYNTHIA HARRISON

MORAL ISSUES FRUSTRATE OUR BENT FOR COMPROMISE

1   For the past two decades, the conflict over abortion has survived every political stratagem to subdue it. Even the usually conclusive policy instrument of a U.S. Supreme Court fueled rather than dampened the debate. In virtually every term, the court hears cases involving new state laws intended to restrict the right to abortion; opponents of abortion militate for a change on the bench in order to have Roe vs. Wade reversed. Congress has prohibited federal funding for abortion except when the mother's life is in danger.

2   In 1982, the Brookings Institution and the Ford Foundation found the political tactics of abortion activists on both sides worrisome enough to conduct a symposium to examine "the effects of the abortion controversy on the governmental system." Had "the relentless pursuit of a policy objective" through "sometimes novel or unprecedented techniques" jeopardized the functioning of the governmental system? These analysts concluded not.

3   But they might have asked a different question: How does the American political system deal with questions like abortion? The answer: ineffectively.

4   The American political system was not designed to deal with those kind of questions—moral issues that can't be negotiated—where you can't split the difference and have all the players feel that they came out with something. With abortion, no compromise can be acceptable, even temporarily, to both sides. For one side, abortion is murder; for the other, it is an exercise in the fundamental human right to control one's body. So, the outcome of each abortion battle is determined not by compromise but by the number of votes on each side in a legislature. The loser's position is never respected and never accommodated. Because of the character of the dispute, it can't be.

5   But the persistence of the abortion dispute also grows out of the most esteemed qualities of the American system. One is respect for a multiplicity of religious expressions incorporated in the separation of church and state. From the beginning, Americans deliberately excluded the church, the very institution designed to grapple with questions of individual morality, from governmental decision-making. European nations historically have had no such bar. Middle Eastern nations make no pretense of separating religious and civil authority. In the most theocratic states, moral questions are resolved by fiat.

6   But the United States was too diverse even in the 18th Century to choose one church to establish; the American response was to decree that individual morality was (within some limits) a matter of individual conscience, not for

the state to define. The upshot of such a policy has been that the state en-
forces only those moral positions that are virtually unanimous. When the
country has been riven by deeply felt divisions on moral questions, like slavery or Prohibition, abortion or homosexuality, government attempts to
compel obedience to laws banning particular kinds of behavior have not
succeeded.

7   But this incapacity also derives from American strengths: a commitment
to free political expression and to the principle of a nonintrusive state. Enforcement of morality laws requires both repressive and invasive police procedures that America traditionally eschew. During Prohibition, federal
agents complained to Congress that they could not catch law-breakers unless
allowed to conduct warrantless searches which are banned by the Fourth
Amendment. Congress nonetheless rejected the proposal. Vocal opponents of
laws may encourage violations, but the courts continue to expand free-speech
protection.

8   Constrained by such legal barriers, states rarely even try to enforce
morals statutes. When it was struck down by the Supreme Court in 1965,
Connecticut's law Prohibiting the use of birth-control devices, even by married couples, had never been used against a married couple despite the
widespread and open sale of contraceptives.

9   Conflicts as bitter as the one over abortion have been rare in U.S. history. To crib from political scientist Louis Hartz: Americans are used to
taking their ethics for granted; our debates are more likely to be over technique, not ends. The abortion argument is certainly over moral imperatives,
not strategy. And, as with the issues of slavery and Prohibition, both the
pro-choice and the anti-abortion positions are emblems of larger world
views, each of them turning on the place of women in that world.

10   But as long as we endorse the right of citizens to voice their political
opinions and to bring pressure to bear upon policy makers, and confirm
our belief in limited government intrusion in personal behavior, two things
will be true of this controversy: If abortion once again becomes illegal,
women will certainly continue to have them (albeit dangerously and expen-
sively) and the dissension over these fundamental moral differences will
stay with us for a long time to come. Free expression and conflict come
together in a single package.

1. The opening paragraph is mostly subjective.

   a. True

   b. False

2. The author's attitude toward the effectiveness of the government's ability to deal with questions like abortion is positive.

   a. True

   b. False

3. Which paragraphs in the essay support your answer to Question 2?

    a. Paragraph 1

    b. Paragraph 2

    c. Paragraph 3

    d. Paragraph 4

    e. Paragraph 5

4. What author bias or subjectivity is shown in paragraph 7?

    _____

    _____

5. We can infer that the author believes abortion is a moral, not a legal issue.

    a. True

    b. False

6. Paragraph 8 is mostly objectively stated.

    a. True

    b. False

7. The author is for abortion.

    a. True

    b. False

    c. Unable to determine from the reading

8. The tone of the essay is best described as

    a. serious.

    b. humorous.

c. sarcastic.

d. impersonal.

e. confused.

Application 3.   Examining your attitude and bias: "The Case for Torture" by Michael Levin

Directions: Read the following essay looking for the author's thesis, support, attitude, tone and bias. When finished reading, on a separate sheet of paper, write your own essay either in support or against the author's thesis.

MICHAEL LEVIN

THE CASE FOR TORTURE

1   It is generally assumed that torture is impermissible, a throwback to a more brutal age. Enlightened societies reject it outright, and regimes suspected of using it risk the wrath of the United States.

2   I believe this attitude is unwise. There are situations in which torture is not merely permissible but morally mandatory. Moreover, these situations are moving from the realm of imagination to fact.

3   **Death:** Suppose a terrorist has hidden an atomic bomb on Manhattan Island which will detonate at noon on July 4 unless . . . (here follow the usual demands for money and release of his friends from jail). Suppose, further, that he is caught at 10 a.m. of the fateful day, but—preferring death to failure—won't disclose where the bomb is. What do we do? If we follow due process—wait for his lawyer, arraign him—millions of people will die. If the only way to save those lives is to subject the terrorist to the most excruciating possible pain, what grounds can there be for not doing so? I suggest there are none. In any case, I ask you to face the question with an open mind.

4   Torturing the terrorist is unconstitutional? Probably. But millions of lives surely outweigh constitutionality. Torture is barbaric? Mass murder is

Reprinted with permission of Michael Levine, Professor of Philosophy, City University of New York.

far more barbaric. Indeed, letting millions of innocents die in deference to one who flaunts his guilt is moral cowardice, an unwillingness to dirty one's hands. If *you* caught the terrorist, could you sleep nights knowing that millions died because you couldn't bring yourself to apply the electrodes?

5   Once you concede that torture is justified in extreme cases, you have admitted that the decision to use torture is a matter of balancing innocent lives against the means needed to save them. You must now face more realistic cases involving more modest numbers. Someone plants a bomb on a jumbo jet. He alone can disarm it, and his demands cannot be met (or if they can, we refuse to set a precedent by yielding to his threats). Surely we can, we must, do anything to the extortionist to save the passengers. How can we tell 300, or 100, or 10 people who never asked to be put in danger, "I'm sorry, you'll have to die in agony, we just couldn't bring ourselves to . . ."

6   Here are the results of an informal poll about a third, hypothetical, case. Suppose a terrorist group kidnapped a newborn baby from a hospital. I asked four mothers if they would approve of torturing kidnappers if that were necessary to get their own newborns back. All said yes, the most "liberal" adding that she would like to administer it herself.

7   I am not advocating torture as punishment. Punishment is addressed to deeds irrevocably past. Rather, I am advocating torture as an acceptable measure for preventing future evils. So understood, it is far less objectionable than many extant punishments. Opponents of the death penalty, for example, are forever insisting that executing a murderer will not bring back his victim (as if the purpose of capital punishment were supposed to be resurrection, not deterrence or retribution). But torture, in the cases described, is intended not to bring anyone back but to keep innocents from being dispatched. The most powerful argument against using torture as a punishment or to secure confessions is that such practices disregard the rights of the individual. Well, if the individual is all that important—and he is—it is correspondingly important to protect the rights of individuals threatened by terrorists. If life is so valuable that it must never be taken, the lives of the innocents must be saved even at the price of hurting the one who endangers them.

8   Better precedents for torture are assassination and pre-emptive attack. No Allied leader would have flinched at assassinating Hitler, had that been possible. (The Allies did assassinate Heydrich.) Americans would be angered to learn that Roosevelt could have had Hitler killed in 1943—thereby shortening the war and saving millions of lives—but refused on moral grounds. Similarly, if nation A learns that nation B is about to launch an unprovoked attack, A has a right to save itself by destroying B's military capability first. In the same way, if the police can by torture save those who would otherwise die at the hands of kidnappers or terrorists, they must.

9   **Idealism:** There is an important difference between terrorists and their victims that should mute talk of the terrorists' "rights." The terrorist's victims are at risk unintentionally, not having asked to be endangered. But the terrorist knowingly initiated his actions. Unlike his victims, he volunteered for the risks of his deed. By threatening to kill for profit or idealism, he

renounces civilized standards, and he can have no complaint if civilization tries to thwart him by whatever means necessary.

10   Just as torture is justified only to save lives (not extort confessions or recantations), it is justifiably administered only to those *known* to hold innocent lives in their hands. Ah, but how can the authorities ever be sure they have the right malefactor? Isn't there a danger of error and abuse? Won't We turn into Them?

11   Questions like these are disingenuous in a world in which terrorists proclaim themselves and perform for television. The name of their game is public recognition. After all, you can't very well intimidate a government into releasing your freedom fighters unless you announce that it is your group that has seized its embassy. "Clear guilt" is difficult to define, but when 40 million people see a group of masked gunmen seize an airplane on the evening news, there is not much question about who the perpetrators are. There will be hard cases where the situation is murkier. Nonetheless, a line demarcating the legitimate use of torture can be drawn. Torture only the obviously guilty, and only for the sake of saving innocents, and the line between Us and Them will remain clear.

12   There is little danger that the Western democracies will lose their way if they choose to inflict pain as one way of preserving order. Paralysis in the face of evil is the greater danger. Some day soon a terrorist will threaten tens of thousands of lives, and torture will be the only way to save them. We had better start thinking about this.

Application 4.   Summarizing what you have learned

Directions: On a separate sheet of paper, summarize what you have learned from reading this chapter (a) about yourself, (b) about skills you can apply to your reading, and (c) questions you still have that need answering. Turn this in to your instructor when finished.

Reading literature

8

R¹   *Reading beyond words*

The previous chapters all deal with reading expository writing—textbooks, essays, newspaper items and the like. This chapter deals with the reading of creative literature. In a sense, all writing is creative, but here we refer specifically to poetry and fiction which includes short stores and novels. Most college English courses, even composition courses, require the reading of some poetry and fiction.

Although poetry and fiction are "made up," writers of such literature, if they are good, manage to capture a significant moment, a mood, or a revelation in the life of a person that readers recognize as true to life, something they too know or have felt. It is said that literature is the substance of everything that man has thought, felt, or created. But to understand that substance requires that a reader know how to approach the reading of creative literature, because such understanding truly requires reading beyond words. This chapter serves that end.

1. Read the following poem and in your own words explain what you think the author is writing about. You will need to read the poem several times before you get beyond the words.

SYLVIA PLATH

METAPHORS

I'm a riddle in nine syllables,
An elephant, a ponderous house,
A melon strolling on two tendrils.
O red fruit, ivory, fine timbers!
This loaf's big with its yeasty rising.
Money's new-minted in this fat purse.
I'm a means, a stage, a cow in calf.
I've eaten a bag of green apples,
Boarded the train there's no getting off.

"Metaphors" from Crossing the Water *by Sylvia Plath. Copyright © 1971 by Ted Hughes. Reprinted by permission of Harper & Row, Publishers, Inc.*

2. Explain the point behind the following cartoon.

By permission of John Hart and NAS, Inc.

_____

_____

_____

_____

R² *Reading actively*

A. Vocabulary preview

Directions: For questions 1–5, find the numbered definition in the dictionary entry that best fits the way the italicized word is used in the sentences below.

1. The *setting* of the novel *The French Lieutenant's Woman*, by John Fowles, is Lyme Regis, England.

   set·ting (sĕt′ĭng) *n.* **1.** The act of a person or thing that sets. **2.** The context in which a situation is set. **3.** A jewelry mounting. **4.** The scenery for a theatrical performance. **5.** The descent of the sun or other celestial body below the horizon.

   _____

2. One of the *themes* of Shakespeare's *Othello* is that passion clouds reason.

> **theme** (thēm) *n*. **1.** A topic of discourse or discussion. **2.** The subject of an artistic work. **3.** A short written composition. **4.** *Mus.* A melody forming the basis of variations or other development in a composition. [<Gk *thema*, "thing placed," proposition.]

3. The *character* of Willy Loman in *Death of a Salesman* is so well developed that we can empathize with him without having shared his particular experiences.

> **char·ac·ter** (kăr′ĭk-tər) *n*. **1.** A distinguishing feature or attribute; a characteristic. **2.** The moral or ethical structure of a person or group. **3.** Moral strength; integrity. **4.** Reputation. **5.** *Informal.* An eccentric person. **6.** A person portrayed in a drama, novel, etc. **7.** A symbol in a writing system. **8.** Any structure, function, or attribute determined by a gene or group of genes. [<Gk *kharaktēr*, engraved mark, brand.]

4. The *conflict* the barber in the story goes through is not one I'd care to have.

> **con·flict** (kon′flikt) *n*. **1.** Prolonged warfare. **2.** A clash of opposing ideas, interests, etc.; disagreement.—*v*. (kən-flickt′). To be in opposition; differ. [<Lat. *confligere*, to strike together.]—**con·flic′tive** *adj*.

5. The *irony* is that the student didn't realize he was criticizing someone like himself.

> **i·ron·y** (i′rə-ne) *n., pl.* **-nies. 1.** The use of words to convey the opposite of their literal meaning. **2.** Incongruity between what might be expected and what actually occurs. [<Gk. *eironeia*, feigned ignorance.]

For the following italicized words in the sentences, write a definition of their meaning as used. If you need to, use your dictionary.

6. I was passing the best of my razors back and forth on a *strop*.

   _____

7. I asked him a question, *feigning* interest.

   _____

8. Under the stroke of my razor, Torres was being *rejuvenated* because I was a good barber.

   _____

9. What he had done was *ineradicable* from my memory.

   _____

10. It was likely that many of our *faction* had seen him enter.

    _____

B.   Thought provokers

1. How is a fictional story different from an essay?

   _____

   _____

   _____

2. What point or value is there in reading poetry?

   _____

   _____

   _____

3. What point or value is there in reading fiction?

   _____

   _____

   _____

C.   Reading practice

Previous chapters show how to survey or look over what you read before reading closely. Doing so helps you focus on what you are going to read, helps you concentrate on the subject while reading, and gives you a purpose for reading. But when you read a poem or fiction, you don't want to survey first. That would ruin the enjoyment of the story. In most cases a story writer's first purpose is to entertain, but along with that is the desire to make a true or meaningful statement about life and people, to give us a new perspective or a reminder of life's values. As you read the following story, see if you understand what the author is saying beyond the words.

HERNANDO TELLEZ

JUST LATHER, THAT'S ALL

1   He said nothing when he entered. I was passing the best of my razors back and forth on a strop. When I recognized him I started to tremble. But he didn't notice. Hoping to conceal my emotion, I continued sharpening the razor. I tested it on the meat of my thumb, and then held it up to the light. At that moment he took off the bullet-studded belt that his gun holster dangled from. He hung it up on a wall hook and placed his military cap over it. Then he turned to me, loosening the knot of his tie, and said, "It's hot as hell. Give me a shave." He sat in the chair.

2   I estimated he had a four-day beard. The four days taken up by the latest expedition in search of our troops. His face seemed reddened, burned by the sun. Carefully, I began to prepare the soap. I cut off a few slices, dropped them into the cup, mixed in a bit of warm water, and began to stir with the brush. Immediately the foam began to rise. "The other boys in the group should have this much beard, too." I continued stirring the lather.

3   "But we did all right, you know. We got the main ones. We brought back some dead, and we've got some others still alive. But pretty soon, they'll all be dead."

4   "How many did you catch?" I asked.

5   "Fourteen. We had to go pretty deep into the woods to find them. But we'll get even. Not one of them comes out of this alive, not one."

6   He leaned back in the chair when he saw me with the lather-covered brush in my hand. I still had to put the sheet over him. No doubt about it, I was upset. I took a sheet out of a drawer and knotted it around my

customer's neck. He wouldn't stop talking. He probably thought I was in sympathy with his party.

7   "The town must have learned a lesson from what we did the other day," he said.

8   "Yes," I replied, securing the knot at the base of his dark, sweaty neck.

9   "That was a fine show, eh?"

10   "Very good," I answered, turning back for the brush. The man closed his eyes with a gesture of fatigue and sat waiting for the cool caress of the soap. I had never had him so close to me. The day he ordered the whole town to file into the patio of the school to see the four rebels hanging there, I came face to face with him for an instant. But the sight of the mutilated bodies kept me from noticing the face of the man who had directed it all, the face I was now about to take into my hands. It was not an unpleasant face, certainly. And the beard, which made him seem a bit older than he was, didn't suit him badly at all. His name was Torres. Captain Torres. A man of imagination, because who else would have thought of hanging the naked rebels and then holding target practice on certain parts of their bodies? I began to apply the first layer of soap. With his eyes closed, he continued. "Without any effort I could go straight to sleep," he said, "but there's plenty to do this afternoon." I stopped the lathering and asked with a feigned lack of interest: "A firing squad?" "Something like that, but a little slower." I got on with the job of lathering his beard. My hands started trembling again. The man could not possibly realize it, and this was in my favor. But I would have preferred that he hadn't come. It was likely that many of our faction had seen him enter. And any enemy under one's roof imposes certain conditions. I would be obliged to shave that beard like any other one, carefully, gently, like that of any customer, taking pains to see that no single pore emitted a drop of blood. Being careful to see that the little tufts of hair did not lead the blade astray. Seeing that his skin ended up clean, soft, and healthy, so that passing the back of my hand over it I couldn't feel a hair. Yes, I was secretly a rebel, but I was also a conscientious barber, and proud of the preciseness of my profession. And this four-day's growth of beard was a fitting challenge.

11   I took the razor, opened up the two protective arms, exposed the blade and began the job, from one of the sideburns downward. The razor responded beautifully. His beard was inflexible and hard, not too long, but thick. Bit by bit the skin emerged. The razor rasped along, making its customary sound as fluffs of lather mixed with bits of hair gathered along the blade. I paused a moment to clean it, then took up the strop again to sharpen the razor, because I'm a barber who does things properly. The man, who had kept his eyes closed, opened them now, removed one of his hands from under the sheet, felt the spot on his face where the soap had been cleared off, and said, "Come to the school today at six o'clock." "The same thing as the other day?" I asked horrified. "It could be better," he replied. "What do you plan to do?" "I don't know yet. But we'll amuse ourselves." Once more he leaned back and closed his eyes. I approached him with the razor poised. "Do you plan to punish them all?" I ventured timidly. "All." The soap was drying on his face. I had to hurry. In the mirror I looked toward the street. It was the same as ever: the grocery store with

two or three customers in it. Then I glanced at the clock: two-twenty in the afternoon. The razor continued on its downward stroke. Now from the other sideburn down. A thick, blue beard. He should have let it grow like some poets or priests do. It would suit him well. A lot of people wouldn't recognize him. Much to his benefit, I thought, as I attempted to cover the neck area smoothly. There, for sure, the razor had to be handled masterfully, since the hair, although softer, grew into little swirls. A curly beard. One of the tiny pores could be opened up and issue forth its pearl of blood. A good barber such as I prides himself on never allowing this to happen to a client. And this was a first-class client. How many of us had he ordered shot? How many of us had he ordered mutilated? It was better not to think about it. Torres did not know that I was his enemy. He did not know it nor did the rest. It was a secret shared by very few, precisely so that I could inform the revolutionaries of what Torres was doing in the town and of what he was planning each time he undertook a rebel-hunting excursion. So it was going to be very difficult to explain that I had him right in my hands and let him go peacefully—alive and shaved.

12   The beard was now almost completely gone. He seemed younger, less burdened by years than when he had arrived. I suppose this always happens with men who visit barber shops. Under the stroke of my razor Torres was being rejuvenated—rejuvenated because I am a good barber, the best in town, if I may say so. A little more lather here, under his chin, on his Adam's apple, on this big vein. How hot is it getting! Torres must be sweating as much as I. But he is not afraid. He is a calm man, who is not even thinking about what he is going to do with the prisoners this afternoon. On the other hand, I, with this razor in my hands, stroking and re-stroking this skin, trying to keep blood from oozing from these pores, can't even think clearly. Damn him for coming, because I'm a revolutionary and not a murderer. And how easy it would be to kill him. And he deserves it. Does he? No! What the devil! No one deserves to have someone else make the sacrifice of becoming a murder. What do you gain by it? Nothing. Others come along and still others, and the first ones kill the second ones and they the next ones and it goes on like this until everything is a sea of blood. I could cut his throat just so, zip! zip! I wouldn't give him time to complain and since he has his eyes closed he wouldn't see the glistening knife blade or my glistening eyes. But I'm trembling like a real murderer. Out of his neck a gush of blood would spout onto the sheet, on the chair, on my hands, on the floor. I would have to close the door. And the blood would keep inching along the floor, warm, ineradicable, uncontainable, until it reached the street, like a scarlet stream. I'm sure that one solid stroke, one deep incision, would prevent any pain. He wouldn't suffer. But what would I do with the body? Where would I hide it? I would have to flee, leaving all I have behind, and take refuge far away, far, far away. But they would follow until they found me. "Captain Torres' murderer. He slit his throat while he was shaving him—a coward." And then on the other side. "The avenger of us all. A name to remember. (And here they would mention my name.) He was the town barber. No one knew he was defending our cause."

13   And what of all this? Murderer or hero? My destiny depended on the edge of this blade. I can turn my hands a bit more, press a little harder on

the razor, and sink it in. The skin would give way like silk, like rubber, like the strop. There is nothing more tender than human skin and the blood is always there, ready to pour forth. A blade like this doesn't fail. It is my best. But I don't want to be a murderer, no sir. You came to me for a shave. And I perform my work honorably. . . . I don't want blood on my hands. Just lather, that's all. You are an executioner and I am only a barber. Each person has his own place in the scheme of things. That's right. His own place.

14   Now his chin had been stroked clean and smooth. The man sat up and looked into the mirror. He rubbed his hands over his skin and felt it fresh, like new.

15   "Thanks," he said. He went to the hanger for his belt, pistol, and cap. I must have been very pale; my shirt felt soaked. Torres finished adjusting the buckle, straightened his pistol in the holster, and after automatically smoothing down his hair, he put on the cap. From his pants pocket he took out several coins to pay me for my services. And he began to head toward the door. In the doorway he paused for a moment, and turning to me said:

16   "They told me that you'd kill me. I came to find out. But killing isn't easy. You can take my word for it." And he headed on down the street.

D.   Comprehension check

1. What is the setting, the place where the story takes place?

_____

_____

2. At what time in history do you think the story is taking place? Explain.

_____

_____

3. Who is the main character in the story? Explain why you think so.

_____

_____

4. What is the major conflict in the story?

_____

_____

5. What are your impressions of the barber?

   _____

   _____

6. What are your impressions of Captain Torres?

   _____

   _____

7. Why do you think the author spends so much time describing Torres' skin, hair, and the shave process itself?

   _____

   _____

8. What arguments in his mind does the barber go through, both for and against killing the Captain?

   _____

   _____

9. Why doesn't the barber kill Torres?

   _____

   _____

10. What do you think is the theme or message behind the story that the author wants to convey?

    _____

    _____

E.   Vocabulary check

Directions: On a separate sheet of paper, use each of the following words in sentences that refer in some way to the story.

1. theme   6. strop

2. setting   7. ineradicable

3. conflict   8. feign

4. irony   9. rejuvenate

5. character   10. faction

R³ *Reading skills check*

A.   Understanding fiction

Fiction, or story telling, has been around probably for as long as people have been able to talk. We listen to or read stories because we get pleasure from hearing about imaginary people or events that can sometimes seem more alive than the people we encounter everyday in real life. In fact, sometimes characters in a story seem more real to us than people we know because the author allows us to get inside them, to know what they think and feel, to understand their desires and actions. A good book or short story goes beyond mere pleasure and helps us see and understand ourselves and others. Fiction holds up a mirror to ourselves, not necessarily giving us answers, but implying suggestions, hints, and insights. Of course, for fiction to do that, we have to know how to approach reading it.

Let's look again at the questions you were asked after reading "Just Lather, That's All."

The first question asked is about the *setting* of the story, the place where all the action takes place. Nothing in this story states exactly where the action takes place, but we can infer that the location is a town in a country caught up in a revolution. Because of the description of the "enemy" Captain Torres' military cap, his pistol and gun belt, the naked, mutilated bodies of rebels hung up for target practice, the barber's fear of being known as an informer for the rebels, we begin to visualize a strife-torn country. The exact location, in this case, is not important. In some stories, however, the specific setting may be vital to the theme.

The second question you were asked deals with when in *time* the story takes place. Again, no dates are provided, and whether or not the author intended it so, it makes the story more universal. Revolution has and continues to divide many countries. By not making the story take place in any one

country or revolution, the point of the story becomes broader, more universal. However, based on the references to such things as the Captain's military cap, pistol and holster, we don't place the story too far back in history.

The third question asks who you think is the *main character* and why. In
this case, the barber is the main character, because the story is told through
his **point of view**. In some stories an author writes everything as though an
outside observer, a third person omniscient viewer, sees all and knows all.
This approach is usually used when the author wants us to get inside the
minds of more than one character. At other times an author chooses to tell a
story through a more limited third person point of view, usually centering
on only one character in the story. In this particular story, everything we are
told is from the first person viewpoint of the barber. Our opinions of Captain
Torres, our feelings about the soldiers, in fact everything that happens in the
story is told through the barber's point of view. It is not until the last lines
that we, along with the barber, learn something more about Torres than the
barber knows while giving the shave.

Question 4 asks about the *conflict* in the story. Every story has a conflict. It might be small; it might be so small the main character isn't even
aware of it until the final moments of the story. In "Just Lather, That's All,"
the conflict of which we're most aware is the barber's struggle with himself
as to whether or not he should kill Torres. Of course there is the conflict of
the rebels versus the soldiers, but that's not played up in the story. At the
very end, we discover that Torres was perhaps having a conflict of his own
while being shaved, wondering if the barber would kill him.

Questions 5 and 6 ask for your *impressions* of the barber and the Captain. Answers to these questions are subjective, of course. However, the impressions you receive are based on how you are reading the story. If you are
misreading a story, not aware of author implications or erroneous perceptions of the main characters intentionally provided by the author, you may
get impressions that don't apply to the author's meaning of the story. Our
impression will depend on what we think of the characters and their actions.
For instance, is the barber a coward because he didn't kill Torres? Is that
what the author wants us to believe? Or does the author want us to believe
the barber is a better person for not killing the Captain and becoming a
murderer himself? Is Torres a cruel, evil soldier? Or are his actions with the
rebels justified in a time of war? We only have the point of view of the barber. Is it all right to murder people in war? You can see how our attitudes
about such things can form our impressions of characters in a story.

The point behind Question 7 has to do with an author's use of *description*. The author Tellez provides much description of the shave itself. Why?
First of all, that's what the barber does for a living, saying at one point that
he was "proud of the preciseness of my profession" and at another, ". . . I
am a good barber, the best in town." The description of the shaving procedure lets us know the barber knows how to give a good shave. But Tellez also
weaves descriptions of Torres in between descriptions of the shaving: "The

razor continued on its downward stroke. Now from the other sideburn down. A thick blue beard. He should let it grow like some poets and priests do. It would suit him well. . . . I attempted to cover the neck area smoothly. There, for sure, the razor had to be handled masterfully, since the hair, although softer, grew into little swirls. A curly beard." By using such description, the author puts us inside the barber's head, allowing us to see the barber doing what he knows best, shaving, and at the same time describing Torres. Such description also implies that the barber is not a murderer at heart, just a normal person caught up in the horrors of the revolution.

Questions 8 and 9 ask for the arguments the barber goes through in trying to determine whether or not to kill Torres. He thinks on the one hand that Torres deserves to die because he is a murderer; but on the other hand, "No one deserves to have someone else make the sacrifice of becoming a murderer." He argues that there is nothing to gain by killing because others come along and kill the next one who kills the first one and on and on. Still, he reasons he could kill Torres so easily with a slit from the razor, but reasons that he would then have to run away, leaving everything behind. He would be hunted down and called a coward by some, although others would call him an "avenger." He decides he is a barber, not an executioner. As readers, we are left to place our own value judgments on the barber: Should he have killed Torres when he had the chance?

The correct answer to the last question is dependent upon our understanding of the point of the story. Just as an essay requires a thesis, a good story will have a *theme*, a point for the story. In the case of "Just Lather, That's All," we might say that the theme is stated near the end of the story: "Each person has his own place in the scheme of things." There are those like the barber and there are those like Torres. Or, you might argue that the story is about bravery. Torres shows his bravery by letting the barber shave him; the barber shows his by not killing Torres. However, if you interpret the barber to be a coward, you might see the story as dealing with the power of fear and how it is used by people like Torres against people like the barber. Can you see other possible themes?

Here are some questions you can use to get more deeply into a story after you have read it. They can be used in almost any fiction you read.

Questions on character:

1. Who is the main character?
2. What is that person like?
3. Do you like the main character?
4. What other characters are important in the story?

Questions on conflict:

5. What is the main character's problem or concern?
6. What happens to solve or not solve the problem?

7. Does the main character take action to solve the problem?
8. If so, is it the right thing to do?

Questions on setting or place:

9. Where and when is everything happening?
10. Of what importance is the setting to the events of the story?
11. How well does the author create the story's setting? Can it be visualized?

Questions on theme:

12. What is the point or theme of the story? Is there more than one?
13. What does the story reflect about people or life in general?
14. How does the title relate to the theme?

Try applying these questions after you read a story. More often than not, truly fine stories require more than one reading, just as fine music requires more than one listening, or true art requires more than one look to get the most from it. Read a story through once, letting it take you along with it. Then come back to it and use the questions to help you comprehend even more. A story, remember, is an art form, a way of saying something that has probably been said before but in a new or unusual way. There are truths about people and life to be discovered in stories, if you search for them and think about their themes.

B.   Understanding figurative language

Figurative language refers to those expressions and phrases that use words to mean something other than their literal or contextual meaning. Usually, figurative language creates an image for us by saying one thing in terms of another. For instance, instead of saying "The sun is shining on the lake," we might say "The lake looks like thousands of sparkling diamonds." The effect of the sun on the lake is being described without even using the word sun. Poetry, as you discovered in Sylvia Plath's poem, "Metaphor," uses figurative language. So does most fiction. To understand figurative language is to truly be reading beyond the words.

There are two basic types of figurative language that authors use: similes and metaphors. A *simile* compares one thing with another by using words such as *like* or *as*. The following phrases are similes:

> My engine *sounds like a machine gun.*
> He's *as cool as spring rain.*
> "Alan Austen, *as nervous as a kitten,* went up certain dark . . . stairs."

Metaphors also compare two things, but the words *like* or *as* are not used. Here are some examples of metaphors:

Oh, the red rose *is a falcon* and the white rose *is a dove*.
His manner *was wooden*.
Old Stone Face, my piano teacher, never smiles.

As you can see, both similes and metaphors compare things by giving us images or pictures in our minds. Figurative language, especially in fiction, is used to help us see in our minds the way the author sees. It is used to paint pictures with words rather than colored paints.

Some figurative language has been used so much they have become **clichés**. Clichés, as you probably know, are expressions that have been used so much they no longer hold much descriptive power. Below are some examples of figurative language, some of which are clichés. Circle the ones that are clichés.

1. It's always hard to nail down what Irving really means.
2. Ethel sat on pins and needles waiting for the test results.
3. The boat cut through the water like a knife through dough.
4. We'll cross that bridge when we come to it.
5. Too old too soon; too wise too late.
6. Be careful not to throw out the baby with the bath water.
7. Last night I slept like a log.

Except for items 3 and 5, the rest can be classified as clichés. Most people have heard or read these figurative figures so often they will immediately understand that the literal meaning is not what is intended.

EXERCISE A

Directions: Write S for simile or M for metaphor in the blank in front of each phrase or sentence below.

_____ 1. The flames, like a form of wildlife, crept as a lion creeps on its belly toward its prey.

_____ 2. Like a surfer, he sat as though he were waiting for that wave of the day.

_____ 3. She painted her nails a funny orange, like the tip of a hot soldering iron.

_____ 4. The pen is mightier than the sword.

_____ 5. With his rattlesnake reach, he grabbed the cookie and ran.

_____ 6. From the burning look in his eye, I knew he was angry with me.

EXERCISE B

Directions: Below are some passages from short stories. Some of the similes and metaphors are obvious, some are not. Read each set and answer the questions that follow.

1. "He put his shoulder against the door, and his long black body slanted like a ramrod. He pushed." (Langston Hughes, "On the Road.")

    A. What kind of figurative language is being used? _____

    B. What is being described? _____

    _____

    C. What can you infer about the door? _____

    _____

2. "The wind was lifting his coattails and tossing his white hair about in tufts, like those of the bunch grass she had known as a girl in the Dakotas." (Jessamyn West, "Love, Death, and the Ladies' Drill Team.")

    A. What kind of figurative language is being used? _____

    B. What is being described? _____

    _____

    C. What is the image the author wants you to see? _____

    _____

    _____

3. ". . . She lay back among the whispering blue flowers." (Tennessee Williams, "The Field of Blue Children.")

    A. What image does this line create in your head? _____

    _____

B. How important is the word *whispering* in this passage? _____

_____

_____

4. "Harrison tore the straps of his handicap harness like wet tissue paper, tore straps guaranteed to support five thousand pounds." (Kurt Vonnegut, Jr., "Harrison Bergeron.")

   A. What can we gather about Harrison's strength?

   _____

   _____

   B. Explain why "wet tissue paper" is used here.

   _____

   _____

EXERCISE C

Directions: In the following sentences, underline the two ideas or things that are being compared. Circle the number of any clichés.

1. The basement in the old house smelled as foul as an Egyptian tomb being opened for the first time in a thousand years.

2. The new father held his baby as though he were holding delicate flowers.

3. Kip's stomach seems to be expanding like a balloon.

4. The shirt fit Jake like a glove.

5. The wind forced the row of flowers to sway like ballerinas, twisting and turning to an unheard tune.

6. During the fire, pieces of exploding trees were hurled through the air like bomb fragments.

7. Bob's handwriting looked like the web of a spider gone mad.

8. After the earthquake, I felt I'd been in the grip of an angry giant.

9. Jan waited, rocklike, for the news.

10. March comes in like a lion and goes out like a lamb.

EXERCISE D

Directions: Read each of the following selections, underline the figurative expressions used, and then answer the questions that follow each selection.

1. His bat flashed in the sun. It caught the sphere where it was biggest. A noise like a twenty-one-gun salute cracked the sky. There was a straining, ripping sound and a few drops of rain spattered to the ground. The ball screamed toward the pitcher and seemed suddenly to dive down at his feet. He grabbed it to throw to first and realized to his horror that he held only the cover. The rest of it, unraveling cotton thread as it rode, was headed into the outfield. (Bernard Malamud, *The Natural*, New York: Farrar, Straus and Giroux, 1952.)

    a. What figurative phrase lets us know the ball was hit with terrific force?

    _____

    _____

    b. How else does the author let us know how hard the ball was hit without telling us directly? _____

    _____

    c. Describe how the ball must have looked by the time it reached the outfield: _____

    _____

2. My dancing shadow rollicks on the walls; our voices rock the chinaware; we giggle: as if unseen hands were tickling us. Queenie rolls on her

back, her paws plow the air, something like a grin stretches her black lips. Inside myself, I feel warm and sparky as those crumbling logs, carefree as the wind in the chimney. My friend waltzes round the stove, the hem of her poor calico skirt pinched between her fingers as though it were a party dress: *Show me the way to go home,* she sings, tennis shoes squeaking on the floor. *Show me the way to go home.* (Truman Capote, "A Christmas Memory," New York: Random House, 1956.)

a. Explain the phrase "her paws plow the air": _____

_____

b. With what is the "I" comparing himself? _____

_____

c. Explain who Queenie is: _____

_____

d. Describe the atmosphere created in this paragraph: _____

_____

3. The fresh-plowed earth heaved, the wild plum buds puffed and broke. Springs and streams leapt up singing. He could hear the distant roar of the river swelling in the gorge. The clear blue skies stretched out above him like the skin of a puffed fiesta balloon. The whole earth strained and stretched with new life. (Frank Waters, *The Man Who Killed the Deer,* Chicago: The Swallow Press, 1970.)

a. What time of year is it? How can you tell? _____

_____

b. Rewrite the paragraph, leaving out the figurative language: _____

_____

_____

_____

_____

_____

_____

EXERCISE E

Directions: Scan back over "Just Lather, That's All." In the space below, copy down any figurative words or phrases that Hernando Tellez uses in his story.

_____

_____

_____

_____

_____

C.   Reading a short story

In this section you can apply what you have learned about reading short stories.

SHIRLEY JACKSON

THE LOTTERY

The morning of June 27th was clear and sunny, with the fresh warmth of a full-summer day; the flowers were blossoming profusely and the grass was richly green. The people of the village began to gather in the square, between the post office and the bank, around ten o'clock; in some towns there were so many people that the lottery took two days and had to be started on June 26th, but in this village, where there were only about three hundred people, the whole lottery took less than two hours, so it could begin at ten o'clock in the morning and still be through in time to allow the villagers to get home for noon dinner.

2   The children assembled first, of course. School was recently over for the summer, and the feeling of liberty sat uneasily on most of them; they tended to gather together quietly for a while before they broke into boisterous play, and their talk was still of the classroom and the teacher, of books and reprimands. Bobby Martin had already stuffed his pockets full of stones, and the other boys soon followed his example, selecting the smoothest and roundest stones; Bobby and Harry Jones and Dickie Delacroix—the villagers pronounced this name "Dellacroy"—eventually made a great pile of stones in one corner of the square and guarded it against the raids of the other boys. The girls stood aside, talking among themselves, looking over their shoulders at the boys, and the very small children rolled in the dust or clung to the hands of their older brothers or sisters.

3   Soon the men began to gather, surveying their own children, speaking of planting and rain, tractors and taxes. They stood together, away from the pile of stones in the corner, and their jokes were quiet and they smiled rather than laughed. The women, wearing faded house dresses and sweaters, came shortly after their menfolk. They greeted one another and exchanged bits of gossip as they went to join their husbands. Soon the women, standing by their husbands, began to call to their children, and the children came reluctantly, having to be called four or five times. Bobby Martin ducked under his mother's grasping hand and ran, laughing, back to the pile of stones. His father spoke up sharply, and Bobby came quickly and took his place between his father and his oldest brother.

4   The lottery was conducted—as were the square dances, the teenage club, the Halloween program—by Mr. Summers, who had time and energy to devote to civic activities. He was a roundfaced, jovial man and he ran the coal business, and people were sorry for him, because he had no children and his wife was a scold. When he arrived in the square, carrying the black wooden box, there was a murmur of conversation among the villagers and he waved and called, "Little late today, folks." The postmaster, Mr. Graves, followed him, carrying a three-legged stool, and the stool was put in the center of the square and Mr. Summers set the black box down on it. The villagers kept their distance, leaving a space between themselves and the stool, and when Mr. Summers said, "Some of you fellows want to give me a hand?" there was a hesitation before two men, Mr. Martin and his oldest son, Baxter, came forward to hold the box steady on the stool while Mr. Summers stirred up the papers inside it.

5   The original paraphernalia for the lottery had been lost long ago, and the black box now resting on the stool had been put into use even before Old Man Warner, the oldest man in town, was born. Mr. Summers spoke frequently to the villagers about making a new box, but no one liked to upset even as much tradition as was represented by the black box. There was a story that the present box had been made with some pieces of the box that had preceded it, the one that had been constructed when the first people settled down to make a village here. Every year, after the lottery, Mr.

Summers began talking again about a new box, but every year the subject was allowed to fade off without anything's being done. The black box grew shabbier each year; by now it was no longer completely black but splintered badly along one side to show the original wood color, and in some places faded or stained.

6   Mr. Martin and his oldest son, Baxter, held the black box securely on the stool until Mr. Summers had stirred the papers thoroughly with his hand. Because so much of the ritual had been forgotten or discarded, Mr. Summers had been successful in having slips of paper substituted for the chips of wood that had been used for generations. Chips of wood, Mr. Summers had argued, had been all very well when the village was tiny, but now that the population was more than three hundred and likely to keep on growing, it was necessary to use something that would fit more easily into the black box. The night before the lottery, Mr. Summers and Mr. Graves made up the slips of paper and put them in the box, and it was then taken to the safe of Mr. Summer's coal company and locked up until Mr. Summers was ready to take it to the square next morning. The rest of the year, the box was put away, sometimes one place, sometimes another; it had spent one year in Mr. Graves's barn and another year underfoot in the post office, and sometimes it was set on a shelf in the Martin grocery and left there.

7   There was a great deal of fussing to be done before Mr. Summers declared the lottery open. There were lists to make up—of heads of families, heads of households in each family, members of each household in each family. There was the proper swearing-in of Mr. Summers by the postmaster, as the official of the lottery; at one time, some people remembered, there had been a recital of some sort, performed by the official of the lottery, a perfunctory, tuneless chant that had been rattled off duly each year; some people believed that the official of the lottery used to stand just so when he said or sang it, others believed that he was supposed to walk among the people, but years and years ago this part of the ritual had been allowed to lapse. There had been, also, a ritual salute, which the official of the lottery had had to use in addressing each person who came up to draw from the box, but this also had changed with time, until now it was felt necessary only for the official to speak to each person approaching. Mr. Summers was very good at all this; in his clean white shirt and blue jeans, with one hand resting carelessly on the black box, he seemed very proper and important as he talked interminably to Mr. Graves and the Martins.

8   Just as Mr. Summers finally left off talking and turned to the assembled villagers, Mrs. Hutchinson came hurriedly along the path to the square, her sweater thrown over her shoulders, and slid into place in the back of the crowd. "Clean forgot what day it was," she said to Mrs. Delacroix, who stood next to her, and they both laughed softly. "Thought my old man was out back stacking wood," Mrs. Hutchinson went on, "and then I looked out the window and the kids were gone, and then I remembered it was the twenty-seventh and came a-running." She dried her hands on her apron, and Mrs. Delacroix said, "You're in time, though. They're still talking away up there."

9   Mrs. Hutchinson craned her neck to see through the crowd and found her husband and children standing near the front. She tapped Mrs.

Delacroix on the arm as a farewell and began to make her way through the crowd. The people separated good-humoredly to let her through; two or three people said, in voices just loud enough to be heard across the crowd, "Here comes your Missus, Hutchinson," and "Bill, she made it after all." Mrs. Hutchinson reached her husband, and Mr. Summers, who had been waiting, said cheerfully, "Thought we were going to have to get on without you, Tessie." Mrs. Hutchinson said, grinning, "Wouldn't have me leave m'dishes in the sink, now would you, Joe?," and soft laughter ran through the crowd as the people stirred back into position after Mrs. Hutchinson's arrival.

10   "Well, now," Mr. Summers said soberly, "guess we better get started, get this over with, so's we can go back to work. Anybody ain't here?"

11   "Dunbar," several people said. "Dunbar, Dunbar."

12   Mr. Summers consulted his list. "Clyde Dunbar," he said. "That's right. He's broke his leg, hasn't he? Who's drawing for him?"

13   "Me, I guess," a woman said, and Mr. Summers turned to look at her. "Wife draws for her husband," Mr. Summers said. "Don't you have a grown boy to do it for you, Janey?" Although Mr. Summers and everyone else in the village knew the answer perfectly well, it was the business of the official of the lottery to ask such questions formally. Mr. Summers waited with an expression of polite interest while Mrs. Dunbar answered.

14   "Horace's not but sixteen yet." Mrs. Dunbar said regretfully. "Guess I gotta fill in for the old man this year."

15   "Right," Mr. Summers said. He made a note on the list he was holding. Then he asked, "Watson boy drawing this year?"

16   A tall boy in the crowd raised his hand. "Here," he said. "I'm drawing for m'mother and me." He blinked his eyes nervously and ducked his head as several voices in the crowd said things like "Good fellow, Jack," and "Glad to see your mother's got a man to do it."

17   "Well," Mr. Summers said, "guess that's everyone. Old Man Warner make it?"

18   "Here," a voice said, and Mr. Summers nodded.

19   A sudden hush fell on the crowd as Mr. Summers cleared his throat and looked at the list. "All ready?" he called. "Now, I'll read the names—heads of families first—and the men come up and take a paper out of the box. Keep the paper folded in your hand without looking at it until everyone has had a turn. Everything clear?"

20   The people had done it so many times that they only half listened to the directions; most of them were quiet, wetting their lips, not looking around. Then Mr. Summers raised one hand high and said, "Adams." A man disengaged himself from the crowd and came forward. "Hi, Steve," Mr. Summers said, and Mr. Adams said, "Hi, Joe." They grinned at one another humorlessly and nervously. Then Mr. Adams reached into the black box and took out a folded paper. He held it firmly by one corner as he turned and went hastily back to his place in the crowd, where he stood a little apart from his family, not looking down at his hand.

21   "Allen," Mr. Summers said. "Anderson. . . . Bentham."

22   "Seems like there's no time at all between lotteries any more," Mrs. Delacroix said to Mrs. Graves in the back row. "Seems like we got through with the last one only last week."

23   "Time sure goes fast," Mrs. Graves said.

24   "Clark. . . . Delacroix."

25   "There goes my old man," Mrs. Delacroix said. She held her breath while her husband went forward.

26   "Dunbar," Mr. Summers said, and Mrs. Dunbar went steadily to the box while one of the women said, "Go on, Janey," and another said, "There she goes."

27   "We're next," Mrs. Graves said. She watched while Mr. Graves came around from the side of the box, greeted Mr. Summers gravely, and selected a slip of paper from the box. By now, all through the crowd there were men holding the small folded papers in their large hands, turning them over and over nervously. Mrs. Dunbar and her two sons stood together, Mrs. Dunbar holding the slip of paper.

28   "Harburt. . . . Hutchinson."

29   "Get up there, Bill," Mrs. Hutchinson said, and the people near her laughed.

30   "Jones."

31   "They do say," Mr. Adams said to Old Man Warner, who stood next to him, "that over in the north village they're talking of giving up the lottery."

32   Old Man Warner snorted, "Pack of crazy fools," he said. "Listening to the young folks, nothing's good enough for *them*. Next thing you know, they'll be wanting to go back to living in caves, nobody work any more, live *that* way for a while. Used to be a saying about 'Lottery in June, corn be heavy soon.' First thing you know, we'd all be eating stewed chickweed and acorns. There's *always* been a lottery," he added petulantly. "Bad enough to see young Joe Summers up there joking with everybody."

33   "Some places have already quit lotteries," Mrs. Adams said.

34   "Nothing but trouble in *that*," Old Man Warner said stoutly. "Pack of young fools."

35   "Martin." And Bobby Martin watched his father go forward. "Overdyke. . . . Percy."

36   "I'd wish they'd hurry," Mrs. Dunbar said to her older son. "I wish they'd hurry."

37   "They're almost through," her son said.

38   "You get ready to run tell Dad," Mrs. Dunbar said.

39   Mr. Summers called his own name and then stepped forward precisely and selected a slip from the box. Then he called, "Warner."

40   "Seventy-seventh year I been in the lottery," Old Man Warner said as he went through the crowd. "Seventy-seventh time."

41   "Watson." The tall boy came awkwardly through the crowd. Someone said, "Don't be nervous, Jack," and Mr. Summers said, "Take your time, son."

42   "Zanini."

43   After that, there was a long pause, a breathless pause, until Mr. Summers, holding his slip of paper in the air, said, "All right, fellows." For a minute, no one moved, and then all the slips of paper were opened. Suddenly, all women began to speak at once, saying, "Who is it?," "Who's got it?," "Is it the Dunbars?," "Is it the Watsons?" Then the voices began to say,

"It's Hutchinson. It's Bill." "Bill Hutchinson's got it."

44   "Go tell your father," Mrs. Dunbar said to her older son.

45   People began to look around to see the Hutchinsons. Bill Hutchinson was standing quiet, staring down at the paper in his hand. Suddenly, Tessie Hutchinson shouted to Mr. Summers, "You didn't give him time enough to take any paper he wanted. I saw you. It wasn't fair!"

46   "Be a good sport, Tessie," Mrs. Delacroix called, and Mrs. Graves said, "All of us took the same chance."

47   "Shut up, Tessie," Bill Hutchinson said.

48   "Well, everyone," Mr. Summers said, "that was done pretty fast, and now we've got to be hurrying a little more to get done in time." He consulted his next list. "Bill," he said, "you draw for the Hutchinson family. You got any other households in the Hutchinsons?"

49   "There's Don and Eva," Mrs. Hutchinson yelled. "Make *them* take their chance!"

50   "Daughters draw with their husbands' families, Tessie," Mr. Summers said gently. "You know that as well as anyone else."

51   "It wasn't fair," Tessie said.

52   "I guess not, Joe," Bill Hutchinson said regretfully. "My daughter draws with her husband's family, that's only fair. And I've got no other family except the kids."

53   "Then, as far as drawing for families is concerned, it's you," Mr. Summers said in explanation, "and as far as drawing for households is concerned, that's you, too. Right?"

54   "Right," Bill Hutchinson said.

55   "How many kids, Bill?" Mr. Summers asked formally.

56   "Three," Bill Hutchinson said. "There's Bill, Jr., and Nancy, and little Dave. And Tessie and me."

57   "All right, then," Mr. Summers said, "Harry, you got their tickets back?"

58   Mr. Graves nodded and held up the slips of paper. "Put them in the box, then," Mr. Summers directed. "Take Bill's and put it in."

59   "I think we ought to start over," Mrs. Hutchinson said, as quietly as she could. "I tell you it wasn't *fair*. You didn't give him time enough to choose. *Everybody* saw that."

60   Mr. Graves had selected the five slips and put them in the box, and he dropped all the papers but those onto the ground, where the breeze caught them and lifted them off.

61   "Listen, everybody," Mrs. Hutchinson was saying to the people around her.

62   "Ready, Bill?" Mr. Summers asked, and Bill Hutchinson, with one quick glance around at his wife and children, nodded.

63   "Remember," Mr. Summers said, "take the slips and keep them folded until each person has taken one. Harry, you help little Dave." Mr. Graves took the hand of the little boy, who came willingly with him up to the box. "Take a paper out of the box, Davy," Mr. Summers said. Davy put his hand into the box and laughed. "Take just *one* paper," Mr. Summers said. "Harry, you hold it for him." Mr. Graves took the child's hand and removed the folded paper from the tight fist and held it while little Dave stood next to him and looked up at him wonderingly.

64   "Nancy next," Mr. Summers said. Nancy was twelve, and her school friends breathed heavily as she went forward, switching her skirt, and took a slip daintily from the box. "Bill, Jr.," Mr. Summers said, and Billy, his face red and his feet over-large, nearly knocked the box over as he got a paper out. "Tessie," Mr. Summers said. She hesitated for a minute, looking around defiantly, and then set her lips and went up to the box. She snatched a paper out and held it behind her.

65   "Bill," Mr. Summers said, and Bill Hutchinson reached into the box and felt around, bringing his hand out at last with the slip of paper in it.

66   The crowd was quiet. A girl whispered, "I hope it's not Nancy," and the sound of the whisper reached the edges of the crowd.

67   "It's not the way it used to be," Old Man Warner said clearly. "People ain't the way they used to be."

68   "All right," Mr. Summers said. "Open the papers. Harry, you open little Dave's."

69   Mr. Graves opened the slip of paper and there was a general sigh through the crowds as he held it up and everyone could see that it was blank. Nancy and Bill, Jr., opened theirs at the same time, and both beamed and laughed, turning around to the crowd and holding their slips of paper above their heads.

70   "Tessie," Mr. Summers said. There was a pause, and then Mr. Summers looked at Bill Hutchinson, and Bill unfolded his paper and showed it. It was blank.

71   "It's Tessie," Mr. Summers said, and his voice was hushed. "Show us her paper, Bill."

72   Bill Hutchinson went over to his wife and forced the slip of paper out of her hand. It had a black spot on it, the black spot Mr. Summers had made the night before with the heavy pencil in the coal-company office. Bill Hutchinson held it up, and there was a stir in the crowd.

73   "All right, folks," Mr. Summers said, "let's finish quickly."

74   Although the villagers had forgotten the ritual and lost the original black box, they still remembered to use stones. The pile of stones the boys had made earlier was ready; there were stones on the ground with the blowing scraps of paper that had come out of the box. Mrs. Delacroix selected a stone so large she had to pick it up with both hands and turned to Mrs. Dunbar. "Come on," she said. "Hurry up."

75   Mrs. Dunbar had small stones in both hands, and she said, gasping for breath, "I can't run at all. You'll have to go ahead and I'll catch up with you."

76   The children had stones already, and someone gave little Davy Hutchinson a few pebbles.

77   Tessie Hutchinson was in the center of a cleared space by now, and she held her hands out desperately as the villagers moved in on her. "It isn't fair," she said. A stone hit her on the side of the head.

78   Old Man Warner was saying, "Come on, come on, everyone." Steve Adams was in the front of the crowd of villagers, with Mrs. Graves beside him.

79   "It isn't fair, it isn't right," Mrs. Hutchinson screamed, and then they were upon her.

Now answer these questions:

1. What is your immediate reaction to the story? _____

   _____

   _____

   _____

2. What is the setting for the story? Be as specific as you can. _____

   _____

   _____

   _____

3. When is the story taking place; that is, past, future, or current times?

   Explain your answer. _____

   _____

   _____

4. Is there a main character in this story? Explain.

   _____

   _____

5. Most of us are surprised or shocked by the story's ending. The author has deliberately provided great detail in the story to make us believe in the events that are described on the morning of June 27th. Everything seems commonplace and ordinary until we discover what the lottery is all about. Yet, if we look carefully at some of the events given, clues to what is going to happen are given. What are some of them? (Hint: Look especially at Paragraphs 2, 3, 32, and 72.)

   _____

   _____

   _____

   _____

6. What do you think is the theme of the story; that is, what is the author trying to say about people or life?

_____

_____

_____

_____

7. Here, in part, is one interpretation of the story:
"This contrast between the matter-of-factness and the cheery atmosphere, on one side, and the grim terror, on the other, gives us a dramatic shock. But it also indicates that the author's point in general has to do with the awful doubleness of the human spirit—a doubleness that expresses itself in the blended good neighborliness and cruelty of the community's action." (Cleanth Brooks and Robert Penn Warren, *The Scope of Fiction*, Appleton-Century-Crofts, 1960, p. 50).
    What do you think is meant by "the awful doubleness of the human spirit"? Does this interpretation seem to fit the story and one possible meaning?

_____

_____

_____

_____

8. Would you call this a realistic or a metaphorical story? Explain. _____

_____

_____

D.   Reading a poem

If anything requires the ability to read beyond words, it is probably poetry. For many students, poetry seems "above" them, a mysterious mixture of words with "hidden meanings." Some poems, of course, do seem that way and do require many hours of study in order to "crack their code," so to speak. But when you think about it, poetry, in some shape or form, good or bad, appears in your everyday life. You've heard poetry since you were a child:

> Jack and Jill went up a hill
> To fetch a pail of water.
> Jack fell down
> And broke his crown,
> And Jill came tumbling after.

It's in the lyrics of music you hear, as in "Bullet the Blue Sky" sung by the group U2:

> In the howling wind comes a stinging rain
> See it driving nails into souls on the tree of pain
> From the firefly, a red orange glow
> See the face of fear running scared in the valley below

It's in the advertisements in newspapers and magazines:

> It Moves Against
> The Prevailing Current.
> The Alternate Route.
> Audi.

It's on TV and radio spot announcements:

> A new soft drink has come to town
> With a taste from Sunkist
> That'll turn you around.
> I'm drinking up
> Good vibrations
> Sunkist orange taste sensations.

Most of the poetry you are required to read in English classes is just an extension to what you already know.

In his book *Elements of Poetry*, Robert Scholes says, "Poetry is essentially a game, with artificial rules, and it takes two—a writer and a reader—to play it. If the reader is reluctant, the game will not work." What Scholes means is that poetry is a language game that exercises the imagination portion of the brain. If we aren't willing to develop this part of our minds, the part that requires our playing with words, their meanings, their arrangements, their sounds, and learn of the pleasure that comes with it, then we can't—or won't—play the game. The result: very little understanding of the power of words.

Like fictional stories, poetry puts our real-life situations and feelings into words. A poet can take thoughts and emotions that we cannot describe ourselves and put words in such a way that we say to ourselves as we read, "Yes, I know that; I've felt that way." As Marianne Moore said about poetry in one of her own poems:

> I, too, dislike it.
>   Reading it, however, with a perfect contempt for it,
>   one discovers in
>   it after all, a place for the genuine.

While poems can come in assorted sizes and shapes, there are two basic ingredients of most poems: the sounds of figurative language and a musical rhythm. You've already done some work with figurative language. As to musical rhythm, this doesn't mean all poems will have a rhyme scheme with every line or every other line rhyming. Many poems have no rhyme to them. But they will have a rhythm, an arrangement of words and lines that creates a type of musical movement. In fact, poems are meant to be read aloud. When you are assigned poetry to read, read it aloud to yourself or have someone read to you. Your appreciation and understanding will be greater.

Someone once said that reading a poem for the first time is a little like meeting a person for the first time. The initial reaction may be one of love at first sight or immediate dislike, a desire to meet again or complete indifference. But in order to understand that person or poem more fully, we need further encounters, a willingness to devote time to the friendship.

Here is a poem that appears in many English literature textbooks. Read it aloud and then answer the questions that follow.

THEODORE ROETHKE

MY PAPA'S WALTZ

The whiskey on your breath
Could make a small boy dizzy;
But I hung on like death:
Such waltzing was not easy.

We romped until the pans
Slid from the kitchen shelf;
My mother's countenance
Could not unfrown itself.

The hand that held my wrist
Was battered on one knuckle;

At every step you missed
My right ear scraped a buckle.

You beat time on my head
With a palm caked hard by dirt,
Then waltzed me off to bed
Still clinging to your shirt.

1. What is your initial reaction to the poem? Explain why. _____

_____

_____

_____

2. Describe what is happening in the poem. _____

_____

_____

3. How does the narrator feel about what is happening? _____

_____

_____

4. What words or phrases are used for special effects or meanings? _____

_____

_____

_____

R⁴ *Reading applications*

Application 1. Applying what you have learned: "The Story of an Hour" by Kate Chopin

Directions: Read the following short story.

KATE CHOPIN

THE STORY OF AN HOUR

1   Knowing that Mrs. Mallard was afflicted with a heart trouble, great care was taken to break to her as gently as possible the news of her husband's death.

2   It was her sister Josephine who told her, in broken sentences; veiled hints that revealed in half concealing. Her husband's friend Richards was there, too, near her. It was he who had been in the newspaper office when intelligence of the railroad disaster was received, with Brently Mallard's name leading the list of "killed." He had only taken the time to assure himself of its truth by a second telegram, and had hastened to forestall any less careful, less tender friend in bearing the sad message.

3   She did not hear the story as many women have heard the same, with a paralyzed inability to accept its significance. She wept at once, with sudden, wild abandonment, in her sister's arms. When the storm of grief had spent itself she went away to her room alone. She would have no one follow her.

4   There stood, facing the open window, a comfortable, roomy armchair. Into this she sank, pressed down by a physical exhaustion that haunted her body and seemed to reach into her soul.

5   She could see in the open square before her house the tops of trees that were all aquiver with the new spring life. The delicious breath of rain was in the air. In the street below a peddler was crying his wares. The notes of a distant song which some one was singing reached her faintly, and countless sparrows were twittering in the eaves.

6   There were patches of blue sky showing here and there through the clouds that had met and piled one above the other in the west facing her window.

7   She sat with her head thrown back upon the cushion of the chair, quite motionless, except when a sob came up into her throat and shook her, as a child who has cried itself to sleep continues to sob in its dreams.

8   She was young, with a fair, calm face, whose lines bespoke repression and even a certain strength. But now there was a dull stare in her eyes, whose gaze was fixed away off yonder on one of those patches of blue sky. It was not a glance of reflection, but rather indicated a suspension of intelligent thought.

9   There was something coming to her and she was waiting for it, fearfully. What was it? She did not know; it was too subtle and elusive to name. But she felt it, creeping out of the sky, reaching toward her through the sounds, the scents, the color that filled the air.

10   Now her bosom rose and fell tumultuously. She was beginning to recognize this thing that was approaching to possess her, and she was striving to

beat it back with her will—as powerless as her two white slender hands would have been.

11   When she abandoned herself a little whispered word escaped her slightly parted lips. She said it over and over under her breath: "free, free, free!" The vacant stare and the look of terror that had followed it went from her eyes. They stayed keen and bright. Her pulses beat fast, and the coursing blood warmed and relaxed every inch of her body.

12   She did not stop to ask if it were or were not a monstrous joy that held her. A clear and exalted perception enabled her to dismiss the suggestion as trivial.

13   She knew that she would weep again when she saw the kind, tender hands folded in death; the face that had never looked save with love upon her fixed and gray and dead. But she saw beyond that bitter moment a long procession of years to come that would belong to her absolutely. And she opened and spread her arms out to them in welcome.

14   There would be no one to live for her during those coming years; she would live for herself. There would be no powerful will bending hers in that blind persistence with which men and women believe they might have a right to impose a private will upon a fellow-creature. A kind intention or a cruel intention made the act seem no less a crime as she looked upon it in that brief moment of illumination.

15   And yet she had loved him—sometimes. Often she had not. What did it matter! What could love, the unsolved mystery, count for in face of this possession of self-assertion which she suddenly recognized as the strongest impulse of her being!

16   "Free! Body and soul free!" she kept whispering.

17   Josephine was kneeling before the closed door with her lips to the keyhole, imploring for admission. "Louise, open the door! I beg; open the door—you will make yourself ill. What are you doing, Louise? For heaven's sake open the door."

18   "Go away. I am not making myself ill." No; she was drinking in a very elixir of life through that open window.

19   Her fancy was running riot along those days ahead of her. Spring days, and summer days, and all sorts of days that would be her own. She breathed a quick prayer that life might be long. It was only yesterday she had thought with a shudder that life might be long.

20   She rose at length and opened the door to her sister's importunities. There was a feverish triumph in her eyes, and she carried herself unwittingly like a goddess of victory. She clasped her sister's waist, and together they descended the stairs. Richards stood waiting for them at the bottom.

21   Some one was opening the front door with a latchkey. It was Brently Mallard who entered, a little travel-stained, composedly carrying his gripsack and umbrella. He had been far from the scene of the accident, and did not even know there had been one. He stood amazed at Josephine's piercing cry; at Richards' quick motion to screen him from the view of his wife.

22   But Richards was too late.

23   When the doctors came they said she had died of heart disease—of joy that kills.

Now read the story again, this time answering the guide questions on pages 279–280.

Application 2. Reacting to what you read: "Stone Throwing an Annual Bash in India Town," by Mark Fineman

Directions: Earlier in this chapter you read Shirley Jackson's short story, "The Lottery." You may or may not know that a few years ago the story was made into a short film. Faithful to the story itself, the film was not appreciated by some parents who had the film and story banned from their children's schools where it was sometimes shown as part of a literature course. The story has and continues to create a stir among some people who feel the story destroys the concept of mother love, that it destroys the concept of following traditions, that it teaches human sacrifice, or that the story itself is ridiculous, that such things can't happen in real life.

Following is a news article that appeared in the *Los Angeles Times* in September 1989. Do you see any connection between it and "The Lottery"?

Stone-Throwing an Annual Bash in India Town

By MARK FINEMAN

PANDHURNA, India—To most of the 45,000 seemingly normal residents of this sleepy little town on the banks of the River Jam, Anil Sambare is nothing more than a spoilsport.

To some, he is something worse. A troublemaker, some say. An idealistic radical, according to others. Some even think him a traitor to his hometown.

And all because the 27-year-old high school teacher has dedicated his life to stopping his entire town from going completely berserk once a year in a frenzied festival of destruction—a day-long event in which thousands of people try to stone each other to death in the name of fun, tradition and, now, stardom.

The annual event is called the Gotmaar Festival—literally, "stone-hitting" —and it is an ancient Pandhurna tradition, unique and brutal even by Indian standards.

No one here remembers exactly how ancient it is, although older people say that it dates back at least three centuries. And no one knows exactly why they do it every year, year after year, despite scores of deaths and thousands of injuries, although the myth behind it is a compelling one.

All the Pandhurnans really know for sure is that once a year, on the day of the new moon in the Hindu month of Sharawan, when the drums start beating along the River Jam, the time for the madness has begun again.

Within minutes, thousands of male Pandhurnans, ranging in age from 6 to 60, many of them deeply scarred or limping from festivals of years past, divide into two groups, gather their huge piles of stones on opposite sides of the river and, for the next 6½ hours, try to kill, maim and mangle as many fellow townsfolk as they can.

When sunset comes, and the drumbeat stops, the two sides drop their rocks, come together, shake hands, nurse each other's wounds and return to the peaceful monotony of rural Indian life.

This year, the Gotmaar carnage, which took place two weeks ago, left four dead and 612 injured. But there were a few new twists this year that speak volumes about India's struggle to enter the modern age.

First, there was Anil Sambare and his signature drive to end the carnage, which drew the ire of almost everyone. Second, this is an election year in India, which meant that Sambare's signature campaign was doomed to failure. And finally, there was the introduction of a new evil, videotape equipment,

which is likely to ensure that Pandhurna's sadomasochistic ritual will continue for many years to come.

The story of the Pandhurnans and their bizarre, ancient rite of stoning is a living illustration of the paradoxes of a modern-day India, as well as a freeze-frame glimpse at the ironies and distortions resulting from Indian Prime Minister Rajiv Gandhi's five-year-old pledge to modernize rural India.

Pandhurna No Backwater

Pandhurna, in central Madhya Pradesh state, is hardly what one would call a backwater. In many ways it is a model of Rajiv Gandhi's rural modernization plan.

There are 10,000 television sets in Pandhurna, 340 telephones and even 100 videocassette players. More than 90% of the homes have electricity. Everyone has access to clean drinking water. Unemployment is under 5%, and there are even beauty parlors doing booming business.

"There is just this one little thing that sets us apart," said Bhargao Pandurang Bhagwatkar, who has taught in the local high school for the last 41 years. "We all know it is barbaric. It is a kind of madness. And it has no reason at all. But it has been with us since Day 1, and, on that day every year, we just cannot help ourselves."

Day 1, as myth has it, was sometime in the 1600s, according to local historians, police and other local officials, who say they and their predecessors have been trying to stop it every year for the last half-century.

On Day 1, it seems, Pandhurna's brutal battle began as a love story.

Began With Elopement

"The way the old ones tell it," town official M.M. Singh explained, "a boy from the Pandhurna side of the river eloped with a girl from the village on the other side, which was then known as Sawargaon but since has merged into Pandhurna.

"As the amorous young couple was trying to flee across the river, the

Sawargaon people began throwing stones at them. The Pandhurnans heard about this and quickly ran to the river bank, where they began stoning the Sawargaons.

"The couple, of course, died in the cross-fire. And it's on the spot where they died that the people now put the tree every year."

"The tree?" the stranger asked.

"Oh, the tree. The tree is the main object of the game."

The Pandhurnans who actually play "the game," which is what everyone here except Sambare calls the annual stoning battle, explained that the tree is cut the day before the festival from a special grove of flame trees beside a temple to the Hindu god of destruction, which is where legend states that the mythical young couple first met.

The tree is then "planted" in the middle of the River Jam, and the object of "the game" is to chop down the tree with an ax, without, of course, getting stoned to death in the process.

Enter the videotape.

Unlike previous years, in which an average of two or three Pandhurnans were stoned to death during the festival, the four deaths this year were from drowning.

"These boys had climbed the tree and were posing for the camera," Sambare explained. "They were so preoccupied with the video camera, they didn't see the stones coming. They got hit in the head, fell into the river and drowned."

Sambare knows what he's talking about. He lives on Stone-hitting Road, in a riverfront house with a view of the battle zone. And he jumped into the river and saved four other "players" from the same fate this year, getting hit in the back with stones in the process.

But that's not why Sambare is so committed to ending the carnage of Gotmaar. It's not even because his uncle was stoned to death 27 years ago, or because he cannot stop his own younger brother from joining in—"Imagine, my own brother bought five different outfits and changed clothes five times during the stone-hitting this year because he wanted to look good for the camera.

"No, I am fighting this because it is a perversion, because it is barbaric and because it puts all of India in a very poor light," said Sambare, who has a masters degree in mathematics.

"This is not a game. This is madness. And now, with this videotape, there is all of a sudden a renewed interest in joining in. Everyone wants to show off their bravado."

Enter Rajiv Gandhi's high-tech revolution.

The videotape was the government's idea. And the local police actually paid 5,000 rupees (about $300) in government funds to a local video contractor to film the festival this year.

"The idea was to minimize the killing," said Krishna Kohle, the enterprising Pandhurnan who got the video contract. "It was, how do you call it, a compromise."

For decades, local officials said, the authorities have attempted to end the festival. Two years ago, the police even opened fire on the festival, killing two Pandhurnans, in an attempt to end it after a passing constable was accidentally stoned to death.

"I myself have seen too many deaths and very much want this madness to end," said Dr. Ratan Singhvi, a local physician who is Pandhurna's equivalent of mayor and the local head of Gandhi's ruling Congress-I party.

"I have seen people with eyes bulging out, ears sheared off, noses broken, teeth shattered, skulls and legs fractured to bits. But we've never been able to stop it. My God, the people like it.

"Of course, an additional problem is these people are all dead drunk when they're playing the game, and the game gives them a good excuse to get drunk. They look forward to it all year long."

Enter politics.

"The people of Pandhurna, you see, are very sentimental about this festival," Singhvi said. "And such things are very important to our local voters. Had we stopped the Gotmaar this year, for example, the Congress Party definitely would be sent away in the next elections. So what we did instead was try to cut down on the deaths—we banned the slingshot."

Called *gofans*, the handmade slingshots came into vogue two years ago and clearly escalated the conflict. They turned the stones into speeding bullets, tripling the death toll and ultimately forcing the police to step in. The *gofan* was outlawed. And, in an effort to enforce that ban, police hired the video man to film violators for prosecution.

"I guess it backfired," said Kohle, who conceded he is now making a tidy profit renting out copies of the Gotmaar video to townspeople who want to relive their moments of bravery and endurance.

1. Besides the stone-throwing itself, what else do the villagers in the story "The Lottery" have in common with the people of Pandhurna, India?

2. What new innovation has been added to the stone-throwing in Pandhurna?

3. Which has more of an effect on your emotions, the short story "The Lottery" or the news article? Why?

4. Do you think the story and film of "The Lottery" should be banned from high schools? Explain.

Application 3.   Reacting to a poem: "We Real Cool" by Gwendolyn Brooks

Directions: Read the following poem aloud two or three times. Then answer the questions that follow.

GWENDOLYN BROOKS

WE REAL COOL

The Pool Players.
Seven at the Golden Shovel.

We real cool. We
Left school. We

Lurk late. We
Strike straight. We

Sing sin. We
Thin gin. We

Jazz June. We
Die soon.

1. How would you describe the rhythm in this poem? _____

_____

2. Who are the "we" in the poem? _____

_____

3. What does the poet think of their "cool" philosophy of life? _____

_____

4. Write an expository statement that says what the poem is saying.

_____

Application 4.   Writing a short story or poem

Part A

Directions: Here are some opening lines. Pick *one* and try finishing the story yourself. If you don't like any of these openings, go to Part B.

1. Descending the slippery rocks, I found the cave again. Entering, there suddenly appeared a strange light, and I saw . . .

2. "Nobody understands me. Nobody! Why can't you all just go away and leave me alone."

3. The last man on earth sat in his lonely room. Suddenly, there was a knocking at the door.

4. Starting all over again was the hardest thing she'd ever had to do in her life.

5. Chuck hated to admit it, but what he really felt at the funeral, more than anything, was boredom.

Part B

Directions: Choose a starting sentence from the column on the left. Write a short story and end it with one of the sentences from the column on the right. (Each comes from a famous short story.)

Openings

And after all the weather was ideal.

In walks these three girls in nothing but bathing suits.

I sit in the sun drinking gin.

The morning of June 27th was clear and sunny, with the fresh warmth of a full-summer day; the flowers were blossoming profusely and the grass was richly green.

Endings

The wind flung the snow into my face and so, singing and jingling the car keys, I walked to the train.

"Isn't it, darling?" said Laurie.

. . . and my stomach kind of fell as I felt how hard the world was going to be to me hereafter.

"It isn't fair, it isn't right," Mrs. Hutchinson screamed, and then they were upon her.

Part C

Directions: Use one of the lines from Part B, or use your imagination and write a poem using figurative language.

Application 5.   Summarizing what you have learned

Directions: On a separate sheet of paper, summarize what you have learned from reading this chapter (a) about yourself, (b) about skills you can apply to your reading, and (c) questions you still have that need answering. Turn this in to your instructor when finished.

Reading the newspaper

9

R¹ *Reading beyond words*

Explain what you think the following statements mean and how they might apply to you.

A. "It is the responsibility of the press to insure that competing views are presented, and it is our responsibility as citizens to object to actions of the government which prevent the press from fulfilling this constitutional role."—Sam Ervin

_____

_____

_____

_____

B. "In a free society each individual is free to determine for himself what he wishes to read, and each group is free to determine what it will recommend to its freely associated members. But no group has the right to take the law into its own hands, and to impose its concept of politics or morality upon other members of a democratic society. Freedom is no freedom if it is accorded [given] only to the accepted and the inoffensive."—American Library Association and the Association of American Publishers.

_____

_____

_____

_____

R² *Reading actively*

A. Vocabulary preview

Directions: The italicized words in the sentences below appear in the newspaper article you are about to read. First, see if you can define the

words from the context in which they are used. For those you can't, use
your dictionary. Knowing these words before you read will help your
comprehension.

1. At the time of his inauguration, Vartan Gregorian, the new president of
   Brown University, *assailed* American schools that do not adequately prepare students for higher education.

   _____

2. College remedial courses and programs are routinely *vilified* by many
   educators.

   _____

3. The Harvard faculty *lamented* the spending of "much time, energy and
   money" teaching students "what they ought to have learnt already."

   _____

4. This kind of talk distorts the historical and social reality of American
   higher education, *quelling* rather than encouraging careful analysis of
   higher education in a pluralistic democracy.

   _____

5. To *temper* any idealism sparked by this broadening of opportunity to
   education, let us remember the history of the American college from the
   early 19th century on.

   _____

6. If we are going to admit people to college for pure or *pragmatic* reasons,
   then we are obliged to do everything possible to retain them.

   _____

7. Academics need to check their *apocalyptic,* angry, dig-in-the-heels language, for it narrows the discussion of the function of higher education.

   _____

8. What we fail to see, for it is so often *castigated,* is that remedial work
   can also yield rich information for our colleges and universities.

   _____

9. We need to think about our colleges and universities in deep and *generative* ways.

_____

10. Remedial courses serve as a corrective to the impersonal *dispensary* that lower-division education has become.

_____

11. If the hope of some to eliminate remediation from college campuses is that such action will straighten out secondary schools, then we have an act of either great *hubris* or great innocence.

_____

B. Thought provokers

1. After reading the sentences in the **Vocabulary preview** above and then looking at the title of the newspaper article below, what do you think the essay will be about and what position do you think the author will take?

_____

_____

_____

_____

2. Why do you think some legislators and educators are against remedial courses at the college and university levels? Are these good reasons?

_____

_____

_____

_____

3. What are your biases about so-called "remedial" courses at the college level? Should they be part of the college and university curriculum? Explain.

_____

_____

_____

_____

C.   Reading practice

Directions: The author of the following newspaper selection is Associate Director of UCLA Writing Programs and author of *Lives on the Boundary: The Struggles and Achievements of America's Underprepared.* The article appeared in the *Los Angeles Times* at a time when state legislators were thinking about cutting funding for remedial programs and/or eliminating them from state funded colleges and universities altogether. Read the article looking for the thesis and the arguments used to support it, as well as attitudes, bias, and tone.

What's Right with Remedy: A College Try

By MIKE ROSE

1   At the time of his inauguration two weeks ago, Vartan Gregorian, the new president of Brown University, assailed American schools that do not adequately prepare students for higher education. "Everybody wants to put as much as possible on the shoulders of the university," Gregorian told an interviewer. "The first two years, colleges are expected to do remedial work for the whole nation."

2   "Remedial work." Correcting somebody else's mistakes. Gregorian is a bit extreme (though not alone) in viewing as remedial the first two years of college courses, but the gist of his complaint is much with us these days. Courses and programs in writing, mathematics, the sciences, learning and study skills, critical reasoning aimed at preparing students for the demands of higher learning are routinely vilified. Many college presidents, legislators and commentators on culture talk this way about remediation: urgent, apocalyptic, angry—just anger, the anger of men at the bastions watching civilization decay.

3   Gregorian is Brown's 16th president. Its fourth, Francis Wayland, also an outspoken man, complained in 1841 that "students frequently enter college almost wholly unacquainted with English grammar." In 1896, the *Nation* ran an article entitled "The Growing Illiteracy of American Boys," which reported on a study of underpreparation at Harvard. The Harvard faculty lamented the spending of "much time, energy and money" teaching students "what they ought to have learnt already."

4   And so it goes. Academicians have been talking about the decline of higher education for a long time, even though colleges and universities have been growing in remarkable ways. There is a certain kind of talk, a crisis talk, serious and powerful. And troubling. It distorts the historical and social reality of American higher education, quelling rather than encouraging careful analysis of higher learning in a pluralistic democracy.

5   It is important to get a sense of the history of the preparatory and remedial function in American higher education, for we are not facing a new and unprecedented danger. Colleges were in the remediation business before they had yell leaders and fight songs.

6   The history of American higher education is one of expansion: in the beginning, the sons of the elite families, later the sons of the middle class, then the daughters, the American poor, the immigrant poor, veterans with less-than-privileged educations, the racially segregated, the disenfranchised. The economic and educational environments from which these students came varied dramatically; if they were to be given access to higher education, much would have to be done to ensure their success. The remedial function, then, has been a force within the college to advance our version of democracy.

7   To temper any idealism sparked by this broadening of opportunity, let us also remember that the history of the American college from the early 19th Century on could also be read as a history of changes in admissions, curriculum and public image in order to keep enrollments high and institutions solvent.

8   One reason U.S. colleges and universities increased admissions of "non-traditional" students in the early 1970's was because campuses had grown so rapidly in the '50s and '60s that, after the peak of the post-war student influx, administrators had to scramble to fill classrooms. American institutions of higher learning as we know them are made

possible by robust undergraduate enrollments. And if we're going to admit people, for pure or pragmatic reasons, then we're obliged to do everything we can do to retain them.

9   In saying this, I am not trying to be cynical or dismissive about standards and requirements. Much work needs to be done to improve the education of school teachers, the curricula they're given and the conditions in which they teach. But university officials are shortsighted and simplistic when they brush aside responsibility for remedial courses and programs: The overlap of secondary and higher education has been, and remains, necessary in an open educational system.

10   Academics need, as well, to check their apocalyptic, angry, dig-in-the-heels language, for it narrows discussion of the function of higher education in American society. Let's engage this issue by sketching out some of the things a good freshman education should provide.

11   Young people entering college need multiple opportunities to write about what they're learning and to develop what has come to be called critical literacy: comparing, synthesizing, analyzing. They need opportunities to talk about what they're learning: to test their ideas, reveal their assumptions, talk through the places where new knowledge clashes with ingrained belief. They need a chance, too, to talk about the ways they may have felt excluded from all this in the past and may feel threatened by it in the present. They need occasion to rise above the fragmented learning encouraged by the lower-division curriculum, a place to reflect on the way particular disciplines conduct their inquiries and the way seemingly isolated disciplines can interconnect.

12   The fact is that one of the few places in the first year of college where a student gets a chance to do such things is *precisely* in those programs and courses labeled preparatory or remedial: tutoring centers, writing labs, remedial classes. Seen in this light, the word *remedial* tells only half the truth. It carries the implication that colleges are correcting someone else's mistakes, are "remedying" the deficiencies and deficits of the schools or of the students themselves.

13   So-called remedial work, when well applied, also helps to make up for the weaknesses in the way *higher* education is dispensed to its initiates. It enables students to do what all the current blue-ribbon reports on liberal education say they should do: engage ideas, use language, develop a sense of how intellectual work is conducted, test personal values against a tradition. Freshmen don't get much chance to do these things in their standard fare of distant lecturers, large classes and short-answer tests. Ask them. It's clear that remedial courses help students. What we fail to see—for it is so often castigated—is that such work can also yield rich information for our colleges and universities.

14   Remedial courses and programs are a kind of boundary area, a transitional domain that allows us—if we are willing to look and

listen—to get a keen sense of what it means to do certain kinds of intellectual work. We could gain significant knowledge, for example, about the social and cognitive processes involved in the complex literacy tasks we routinely ask our students to do: Interpret literature, analyze a political or philosophical argument, synthesize a range of sources. Such knowledge would assist institutions in examining the uses of—and assumptions about—writing in the college curriculum. And everyone would benefit from that.

15   We need to think about our colleges and universities today in deep and generative ways. What does it mean to enter higher education in America? What *truly* is the relationship between the research and undergraduate teaching missions of the university? How is knowledge best developed and incorporated into the social structure of a pluralistic democracy?

16   What we hear instead are impatient, contemptuous calls to kick remediation off campus. If the hope is that such an action will straighten out secondary schools, then we have an act of either great hubris or great innocence: pressure from the college is but one of many problems—and hardly the greatest—that schools face today. Kick remediation off campus and the primary thing you will achieve is the greater exclusion of American youth from higher education.

17   We need remedial programs. They are a part of our history. They are necessary if we want to further develop our democracy. They serve as a corrective to the impersonal dispensary that lower-division education has become. And, if we are wise enough to see, they can be a source of rich information.

18   At heart, the issue of remediation is embedded in two central questions: How is higher learning best pursued in a pluralistic democracy, and how many or how few do we want to have access to that learning? We are talking, finally, about the kind of society we want to foster.

D.   Comprehension check

1. What is the author's position on remedial education at the college level?

_____

_____

2. What evidence does the author give that shows remedial education is not something new to contemporary times?

_____

_____

3. Which of the following does the author claim are the functions of higher education and should be provided to students? Circle those that apply.

   a. opportunities to write about what they are learning

   b. a chance to develop their ability to compare, synthesize, and analyze

   c. opportunities to talk about what they are learning

   d. a chance to talk about the ways they have felt excluded and threatened

   e. a place to reflect on the ways seemingly isolated disciplines can inter-connect

   f. a place to engage in ideas, use language, and test personal values against tradition

4. What bias does the author reveal toward most lower-division college classes as taught?

_____

5. What does the author predict will happen if you "kick remediation off campus"?

_____

6. What function does remediation serve on the college campus, according to the author?

_____

_____

7. Is the article mostly fact or opinion? Explain.

_____

_____

8. Does the author convince you of his argument? Why?

_____

_____

9. Does your own bias have anything to do with your answer to Question 8?

_____

E.   Vocabulary check

Directions: Define the following words as used in context. The number after the word is the paragraph where the word appears in the article.

1. assail (1) _____

2. vilified (2) _____

3. lamented (3) _____

4. quelling (4) _____

5. to temper (7) _____

6. pragmatic (8) _____

7. apocalyptic (10) _____

8. castigated (13) _____

9. generative (15) _____

10. hubris (16) _____

R³   *Reading skills check*

A.   Getting the main idea: the 5 Ws

You have no doubt heard the old one-liner joke: "What's black and white and 'red' all over?" Unfortunately the newspaper is *not* "read" all over. Of those who can read the words in a newspaper, many don't know how a news-paper is organized, how to learn from reading newspapers, or how to sepa-rate fact from opinion in news stories.

One of the purposes of this chapter is to teach you the 5 Ws involved in newspaper reading. The 5 Ws refer to *who, what, where, when,* and *why.* Practice in finding the answers to these questions can improve your com-prehension of the main idea of any newspaper article as well as other things you read. Usually, though certainly not always, many of the 5 Ws are written into the *lead,* or the opening sentence of a news story. Notice the following example:

News lead	5 Ws	
LOS ANGELES—Today, a federal grand jury indicted 10 men on charges of operating a drug ring that netted more than $8.7 million in cocaine sales during a six-month period.	who:	federal grand jury
	what:	indicted 10 men
	where:	Los Angeles
	when:	today
	why:	operating a drug ring

The rest of the article would go into more detail, giving names and reasons. However, the news-story lead generally gives the main idea in a short space.

Here is another example of how the 5 Ws are used in news stories.

News lead	5 Ws	
WASHINGTON, D.C.—Today the Supreme Court ruled that an unwed minor may not be forced to obtain her parents' consent to an abortion, nor does a married woman need to obtain her husband's consent.	who:	the Supreme Court
	what:	ruled that minor, unwed mothers or married women do not need parents' or husbands' consent to abortion
	where:	Washington, D.C.
	when:	today
	why:	not mentioned

Notice that not all 5 Ws are always given. Sometimes the *who* is not a per-son, but a group or a report. In the example above, the *who* is the Supreme Court, not a person.

Read the news lead below and fill in the blanks under the 5 Ws column.

News lead   5 Ws

> PROVIDENCE, R.I.—A smooth-
> working U.S. Olympic basketball
> team ran roughshod over a
> professional all-star team, 116–71,
> before an estimated 10,000 fans
> at the Civic Center last night.

who: _____

what: _____

where: _____

when: _____

why: _____

✓ Compare your answers with these:
   who: U.S. Olympic basketball team
   what: beat all-star team 116–71
   where: Civic Center, Providence, R.I.
   when: last night
   why: not mentioned, other than saying "smooth-working" team

Look for the 5 Ws in this news story:

Married Priests Convening Near Papal Retreat

ROME (UPI)—Roman Catholic priests who have married in defiance of church celibacy requirements gathered Saturday for a meeting near Rome to rally support for their attempt to have the ban on marriage lifted.

The meeting, officially designated the second session of the General Synod of Married Catholic Priests and their Wives, formally opens today at Ariccia, a village in the Alban hills 15 miles southeast of Rome near Castel Gandolfo, where Pope John Paul II is spending the summer.

Married priests from 15 nations are taking part in the sessions sponsored by the Vocatio Association, which says it represents an

"Married Priests Convening Near Papal Retreat" from UPI, August 25, 1985. Reprinted by permission of United Press International, Inc.

estimated 70,000 priests who have married in defiance of the church's celibacy standard.

Current Cases First

At a news conference, spokesman Gianni Gennari said the group's first aim will be to formulate a request to the Vatican to grant prompt dispensation to 5,800 priests who have marriage requests pending before church authorities.

It is also trying to obtain a change in canon law that would make priestly celibacy optional, giving every Catholic cleric the choice either to remain celibate or marry. Current rules force a priest who marries to renounce his ministry.

Dutch priest Lambert van Gelder said that an analysis of the 7,000 Italian priests who are married showed that 20% abandoned the church, 30% sought some form of lay service, and 50% would like to continue to be priests.

He said the readmission to the church of married priests would help increase the number of Catholic clerics, who are currently relatively scarce.

Answer the 5 Ws regarding the news story:

who: _____

what: _____

where: _____

when: _____

why: _____

Is the story objective or subjective? _____

✓ Compare your answers with these:
  who: married Roman Catholic priests
  what: got together for a meeting
  where: near Rome
  when: Saturday
  why: to have the ban on marriage lifted

The story is presented objectively with no opinions of the author being given on the subject.

PRACTICE 1.   READING FOR THE MAIN IDEA USING THE 5 Ws

Directions: Below are some news-story leads. Read them and then fill out the 5 W blanks. In some cases, not all 5 Ws are in the lead.

1.

> DETROIT—More than half the city's police officers scheduled for the day shift failed to show up today as a protest against the layoff of 1000 officers in a budget-cutting move.

who: _____

what: _____

where: _____

when: _____

why: _____

2.

> REDWOOD CITY—Close to 2800 fire-fighters battled a 112-square-mile fire to 90 percent containment yesterday, but officials were worried that new winds would bring new trouble spots in California's largest forest blaze in five years.

who: _____

what: _____

where: _____

when: _____

why: _____

3.

> CHICAGO—Reporter Adam Ribb was ready to go to jail today for refusing to disclose a news source after the U.S. Supreme Court ruled against him.

who: _____

what: _____

where: _____

when: _____

why: _____

4.

> WASHINGTON—The Federal
> Energy Administration yesterday
> froze U.S. crude oil prices for at
> least two months to correct a
> price-estimating error that let
> producers collect an excess $60
> million in February.

who: _____

what: _____

where: _____

when: _____

why: _____

5.

> LONDON—The British employee
> of an American armored car
> company wanted for the theft of
> $4.1 million from Heathrow
> Airport last weekend was known
> in the underworld as "the
> Professor" and had a record of 15
> convictions, British newspapers
> reported today.

who: _____

what: _____

where: _____

when: _____

why: _____

B.   Types of newspaper articles

There are at least seven different types of newspaper articles. Here is a list:

1. The straight news story
2. The feature story
3. The column
4. The interpretive story
5. The review
6. The sports story
7. The editorial
8. The editorial cartoon

Each one is described below, with an example.

1.   *The straight news story*

In a straight news story the lead, or first sentence or paragraph, contains all the 5 Ws. The whole main idea is presented in the opening sentences. The rest of the story merely adds detail or support to the 5 Ws. No opinions or judgments are made. The straight news story is an attempt to present facts with no author's name given. Usually, these stories are United Press International or Associated Press "wire stories." Notice, in the example below, the "AP" after "Tallahassee, Fla." That stands for Associated Press wire story.

'Mercy Killer' Criticizes Appeal Ruling

TALLAHASSEE, Fla. (AP)—Roswell Gilbert, the 76-year-old man who lost a bid for freedom during appeal of his conviction in the "mercy killing" of his wife, says the decision by the state Cabinet was "grossly unfair."

Two previously undecided members of the independently elected Cabinet, sitting as the Board of Executive Clemency, refused to go along with Gov. Bob Graham's recommendation for the retired engineer's conditional release.

The officials split on the decision 4–2. Graham needed at least three signatures on the commutation order to free Gilbert.

Asks Compassion

Afterwards, in a news conference at Avon Park Correctional Institution, where he is serving a life sentence for the March slaying of his 73-year-old wife, Emily, Gilbert said, "I didn't do it just to get rid of her. What I need is compassion, I guess, and belief that what I say is the way it happened.

"I'm mad more than anything else and I'm angry. I think the whole thing is rather unfair because morally I had to do what I did. It's very disappointing and I think it's grossly unfair."

Comptroller Gerald Lewis and Agriculture Commissioner Doyle Conner said Gilbert should not be given special consideration because of his age and said he was not justified in taking a life, regardless of motive.

No Special Rights

"The law does not give one person the right to kill another because of illness or age," Lewis said.

Mrs. Gilbert suffered from Alzheimer's disease, which causes a progressive loss of memory, and osteoporosis, a painful ailment that makes the bones brittle.

If Gilbert had been released, he said he would have returned to the Fort Lauderdale condominium where he gave his wife of 51 years a sedative before shooting her twice in the head with a 9mm Luger.

The case has stirred strong emotions nationwide.

"We are receiving messages from all over the country," Conner said. "They're rather indignant. Mr. Gilbert did not have the solution to this serious problem. There were some alternatives. I regret that Mr. Gilbert did not pursue those alternatives."

What is the main idea of this straight news story? Express your answer using the 5 Ws.

_____

_____

_____

_____

_____

_____

2.   *The feature story*

Unlike a news story, the feature story does not always have all the 5 Ws in the lead. It may begin with a catchy title or first sentence. Usually, the feature story is about someone or some event that is unusual. Sometimes it's called a "human interest" story. Notice, in the following example, that the author's name is given and the story "features" an unusual person or event. Both the straight news story and the feature story are factual, but the feature writer writes with a personal style that does not rigidly stick to the 5 W opening. Read the following feature story.

Executions

The South—Nation's Death Belt

by Maura Dolan, *Times Staff Writer*

In Starke, Fla., the executioner wears a black hood and a long black robe. He earns $150 for each person he electrocutes.

In Parchman, Miss., the man who releases cyanide pellets in the gas chamber is a retired custodian who was appointed to the job by the governor and holds the official title of "Mississippi Executioner." Between executions, he sells vegetables at a roadside stand.

In Jackson, Ga., Death Row inmates eye their jailers uneasily, wondering whether the uniformed deputy who delivers their dinner will be the same one who sends a deadly shot of electricity through their limbs. For in Georgia, prison guards can volunteer to do the electrocutions.

Texas offers the "most humane way" to execute—"if there is a humane way of killing a person," said Robert Ott, 42, a member of the state's execution team in Huntsville. The team straps the condemned person to a gurney and injects a fatal solution that causes quick death.

Electric Chairs Nicknamed

The machinations of capital punishment vary from state to state like the nicknames of the electric chairs themselves: Old Sparky in Florida, Yellow Mama in Alabama, Gruesome Gertie in Louisiana. But it is no coincidence that all but three of the 47 people executed since the reinstatement of capital punishment in 1976 went to their deaths in the South.

The South has become what one attorney calls "the death belt" of the nation.

The three men executed outside the South voluntarily waived their appeals and asked to die. Since 1982 no one has been executed north of the Mason-Dixon line, but in the South the pace has quickened: 2 in 1982, 5 in 1983, 21 in 1984 and 15 in the first seven months of this year [1985].

"Our people are tried quicker, our supreme courts don't sit on the cases and our laws were upheld by the U.S. Supreme Court first," said Florida Assistant Atty. Gen. Ray Marky.

The bulk of the executions have been in Florida, Texas, Georgia and Louisiana. Three of these states—Florida, Texas and Georgia—were the first to adopt death penalty laws after the U.S. Supreme Court reinstated capital punishment in 1976. None of the four provides public funds for the legal defense of the condemned after the first post-conviction appeal to the state supreme court, although Florida will set up an office for such appeals under a law passed this year.

There are signs of support for the death penalty throughout the South. Miniature electric chairs adorn the offices of some public officials. The toy chairs emit a tiny jolt to the touch.

Rowdy crowds occasionally turn out for executions, transforming prison surroundings with tailgate parties complete with fireworks, lawn chairs and heavy drinking.

After the bars close in Huntsville, Tex., on execution nights, students from Sam Houston State University often go to the state prison to continue their revelry. When a man who killed a clerk for a six-pack of beer was to be executed, the students carried signs, "This Bud's for You." The students booed when the attorney general announced that the condemned man had received a last-minute reprieve.

During Virginia's most recent execution in June, members of a cheering crowd hollered, "Bring back lynching!" and carried signs saying, "Fry the Nigger."

Supports Capital Punishment

In Florida, Wendy Nelson, 36, packs up her mobile home and drives 125 miles to the state prison on execution mornings. She stands in a cow pasture across from the prison to demonstrate support for capital punishment. Her daughter, Elisa, 10, was slashed and beaten to death by a convicted rapist who is now on Death Row.

Nelson wants him executed as "a statement as to the value of Elisa's life, that the state of Florida feels her life was so valuable that they're willing to commit this negative act."

In Macon, Ga., David's Lounge held an execution party the night a young man was electrocuted for the abduction, rape and murder of a nursing student. When the condemned man's death was announced shortly after midnight, patrons in the dimly lit tavern whooped and hollered. A live band played on a makeshift stage where a Confederate flag hangs.

David Little, 34, owner of the bar, advertised the party on a billboard. "He's just a son of a bitch," Little said of the man whose death he celebrated. "Lucky I didn't catch him in my sight."

But as executions grow more routine, the numbers outside the prison drop. There are usually bands of protesters who carry candles and sing "We Shall Overcome." And sometimes there are relatives of the condemned.

On a hot, humid June afternoon in Huntsville, Tex., a condemned man wrote his last statement, ordered his last meal and considered how to distribute his possessions as he prepared himself to meet the executioner's needle at midnight.

Outside, 15 members of his family, dressed in their finest clothes, sat at a cement table under a tree facing the prison entrance. They sat there hour after hour, adults and children, waiting in the sticky heat. Prison officials, some of whom were to witness the execution, passed by periodically, glancing uneasily at the family scene before averting their eyes.

Charles Milton, 34, was to die for killing Maneree Denton during a 1977 robbery of a Fort Worth liquor store she owned with her husband, Leonard. Leonard Denton, 66, publicly called for Milton's execution and stayed up until the early morning hours watching television so he could go to bed assured that Milton was dead.

During the robbery, Denton grabbed Milton's pistol while Denton's wife hit Milton over the head with a bottle. She was shot as the two men struggled over the gun.

"I believe if we had the money to get a (better) lawyer for Charles it might not have come this far," said Milton's sister, Joyce Smith, 39, weeping and groping for a tissue in her purse as she waited to visit her brother. "I feel there is no justice done."

Milton's three daughters sat next to their aunt. Consuela, 15, cried but said she did not really believe that her dad would die. Gloria, 17, surveyed the others nervously. Natasha, 9, played with her hair ribbons. Their brother, Charles Jr., the eldest at 18, sat quietly and betrayed no emotion.

Inside the prison, Milton had advised his teen-age daughters to finish high school and to go to college. He recommended a military career for his son but asked him to avoid the Marines because too many were getting killed. He told his eldest daughter that she was to have his typewriter after his death. And he made his children promise to watch out for each other and stay out of trouble.

Several hours later, when night breezes cooled the air and unrelenting chant of crickets was everywhere, prison officials strapped Milton to a gurney and injected him with a deadly combination of drugs. His eyes rolled back in his head and he died.

The 15 family members, who had spent the final hours inside a prison lounge, boarded the church van in which they had arrived. A guard tossed in an onion sack containing the dead man's possessions, and the family drove away.

1. What is the main idea of the feature story? _____

_____

_____

_____

2. Why is this article called a feature story rather than a straight news story?

_____

_____

_____

_____

3. *The column*

A columnist is someone who writes stories, articles or essays on a regular basis either for a local paper or for syndication (meaning many newspapers use their columns). A newspaper column does not present the news; its function is to provide everything from entertainment to provoking thought about issues in the news. Usually, the "Letters to the Editor" sections of newspapers are filled with responses from readers who agree or disagree with a columnist's position.

The columnist's style and viewpoints are usually consistent and predictable. For instance, Art Buchwald writes satire on the political scene; Ann Landers writes advice columns in response to her readers' questions and letters; Dave Barry often writes sarcastic humorous pieces; Jack Anderson, James Reston, and Max Lerner write serious essays on world-wide current affairs and controversial topics.

Following is an example of a column written by Alice Kahn, who generally writes homestyle humor about family life. You may already be familiar with her columns.

Wear That Earring Like a Man

Alice Kahn

My daughters are growing up in the post-feminist era. When a guy comes on TV talking about how it's OK to hit a woman as long as you use an open hand, nobody has to teach them what to do. They were born knowing how to hiss. They just tighten their teeth and blow.

When they see a panel of men discussing an important issue on TV, they will instinctively ask: "Why aren't there any girls?" They didn't need to go to consciousness-raising sessions. They didn't need a class in Women's Herstory. They've never even read a single self-esteem book.

And since nobody ever told them that girls aren't supposed to be good at certain things, the older daughter passed me at math when she was 9, and the younger daughter could outrun me almost as soon as she could out-walk me.

When young jock Hannah, 9, and I were riding past a park the other day, I commented on the scene. "Isn't that nice?" I said. "It's a boy and a dad playing baseball."

She was apparently born with the sarcasm gene and said mockingly, "Oh yes, a boy and a dad—how very nice. Why is it always a boy and a dad? A girl and a dad playing baseball would be nice. A girl and a mom playing soccer would be better."

Being a post-feminist mom isn't easy, especially if you were raised to be a pre-feminist klutz. But consider the plight of the post-feminist boy. This brave new role was on exhibit recently in our neighborhood earring store.

I had long ago abandoned my stand against the girls getting their ears pierced. I knew it was a hopelessly old-fashioned attitude on my part, and after throwing out a few lighthearted comments about "primitive mutilation rituals," I took my older daughter to the doctor when she was 11 for a $60 sterile-technique piercing. When she was a little older, she came home and announced that she had gotten a "double pierce" for free from a hippie selling earrings on the street.

The second daughter, benefiting from her sister's pioneer work and community trends, got her ears done at an earring store this year. (After all, Samantha and Danielle and Sarah and Lily all had theirs done.) When she lost all her earrings and the holes closed up, I sprang for a second mutilation ritual last week, keeping my opinions to myself.

In the shop were a man and his 9-year-old son. Both of them were dressed in conventional T-shirts, jeans and boots. If the son had any trouble convincing his dad that all the cool young dudes had pierced ears, there was no sign of the struggle. The dad paid his nonrefundable $16 for the birthstone stud, the antiseptic and the piercing procedure. He signed the release absolving the store from blame should his son die in the cause of trend-following.

However, when the shop clerk went to shoot him in the ear, the boy began to squirm. After several tries, he refused. "I can't do it," he cried out. The father attempted to reason with him. "Look, Jason, we can't get our money back. Now sit still and take your earring like a man."

He actually said that. Can you imagine what he'll say when Jason tries to walk in high heels? "Don't wince, boy. Remember you're a Walton."

But Jason was squirming and appeared close to tears. So my Hannah went ahead of him. It was almost as if she were saying: Well, I'll show this boy how to hang tough at a piercing. She sat perfectly still and took it. Like a girl.

Now the father looked truly humiliated. I tried to console him. "Boys aren't raised to suffer for fashion," I said. He didn't seem consoled.

Hannah stood there right next to Jason, saying, "It doesn't hurt, re-ally." Jason didn't seem convinced.

Finally, Jason's father took him to a corner of the store for a serious dressing-down. I imagined him saying things like, "You get that earring or I'm gonna whup your hide, boy."
I said to my daughter, "Maybe he's afraid he'll cry when it happens. We should leave." Not wanting to witness such an ugly scene, Hannah left looking proud.
I'm sure she pondered the essential mystery of modern life. How can boys be so good at baseball but such sissies at earrings?

1. What is the purpose of such a column in a newspaper? Why would peo-ple read it?

_____

_____

_____

2. How does this column differ from a typical essay, such as those you studied in Chapter 7?

_____

_____

_____

3. Why would you or would you not be interested in reading such columns regularly?

_____

_____

_____

4. *The interpretive story*

Usually the interpretive story, like a feature story, carries a by-line (the name of the person who wrote it). Such stories not only give the facts, but they add opinions and make actual happenings read more like a story. Unlike the style of the straight news story or the feature, writers can give their slants to the news item and use words that reflect their opinions. Notice how this is done in the following article.

Teenage Pregnancy Rising in the U.S.

by Adam Ribb

A recent study raises some alarming questions regarding the teenage pregnancy rate in the United States. The study shows that of U.S. females aged 15–19 is 96 per 1000. In Canada it is 44 per 1000; in France, 43 per 1000; in Sweden, 35 per 1000, and in the Netherlands, only 14 per 1000. Ours is the only developed country in the world where teenage pregnancy has been rising in recent years. In fact, our teenage abortion rate is at least as high as the combined rates for abortion and birth in these countries. Why is it that the U.S. leads almost all other nations in rates of pregnancy and abortion among teenagers?

In an attempt to explain this rise, the Alan Guttmacher Institute and researchers from Princeton University offer some possible explanations. One observation is that "American teenagers at present have inherited the worst of all possible worlds regarding their exposure to the messages about sex." The report claims that the media "tell them that sex is romantic, exciting, titillating . . . yet at the same time teenagers get the message that good girls should say 'no.' Almost nothing they see or hear about sex informs them about contraception or the importance of avoiding pregnancy."

The study points out that those countries that make contraceptives and sex education programs easily available for teenagers have the lowest rate of teenage abortion, pregnancy, and childbearing.

Contrary to what many think, it is not true that teenage pregnancy in the U.S. is primarily among blacks, the study claims. Pregnancy rates for whites is 83 per 1000 and higher here than in any of the countries mentioned above, including England. It is also not true, as some think, that the availability of welfare benefits serves as a motive for teens to have babies.

Reprinted by permission of the author.

> What can we learn from this? If the researchers are correct and teenage pregnancy rates are lower in those countries where birth control and sex education are regularly taught, then we should consider making a bigger push toward this effort rather than cutting down on such services. In the long run, it will benefit us all to follow the lead of those countries that have been successful in reducing teenage pregnancies and abortions.

What makes this article an interpretive one, rather than a straight news story or a feature story? _____

_____

_____

_____

5. *The review*

Newspapers usually carry reviews on TV shows, movies, art shows, and books. The writer gives an opinion on how good, how enjoyable, or how important the subject is, using certain facts to support the opinion or to give background information. The following example provides information about a new book and the reviewer's opinions of it.

"Boston Brawler"

Straight Shooting: What's Wrong with America and How to Fix It

By John Silber
336 pp. New York:
Harper & Row. $22.50

By Leland Miles

IN THE BLEAK WORLD OF JOHN SILBER, the longtime president of Boston University, the only thing that makes his pessimistic heart leap up is the splendor of the Corps of Cadets at West Point, where the roaming ghosts of Generals George S. Patton and Douglas MacArthur still recall past glories. The rest of the country he sees as essentially deformed, undermined by the epidemic of drugs, breakdown of the family, failure of education, emergence of the underclass, growth of litigation, abuse of sex and decline of church influence. The purpose of "Straight Shooting," as its subtitle suggests, is to explain why these problems have arisen and how we should address them.

Mr. Silber's proposals are legion, and pumped out as if from a pom-pom gun. They are variously dated or current, redundant or novel, on target or off. But all are provocative and pungently phrased.

In our schools and colleges, Mr. Silber would terminate bilingual education, stop television from polluting children's sensibilities, break the education schools' monopoly on teacher certification and begin ethics instruction in kindergarten. On the domestic front, he would generally deny women's right to abortion, strengthen poor families through a national day-care system and fight poverty through job education for pregnant mothers. Internationally, he advocates support for the Nicaraguan contras and exchanging the property of landowners in El Salvador for bonds to build bridges and schools.

Someone should do a master's thesis on Mr. Silber's argumentative style. It begins with patient research (the old McGuffey's readers, he explains, emphasized heroic lives) and features broad erudition (no one formulated ethical principles more rigorously than Kant), critical analysis (tenure is not limited to the academy), incisive semantic distinctions (ethics is not the same as morals) and the stern application of logic (the fetus is not part of a woman's body). Other characteristics are colorful metaphor (stock markets are automated casinos), biting satire (education schools will produce educators when seminaries produce saints) and a flair for statistical pyrotechnics (welfare since the Johnson Administration has cost more than World War II).

Where these sophisticated devices are inadequate, Mr. Silber shifts to blunter weapons like the use of assertion as fact (despite the treatment of Indians and other minorities, the American past was good and just) and dismissive ridicule (opponents' views are rubbish). As a last resort, he rolls out his heavy howitzer to numb an opponent: the outrageous shocker (Ronald Reagan might go down in history as an appeasing Chamberlain).

These techniques account for some of the flaws in this volume. To start with, Mr. Silber is a sort of philosophical Mario Lanza, singing incessantly at full volume, with almost no modulation or change of pace. In some ways, "Straight Shooting" resembles St. Thomas More's 16th-century attacks on heresy. There is the same lack of joy and compassion, the same merciless flogging of enemies, the same exhaustive emptying of every nook and cranny of an argument and the same overkill. Both men use clubs to break butterflies.

Once Mr. Silber gets hold of an idea, no matter how mundane, he tears it to shreds like a bulldog. The chief flaw, however, is lack of balance. Television violence should certainly be condemned, but what about "Sesame Street" and "Captain Kangaroo"? Abortion may be immoral, but what about having children one cannot feed or clothe? It may be ridiculous to trust the Russians, but what about their trusting *us?*

Some of the most provocative ideas in this loosely organized work are contained in the chapter entitled "The Litigious Society." Mr. Silber's solutions for frivolous lawsuits motivated by greed are to make the loser pay all court and attorney fees; require the court rather than the winner to collect all punitive damages; and permit a client to sue his losing lawyer for malpractice. The author's least constructive performance comes in "The Illusion of Peace," where he belittles the 1987 treaty on intermediate-range nuclear forces for banning merely a small subclass of weapons. (But peace must start somewhere.) Most surprising, for a scholar supposedly conversant with modern history, Mr. Silber ignores Hiroshima, which changed the rules of war and made all of us hostage to a nuclear sword of Damocles.

There are so many paradoxes in this book that it is practically two separate works. For example, Mr. Silber supports tolerance as a distinctive feature of American and university life. Yet he is anything but tolerant once he moves into argumentative high gear. He concedes that all consciences have equal claim to moral authority, but adds that some consciences are more equal than others.

In the last analysis, Mr. Silber tolerates only views from the right, often insulting those who hold different positions; and the reader who is told that his favorite opinions are intolerable, tragic, disastrous or absurd is not likely to warm up to the author's proposals. For all his brilliance, Mr. Silber ignores the advice of Ben Franklin to present at least "the appearance of humility." The result is that instead of persuading his opponents, he will, through this book, chiefly reinforce the views of those already convinced.

1. What book is the author reviewing? _____

_____

2. Does the author like the book? _____

How do you know? _____

_____

_____

_____

3. Would you want to read the book? _____

   Why? _____

   _____

   _____

6. *The sports story*

Coverage of sports events is varied. Usually, lots of figurative or colorful language is used, such as "Cards Bomb the Angels" or "Angels Rip Indians." The Cards didn't "bomb" the Angels, nor did the Angels "rip" the Indians. These phrases are figures of speech. The following example is typical of sports stories. Notice some of the language used, both specialized and colorful.

Broncos Roll Early, Halt Bills Late

Denver Takes 21–0 Lead, Then Holds On for 28–14 Victory

ORCHARD PARK, N.Y. (AP)— Denver's big-play defense, sparked by interceptions from Wymon Henderson and Tyrone Braxton, helped the Broncos build a 21–0 lead and they held on for a 28–14 victory over the Buffalo Bills on Monday night.

Denver (2–0), which lost 10 of its last 11 Monday night road games and its last eight games on artificial turf, forced turnovers and converted them into points, as it did in an opening victory over Kansas City.

The defense, which ranked 22nd in

the NFL last year, contributed two points on a first-quarter safety and set up 13 more points. Those points came on Vance Johnson's nine-yard scoring pass from John Elway and field goals of 46 and 24 yards by David Treadwell.

The rookie also hit from 33 and 22 yards.

That same defense began to wilt, though, when Buffalo (1–1) went to a hurry-up offense—the same ploy Bills' Coach Marv Levy criticized as unethical when Cincinnati used it last year. Jim Kelly led the Bills on drives of 77 and 66 yards against a suddenly confused Denver defense.

But the Broncos again came up with crucial plays after Elway's pass was intercepted early in the fourth quarter by Mark Kelso at the Buffalo 31.

Kelly got the Bills to the Denver 41, but Simon Fletcher sacked Kelly, Braxton broke up a pass to Ronnie Harmon in the end zone with a diving swipe and rookie Warren Powers sacked Kelly again.

Denver regained control when Elway hit Johnson for 25 yards on third-and-12 and scrambled for 31 yards to the Buffalo five. Rookie Bobby Humphrey scored from the five to silence the crowd of 78,176.

Buffalo self-destructed under pressure from Denver's revitalized defense. The Broncos play more aggressively without the ball under defensive coordinator Wade Phillips then they did with Joe Collier in charge. Phillips replaced the fired Collier this season.

A Denver turnover actually helped the Broncos to a 2–0 lead. Nate Odomes made a spectacular over-the-shoulder interception and ran into his own end zone, but officials placed the ball on the one.

On the first play, Michael Brooks was not blocked and brought down Jamie Mueller in the end zone for the safety.

Denver took the free kick and marched 34 yards before Treadwell made a 22-yard field goal.

Another mistake hurt the Bills midway through the second period. After Larry Kinnebrew gained 14 yards with a screen pass and Thurman Thomas got 16 with another, Kelly's pass for Andre Reed was tipped high by the receiver. Henderson grabbed it and, though he fumbled when tackled, Denver recovered at its 36.

Humphrey ran for six yards, then burst through the left side of the line behind Melvin Bratton's block for a 33-yard gain.

An illegal contact penalty on Leonard Smith and a 10-yard pass to Mark Jackson set up Johnson's touchdown. Johnson went in motion to the left, hesitated, then continued left. He wasn't covered, and Elway hit him for the score.

The Bills didn't quit making mistakes there. Scott Norwood, who had hit nine straight field goals, missed from 43 yards and Reed fumbled after a 17-yard gain later in the second period.

1. What does the title mean?

_____

_____

_____

2. List some of the specialized language used that requires knowledge of football.

_____

_____

_____

_____

3. List some "colorful" language used, such as "Broncos roll early."

_____

_____

_____

4. Who wrote the sports story?

_____

7. *The editorial*

Often based on an important daily happening, an editorial (a) presents a problem or problems, (b) takes a stand by presenting the writer's opinion on how to interpret the facts, and (c) attempts to get the reader to agree. Ideally, editors' opinions are based on facts, though sometimes they let emotion take over. Notice the editor's opinions in the example that follows:

Smokeless Flying

Congress has temporarily banned smoking on domestic airline flights lasting two hours or less in response to medical evidence that the toxins in tobacco smoke harm not just smokers but the people around them, not the least within the closed environment of an airliner cabin. But if smoking on short flights is now seen as presenting intolerable health dangers to nonsmoking passengers and crew members, then smoking on longer flights obviously poses even greater hazards. The Senate has now recognized that by voting to forbid smoking on all domestic airline flights.

Getting the House to go along with this prohibition won't be easy, given the influence of the well-financed tobacco lobby. But it shouldn't prove impossible, either. The House has already acknowledged the health perils to nonsmokers aboard airliners by voting to make permanent the smoking ban on shorter flights that is due to expire next February. That must be done, but not as a trade-off to banning smoking on longer flights.

It's clear now that the air-filtration systems on passenger planes aren't effective in screening out tobacco smoke pollutants. The result is that the more than 80% of passengers who are nonsmokers are beset by gaseous poisons. A total smoking ban would of course make a cross-country flight uncomfortable for smokers. Millions of Americans who are former smokers can feel compassion for what they face. But the vast majority of passengers are nonsmokers, and they have a right to be protected. The Senate has seen that. The House has no rational reason for not doing so as well.

1. What is the problem the editor discusses?

   _____

   _____

   _____

2. What is the editor's opinion about the problem?

   _____

   _____

   _____

3. Do you agree with the editor's opinion? _____

4. Write a short, one-paragraph letter to the editor explaining why you feel as you do about the editorial.

Dear Editor:

_____

_____

_____

_____

8. *The editorial cartoon*

An editorial cartoon usually occurs on the editorial page and deals with a current news item. Cartoons, like editorials, express the artist's opinions. At the time the following cartoon appeared in the newspapers, much was being written about the so-called "war on drugs" and widely publicized attempts to get young people to "just say no" to drug use.

1. Who is the character in the cartoon supposed to represent?

   _____

   _____

2. What is the artist's opinion about the slogan "Just Say No" to drug use?

   _____

   _____

3. Does the cartoon mean that the artist excuses the selling of drugs for money? Explain.

   _____

   _____

   _____

PRACTICE 2. COMPREHENDING NEWS STORIES

A. *Directions:* Read the following news item and answer the questions that follow.

Knockout Drugs Used on Men, Police Say

DALLAS (AP)—At least six men have reported losing money and valuables after succumbing to drinks doctored by attractive women who gave them strong come-ons in bars, police say.

The victims told officers that when they awoke after sleeping off the effects of what are believed to be Mickey Finns—knockout drops—they found their companions missing along with the valuables.

Used by permission of the Associated Press.

1. Summarize the contents of this news report in a one-sentence statement. Avoid using the words "succumbing to drinks doctored" and "come-ons" in your summary.

_____

_____

_____

_____

_____

2. Why do you think this item made it into the newspapers?

_____

_____

_____

_____

B. *Directions:* Apply the 5 Ws to the following news story and answer the questions that follow.

Doctors' Plot Alleged in Painkiller Sales

NASHVILLE, Tenn. (AP)—Three doctors, a pharmacist and 10 other people have been indicted in a plot to obtain pain-killing prescription drugs for street sale, officials said Tuesday.

The sealed indictments, handed up Monday, accuse the doctors of illegally writing prescriptions for Dilaudid and the pharmacist of illegally filling them, the U.S. attorney's office said in a statement.

The others charged at the end of an 18-month investigation were accused of selling the drug, which produces heroin-like effects when watered down and injected, the statement said.

J. Bernard Redd, an agent in charge of the Drug Enforcement Agency in the area, estimated that more than 100,000 tablets were sold in the operation.

If bought by prescription, the pills cost about 50 cents to 75 cents each, he said.

"On the illicit market, they're worth anywhere from $50 to $75 a tablet, so you can see why the people would get involved with these kind of tablets," said Redd.

Used by permission of the Associated Press.

1. Fill in the 5 Ws:

   who: _____

   what: _____

   where: _____

   when: _____

   why: _____

2. Is the news story fact or interpretation?

   _____

3. Write a one-paragraph summary of the article.

   _____

   _____

   _____

   _____

   _____

   _____

C. *Directions:* Read the following news story and answer the questions that follow.

Reissue a License to Kill

In This War, Lives of Narco-Terrorists Must Be at Stake, Too

By JOSEPH I. LIEBERMAN

Will Colombian drug lords begin attacking Americans now that we've declared war on them and begun to extradite their partners in crime?

The chilling answer from terrorism experts is "yes, if they want to." Oliver B. Revell of the FBI testified before a Senate hearing last week that "if the cartels want to have blood running in the streets of America . . . I can't give you assurances we would be in a position to preempt it."

The question then becomes, how do we respond?

One thing we can do is reconsider the wisdom of Executive Order 12333, signed in 1975, which absolutely bars agencies of the U.S. government from ordering the killing of specific foreign individuals.

In other words, no matter how many acts of terrorism are ordered by leaders of the Medellin drug cartel or any other terrorists around the world, they can rest secure in the knowledge that their lives are safe from American reprisals or preemptive strikes.

The threat of narco-terrorism is quite unlike any we've confronted because of the unprecedented combination of greed, evil and money. It is a volatile mixture that has yielded deadly results. Look at the toll in Colombia: 70 judges killed in this decade, along with dozens of journalists, hundreds of police and a leading candidate for that country's presidency. And look at the toll in America: thousands of lives—often the youngest and most vulnerable among us—ended or permanently damaged by the drugs these cartels ship to our shores.

Unlike terrorists based in the Middle East or Europe, narco-terrorists have a criminal infrastructure in place in America—hundreds of drug traffickers in virtually every city and region of the country—ready to respond to their commands. In 1987, the murder of Drug Enforcement Administration informant Barry Seal in Louisiana was believed to be on the orders of the cartel.

Narco-terrorists have the will and the means to attack not just innocent civilians, but the very institutions that form the foundation of our society. In that sense, they are more than lawbreakers. They are a threat to our national security.

We cannot officially declare war against a group that has no diplomatic status as a country. But we should respond to their behavior as if we were at war. Placed in the context of such a conflict, Executive Order 12333 is an unnecessary and unwise restriction on the President's power to defend against a terrorist threat.

When confronted by such a threat, the President should have the widest array of options available to him. It does not make sense to wage war against terrorists with one hand tied behind our back. Nor does it make sense to telegraph to our enemies what tactics we have already ruled out by law.

Some will say that such a change in our policy would be immoral. I disagree. Is it more moral to let a terrorist carry out an attack that kills innocent civilians when the only thing preventing us from stopping him is an executive order? Is it more moral for us to launch a bombing raid on an area in which terrorists live, thereby threatening the lives of innocent civilians, because a covert mission targeted to those same terrorists cannot be authorized under our laws?

The occasions on which a President would find cause to order a strike against a terrorist would be limited. We should continue to attempt to prevent terrorist acts and bring terrorists to justice through normal channels, if possible. But Executive Order 12333 should be revised to account for those cases in which force is the only means we have to prevent a tragic attack against us. To safeguard against abuse, such action should be taken only with the approval of the President and the leadership of Congress and the intelligence committees, as is done now for other covert operations.

Changing Executive Order 12333 should not be seen as a panacea, but making terrorists susceptible to direct attack would signal the seriousness with which we view their acts and hopefully make them more hesitant to act against us.

As it stands, Executive Order 12333 represents a safe haven for narcoterrorists. While we deepen our involvement in the war against the drug lords, we must recognize that the price of that war will be exacted in blood as well as dollars. Should not their lives, as well as our own, be at stake?

1. The essay is mostly

   a. fact.

   b. opinion.

2. This essay would probably appear on the front page of a newspaper.

   a. True

   b. False, because _____

   _____

3. What is Executive Order 12333?

   _____

   _____

   _____

4. Do you agree with the author's thesis? Why?

_____

_____

_____

_____

D. *Directions:* Read the following piece from a newspaper and answer the questions that follow.

Combatting U.S. Scientific Illiteracy

Isaac Asimov

For a long time now, scientists have been concerned about the low level of scientific and mathematical instruction in American schools. Recent reports in 1988 and 1989 are unanimous in indicating not only that American students are scientifically and mathematically illiterate, but that they are more so than students in any other industrial society studied.

This is depressing in the extreme. The United States is the scientific leader of the world. Partly this may be due to the steady influx of scientists who were educated in other parts of the world. During the 1930s, Nazi oppression drove numerous scientists to Great Britain and the United States, and they were a key factor in the development of the nuclear bomb—a development widely touted in the United States as based on "Yankee know-how." Except that virtually all the Yankees had foreign accents.

And where do we stand today? Must we depend on the continued maintenance of our scientific lead on foreign imports?

Increasingly, our leaders must deal with dangers that threaten the entire world, where an understanding of those dangers and the possible solutions depend on a good grasp of science. The ozone layer, the greenhouse effect, acid rain, questions of diet and heredity—all require scientific literacy. Can Americans choose the proper leaders and support the proper programs if they are scientifically illiterate?

The whole premise of democracy is that it is safe to leave important questions to the court of public opinion—but is it safe to leave them to the court of public ignorance?

Let us take an example. In July, 1988, Jon Miller of the Public Opinion Laboratory at Northern Illinois University conducted a telephone poll of 2,041 adults and asked each about 75 questions on basic science. The results of the questionnaire showed that almost 95% of those questioned were ignorant of basic and simple scientific facts and had to be considered scientifically illiterate. There seemed to be a popular impression, for instance, that laser beams were composed of sound waves (rather than light waves) and that atoms are smaller than electrons (rather than the other way around).

This point might seem a little esoteric, but consider this. Twenty-one percent of those questioned were of the opinion that the sun revolved about the Earth and an additional 7% didn't know which went around which.

Considering that it is now four centuries that science has been unanimous over the fact that the Earth goes about the sun, how is it possible that a quarter of those asked didn't know about i? To my mind, there are three possibilities.

Those who didn't know either:

—Had never gone to school and had never read any book that dealt with science in any significant way.

—Had indeed gone to school and had read some books but had paid no attention whatever.

—Had gone to school and had read books and had paid attention but hadn't been properly taught.

To me the first two possibilities are unthinkable, and I am forced to consider the third.

That Americans aren't properly taught is all too likely considering the fact that a great many teachers must be as scientifically and mathematically illiterate as the general public. Yet how can any teacher, however poorly prepared, not teach the children that the Earth goes around the sun?

Well, there is a passage in the Bible that describes a fight between the Israelites under Joshua and the Gibeonites. The Israelites were winning, but it seemed the Gibeonites might escape under cover of darkness. To complete the victory, Joshua therefore commanded "Sun, stand thou still upon Gibeon. . . . And the sun stood still . . . and hasted not to go down about a whole day." (Joshua 10:12–13).

Now, how can Joshua have ordered the sun to stand still and how could the sun have proceeded to stand still if it weren't moving to begin with? These verses were used by people in the 1500s and 1600s to fight the notion that the Earth was moving around the sun. They kept quoting the passage in Joshua.

In fact, this story was told when everyone in the world thought the sun did move. We now know better. And, even if the passage were divinely inspired, it may simply have been worded in a way that would make sense to the people of that time.

Nevertheless, there are millions of people in the United States who still firmly believe that every word of the Bible is inspired and absolutely, literally true; that the sun is moving and Joshua did command it to stand still, and it did stop moving temporarily.

Perhaps that means that in areas where such views are strong, teachers teach that the sun goes around the Earth, either out of stubborn belief or out of the fear that they will be fired if they don't. And perhaps that is why so many Americans are ignorant of so vital and elementary a point.

Imagine the harm things like this can do! This kind of backward thinking must not continue if America is to keep its role of the world's scientific leader.

---

1. Is this a news story, an editorial, or an essay for a column? Explain.

   _____

   _____

2. Does the author use mostly fact or opinion? _____

3. What is his thesis? _____

   _____

   _____

4. What, according to the author, might the early years of World War II have to do with the U.S. gaining a lead in the scientific community?

   _____

   _____

5. What are some of the problems facing the world today that require scientific understanding and literacy?

_____

_____

_____

6. Is the information used to support the thesis reliable? Explain.

_____

_____

_____

7. What author biases are revealed?

_____

_____

8. Do you agree with the author? Explain.

_____

_____

_____

R⁴   *Reading applications*

Application 1.   Identifying types of news stories

Obtain a copy of today's newspaper for your area. Find an example of each of the following types of newspaper coverage:

a. straight news story
b. feature story

c. a syndicated or local column
d. interpretive story
e. review
f. sports story with figurative language
g. editorial
h. editorial cartoon

Cut them from the paper and bring them to class to share and discuss.

Application 2.   Writing news stories

Directions: Pick *one* of the following news assignments.

1. Write a short editorial on some problem or issue about which you are concerned. It can be a school issue, a city problem, a national problem, or a worldwide problem. Support your opinions with facts. Use the examples in this chapter or your newspaper as a guide.

2. Write a sports story on a sports event you actually saw. It can be a live event or one you saw on television.

3. Write a review of a book, movie, concert, record, or TV program that you saw recently. Try not just to retell the story or plot, but to give your personal evaluation of your subject.

4. Write a news item on something you saw happen recently. Use the 5 Ws in your opening paragraph and write it the way you think it would be done in the newspaper.

5. Write a letter to the editor of your newspaper expressing your opinions/ feelings on some event in local or national news.

Application 3.   Reading today's newspaper

1. *Directions:* Pick a newspaper story from today's paper. Answer the following questions about the article. Cut the article from the paper and attach it to this page.

   a. Name of newspaper: _____

   b. Date: _____ Section of paper: _____ Page: _____

c. Title of article: _____

d. Writer or wire service: _____

e. Who or what is the article about? _____

   _____

   _____

f. What is happening or has happened? _____

   _____

g. Why did it happen? _____

   _____

h. When did it happen? _____

   _____

i. Where did it happen? _____

   _____

j. Is the information mostly fact or opinion? _____

   _____

2. *Directions:* Pick an editorial from today's paper and answer the following questions about it. Cut the editorial from the paper and attach it to this page.

a. Name of newspaper: _____

b. Date: _____ Page: _____

c. Title of editorial: _____

d. What problem or subject was discussed? _____

   _____

e. What are/were the causes of the problem? _____

_____

f. What stand or point of view does the editorial take on the problem?

_____

_____

g. What words are used to show the author's feelings or point of view?

_____

_____

_____

h. Does the author present a solution to the problem? _____

_____

i. Are there points or views the author should have used? _____

_____

j. What is your own solution to or view of the problem? _____

_____

_____

3. *Directions:* Pick an editorial cartoon from a newspaper and answer the following questions about it. Cut the editorial cartoon from the paper and attach it to your answers.

a. What is the subject of the cartoon? _____

_____

_____

   b. What point is being made? _____

   _____

   _____

   c. Do you agree with the artist? _____

   _____

   _____

   d. Who is the artist? _____

   _____

Application 4.   Summarizing what you have learned

Directions: On a separate sheet of paper, summarize what you have learned from reading this chapter (a) about yourself, (b) about skills you can apply to your reading, and (c) questions you still have that need answering. Turn this in to your instructor when finished.

Additional reading selections

The following reading selections are varied in content, difficulty, and length. Rather than have you answer comprehension and vocabulary questions similar to those that appear after the reading selections in each chapter, you will be asked to do something different with each of the following readings. In order for you to do what you are asked, you will need to apply the various reading skills taught in this book. We hope that you will be able to discuss these readings within your class and to share your reactions and answers. For many of the questions there are no "right" answers.

We encourage you to keep a record of the words that give you trouble in these readings. When you can't figure out a word's meaning in context, underline it so that you can look up the word later. If not knowing the word keeps you from understanding a passage, you may want to stop and look it up before reading on. You be the judge, but don't stop to look up every word as you read. Doing so will cause you to lose track of comprehension. Besides, some words become clear as you read on.

Reading Selections

Selection 1. "The Learner's Club" by Frank Smith
Selection 2. "The Sociology Final" by Edward Rivera
Selection 3. "Conformity and Groupthink" by Roger von Oechs
Selection 4. "What Are We Waiting For?" by Ann Wells
Selection 5. "Shame" by Dick Gregory
Selection 6. "We're Not Taught to Hate" by H. Keith H. Brodie
Selection 7. "Stress: Some Good, Some Bad" by Jane Brody
Selection 8. "Single Mothers by Choice" by Howard Halpern
Selection 9. "Putting Something Back" by Brian A. Rosborough

Selection 1

Are you a member of the Learner's Club? Are your brains and intelligence underrated? In the following selection taken from Frank Smith's book *Insult to Intelligence: The Bureaucratic Invasion of Our Classrooms*, Smith has some interesting things to say about how we learn and why learning should not be made as difficult as it is.

FRANK SMITH

THE LEARNER'S CLUB

1   We underrate our brains and our intelligence. Formal education has become such a complicated, self-conscious and overregulated activity that learning is widely regarded as something difficult that the brain would rather not do. Teachers are often inclined to think that learning is an occasional event, requiring special incentives and rewards, not something that anyone would normally engage in given a choice. Such a belief is probably well-founded if the teachers are referring to their efforts to keep children moving through the instructional sequences that are prescribed as learning activities in school. But reluctance to learn cannot be attributed to the brain. Learning is the brain's primary function, its constant concern, and we become restless and frustrated if there is no learning to be done. We are all capable of huge and unsuspected learning accomplishments without effort.

The World of Speech

2   Learning to talk and to understand spoken language is a monumental intellectual achievement. Babies arrive in the world with no prior knowledge or expectations about language. They have no choice but to learn from the artifacts they find around them and from what they see people doing. They must behave like archaeologists and anthropologists from another world. And they do so effortlessly and inconspicuously.

3   Children are so competent in learning that they are usually denied credit for their abilities and achievements. Myths protect adults from the true knowledge of how much children learn, not occasionally but all the time. Indeed, it can be astonishing to adults to discover how much children are learning.

4   Forget the condescending myth that children do not learn very much when they learn spoken language. All children except the most severely

deprived or handicapped acquire a vocabulary of over ten thousand words during the first four or five years of their lives. At the age of four they are adding to their vocabulary at the rate of twenty new words a day. By seven this rate may have increased to nearly thirty words, every day of the year, including holidays, with no allowance for forgetting. By late adolescence the average vocabulary is at least fifty thousand words, perhaps over one hundred thousand, depending upon how the counting is done. How do children manage to learn twenty new words or more a day? Not from formal instruction. Not from flashcards or by filling in the blanks; not from the r-bbit.

5   Teachers have told me it is impossible for children to learn words at such a rate, whatever the research shows. I ask these teachers how they can be so sure. They tell me it takes them an hour to teach children ten words on a word list, they forget five by the next day, and by the end of the week they might remember only two. So how could they possibly be adding to their vocabulary at the rate of twenty words a day? I have to say it must be when the children are not working on the word lists.

6   Children not only learn words, they learn how to put words together into conventional phrases and sentences, so that they can understand and be understood. Every child learns a very specialized grammar. Children may not learn to talk the way their school teachers talk, but they do not see themselves as teachers. Children learn to talk like the people they see themselves as being. They learn to talk the way their friends talk. Children learn the vocabulary and grammar of the language spoken around them, its idioms and jargon, its distinctive patterns of intonation and gesture, and its complex rules of eye contact, body posture, and interruption. And children learn all this with exquisite precision—they learn to be *exactly* like their peers. A complete description of the complexities of language as it is actually used defies the lifetime efforts of professional linguists, yet infants learn the fundamentals in a few short and busy years, without anyone suspecting what they are doing.

7   Forget also the dismissive myth that language is a biological predisposition, that the way we talk is in our genes. Our language is not inherited from our parents. We talk the way our parents talk only if we grow up in the company of our parents. Our biological parents may be English-speaking, but if we are raised in a Chinese community then we will speak that community's dialect of Chinese, and we will have as much trouble later in life trying to learn English as our parents would trying to learn Chinese. Every aspect of language must be learned.

8   Babies are born capable of learning any dialect of any language in the world today. And no one would suggest that the 3,000 or more languages currently spoken on earth constitute a full set, that there are no alternative possibilities. There have been other languages in the past and there will be other languages in the future (at least if the human race survives). Infants are capable of learning languages that do not yet exist.

9   Forget the demeaning myth that children learn about language through imitation. A grain of truth underlies this view, but it is not that children learn by blindly mimicking the behavior of adults. Children no more parrot the noises and gestures of grown-ups than they walk around

the room making sounds like the vacuum cleaner. They don't learn to do what the vacuum cleaner does; they learn to use the vacuum cleaner the way the people around them do. When children emulate the language of adults they do so for purposes of their own. If young children say they want to be taken for a walk, it is because they want to go for a walk, not because they have just heard an adult utter those words. They imitate when it is useful to do so, to achieve a purpose of their own. Indeed, when infants don't know the appropriate way to say something they want to say they invent a way. Children learn in the course of accomplishing their own ends. They are selective and discriminating, and they learn far more about language than they ever could if they blindly imitated the sounds they heard adults making.

10   Forget finally the misleading myth that children learn to talk because adults deliberately set out to teach them language. Parents, like other family members and friends, may indeed be teachers of children, but this is because of what they demonstrate about spoken language, not because of any organized instruction that they provide. Children learn to be users of spoken language by observing and overhearing how other people use it, by becoming apprenticed to language users, and especially by being helped to say things and to understand things themselves. None of this is anything like the way children are expected to learn in school. In the broader world of learning, there is no systematic instruction, and there are no curriculum guides or lesson plans, no workbooks, exercises or drills, no tests or marks, no assignments, no grades, no specified objectives, no formal teacher accountability. There are no r-bbits. . . .

Learning About Language Incidentally

11   If children master spoken language without formal instruction, then how can such learning be best described? Many striking metaphors have been devised to capture the nature of the learning, characterizing children as "inventors" or "scientists," and defining learning as "experimentation" or "hypothesis-testing." George Miller once referred to children as "informavores"—they eat up new knowledge. My alternative is more down to earth. I call it the "Can I have another donut?" system of language learning. Every child learns to say, "Can I have another donut?" not in order to say, "Can I have another donut?" but in order to get another donut. The language learning is incidental, a by-product of the child's attempt to achieve some other end. The child wants to get another donut, and in the course of doing so learns how to ask for it. In fact, neither the child nor anyone else around is likely to be aware that language learning is taking place.

12   A British linguist, Michael Halliday, pointed out in 1973 that children do not learn to talk the way linguists learn language—as an abstract system that can later be used to fulfill a variety of purposes. Children learn language and its uses simultaneously. In fact, it is through its uses that language is learned. Children have difficulty in learning anything that to them seems to have no purpose. This is the reason why the r-bbit is a totally unnecessary and inadequate means of teaching children to talk, and why the drill-and-test type program is such a misguided means of

trying to teach children to read and write. There is no point in filling in
the second letter of r-bbit.

13   Learning is not the occasional and difficult thing it is often thought to
be. That learning requires effort is another myth. The stress and strain
comes from trying to learn and failing. When learning is successful, it is
totally inconspicuous. Children learn all the time, but the only indication
that learning has taken place usually, is the sudden demonstration that they
know something they didn't know before. Parents are for ever saying,
"Where did the child learn to say that?" And the situation is exactly the
same with adults. We learn all the time without suspecting that we are doing so, and the main reason we are unaware of learning is because no effort
is involved. We are painfully aware when we have failed at something we
have deliberately set out to learn, yet we tend to blithely ignore the kind of
learning we do every day.

14   Take some simple examples. Most people can tell you about the last
movie they saw, or the program they watched on television the previous
evening, or the last newspaper or magazine that they read, and they have
almost total recall. They can tell you what they wore yesterday and the day
before, what they ate, and what the weather was like. They can tell you
whether many well-known people are alive or dead. And they learned all of
this without trying, without being aware that they were in fact learning. We
learn every time we make sense of something; we learn in the act of making
sense of the world around us. Understanding takes care of learning. If you
understand what you see in a movie, you will probably remember what you
see, at least for as long as it is important for you to do so.

15   We still learn to talk in the way we learned as babies, and we continue to
be completely unaware that this learning is taking place. In fact, we cannot
help learning in this way. My Canadian friends are always telling me when I
come back from some travels that I've picked up an American accent or that
I'm speaking like a Londoner again. An American friend of mine named
Donald Graves went to Scotland for a few months to study at the University
of Edinburgh. When he came back he had a distinctly Scottish lilt in his
voice which is still there two years after the visit. Don Graves did not go to
Scotland to learn to speak like a Scot, he did not practice or take lessons,
and at the time he was not aware of what he was learning. In fact, he would
just as soon not have learned what he did. He tells me he is still em-
bahrrrrassed by the way he talks.

16   The examples that I have just given are so commonplace that some people want to deny that this is "learning." They want to call it something else,
like "memory." But remembering something in these everyday ways reflects
exactly the same kind of learning that a child accomplishes in first making
sense of spoken language. It is the kind of learning we are normally unaware
of because it takes place continually and effortlessly, while we think we are
doing something else (like enjoying a movie or reading a magazine). If learning does not take place in this way, then we are bored. We find it difficult to
tolerate situations in which there is nothing new to be made sense of, nothing to learn. It is only when we deliberately try to learn (or teach) something
that does not make sense that learning is difficult to accomplish. And what
we are aware of then is not learning, or even the failure to learn, but

the confusion of not being able to make sense of what we are engaged in. The struggle to learn is usually a struggle to comprehend. The moment of comprehension is the moment of learning. Learning is a smooth, continuous flow from one understanding to another, not a series of sporadic lurches from confusion to confusion.

17   Infants constantly find much that is new in the world to do and to understand. They learn whenever someone or something helps them to do something they want to do or to understand something they want to understand. And with spoken language they accomplish all of this enormous amount of learning by the simple device of joining a club, the club of people who use spoken language.

Word Count: 2214

Exercise

1. Summarize the reading selection in one paragraph.

2. Explain why you agree or disagree with Frank Smith.

3. Explain this quote from the selection in terms of yourself and how you learn:

    It is only when we deliberately try to learn (or teach) something that does not make sense that learning is difficult to accomplish. And what we are aware of then is not learning, or even the failure to learn, but the confusion of not being able to make sense of what we are engaged in. The struggle to learn is usually a struggle to comprehend. The moment of comprehension is the moment of learning. Learning is a smooth, continuous flow from one understanding to another, not a series of sporadic lurches from confusion to confusion.

Selection 2

In *Family Installments,* his semi-autobiographical book on Spanish Harlem, Edward Rivera describes the experiences of a Puerto Rican boy growing up in American society. The experience described in this excerpt— taking a final exam in a college course—will be familiar to many students. Rivera writes about the exam from an unusual perspective.

EDWARD RIVERA

THE SOCIOLOGY FINAL

I took a cab up to school, but I was still late. On the way there, I reviewed the "material" in my head: almost total confusion, a jumble of jargon, ordinary things passed off as profundities with the aid of "abstractionists." ("The home then is the specific zone of functional potency that grows about a live parenthood an active interfacial membrane or surface furthering exchange a mutualizing membrane between the family and the society in which it lives. . . .")

The classroom was packed for the first time since the opening day of classes, and filled with smoke. Over forty students were bent over their examination booklets, most of them looking confused by the questions. The professor, puffing an immense pipe, was at his desk (manufactured by Vulcan), reading Riesman on *The Lonely Crowd*, casually, as if it were a murder mystery whose ending he had figured out back on page one. He didn't look pleased when I stepped up to his desk: another pair of lungs in a roomful of carbon dioxide and cigarette smoke.

"Yes?"

I asked him for a question sheet and an examination booklet. They were on the desk, weighted down with the eighth edition of his anthology.

"Are you registered in this course?" he asked.

Yes, I was. He wanted to know my name. I told him. He looked me up in his roll book. Had I been coming to class regularly? Every time. How come I never spoke up in class? Because I sat in the back. It was hard to be heard from back there. I might try sitting up front, he said. I said I would. He said it was a little late for that. For a moment I'd forgotten what day this was. *Dies irae*, according to my paperback dictionary of foreign phrases. Do-or-die day.

There were no empty chairs, so I walked to the back of the room and squatted in a corner, keeping my coat and scarf on.

"Answer one from Part A, one from Part B, and one from Part C." I had no trouble understanding that much. But my mind blanked out on the choices in Parts A, B, and C. There was something about "group membership as the source of individual morality and social health" (Durkheim? I couldn't remember). I must have slept through that lecture, and I couldn't remember any mention of it in the eighth edition. Another one asked for something or other on Weber's contention that "minorities in 19th-century Europe—the roles in Russia, the Huguenots in France, the Nonconformists in England, and the Jews in all countries—had offset their socio-political exclusion by engaging in economic activity whereas the Catholics had not." This one had to be explained in fifteen minutes. I got around it by drawing a blank.

The easiest choice in Part C asked for "a sociological autobiography, demonstrating your command of certain relevant aspects in this course, as well as the terminology of sociology."

"Terminology of sociology." That wasn't even a good rhyme. It was also asking too much for fifteen minutes. It wasn't even enough time for my nerves to calm down. Too bad. I got up and left the room. No one noticed.

I went down to the student cafeteria for a cup of coffee, and while I drank it, I read the opening chapter of Dr. A. Alonso's *El Gibaro*, a Puerto Rican classic which I'd brought with me to reread on the subway back home. "I am one of those," it went, "and this can't matter much to my readers, who are in the habit of not sleeping without first having read something"—another one, I thought, nineteenth-century version—"and this something must be of the sort that requires more than usual seclusion, order and meditation, since I think that at no time other than the night's silence can one withdraw from the real world, to elevate oneself into the imaginary; above all when the day has been spent without affliction, something that a young man achieves from time to time, before he becomes the head of a family, or while he does not have to govern, on his own, the vessel of his future."

In the examination blue book, which I hadn't bothered returning, I translated some of these long, rhythmic sentences as best I could (no dictionary on me, for one thing), just for practice, and then, when I'd finished a second cup of coffee, I shoved the Alonso and the blue book back inside my coat pocket and left for the subway.

Word Count: 758

Exercise

1. Even though Rivera provides explicit details of the exam, he suggests more through his tone than with what he says. What is his tone and how does it help express his main point or thesis?

2. What significance does the title of the book the professor is reading have on what Rivera is describing? Of what significance is the quotation and book that Rivera is reading?

3. Write a description of a memorable final exam you have taken. What effect has it had on you?

Selection 3

The following selection is from the author's book *A Whack on the Side of the Head*, a book about mental blocks that can prevent us from being more innovative. Read to see what the advantages and disadvantages of conformity are and what groupthink is.

ROGER VON OECHS

CONFORMITY AND GROUPTHINK

Scene #1

A man walks into the waiting room of a doctor's office. He looks around and is surprised by what he sees: everybody is sitting around in their underwear. People are drinking coffee in their underwear, smoking cigarettes in their underwear, reading magazines in their underwear, and carrying on conversations in their underwear. The man is shocked at first, but then decides that they must know something he doesn't. After about twenty seconds, he, too, takes off his clothes and sits down in his underwear to wait for the doctor.

Scene #2

A man waits patiently for an elevator in an office building. After a short period, the elevator arrives and the doors open. As he looks in, he notices that everybody is turned around and facing to the rear of the elevator. So, he, too, gets into the elevator and faces to the rear.

These scenes are from Allen Funt's 1960's television series *Candid Camera*. They both confirm what countless psychology tests have found, namely, the best way to get along is to go along.

All of us are subject to group pressures. If you study your own behavior, you will see how much you conform to various situations. Let's suppose that you are driving down the freeway, and everyone around you is going 65 miles per hour. (At this writing, the speed limit is still 55 MPH.) What happens? It is very difficult not to break the law; you get caught up in the "flow of traffic." Or, suppose that you are a pedestrian standing on the corner of an intersection in a major city. Ten or twelve other people are standing there with you. The sign says, "DON'T WALK," but no traffic is coming. Then one of the pedestrians crosses the street against the light. Soon another goes, and then another. In no time at all, all the other pedestrians have crossed the street against the light. And you do too, because you would feel really stupid being the only person still standing there.

Benefits of conformity

Conformity serves at least two practical purposes. First, to live in society requires cooperation among its members. Without conformity, traffic would get tied up, production quotas would be missed, and the fabric of society would come apart. Part of the price we pay for the benefits of our social existence is a piece of our own individuality.

Second, in those situations in which we don't know our way around, what do we do? We look to others for the right way to act and the knowledge to get along. Suppose you are in a laundromat, and you are not quite sure how to operate the washing machine. What do you do? Probably look over to the person next to you and try the approach he is using.

The best example of this is St. Augustine. As a young priest in Milan, Italy, Augustine had a problem, and so he went to his bishop, Ambrose, for advice. It seemed that Augustine was going to spend the weekend in Rome. His problem was that in Rome it was customary to celebrate the Sabbath on Sunday, while in Milan the Sabbath was celebrated on Saturday. Augustine was confused as to which was the appropriate day. Ambrose solved Augustine's problem by telling him,

WHEN IN ROME, DO AS THE ROMANS DO.

Groupthink

New ideas, however, are not born in a conforming environment. Whenever people get together, there is the danger of "groupthink." This is the phenomenon in which group members are more interested in retaining the approval of other members rather than trying to come up with creative solutions to the problems at hand. Group pressure can inhibit originality and new ideas. Thus, when everyone thinks alike, no one is doing very much thinking.

Alfred Sloan knew the dangers of groupthink. In the late 1930's, Sloan was chairing a board meeting at General Motors. An idea was proposed and everyone present became very enthusiastic about it. One person said, "We'll make a lot of money with this proposal." Another said, "Let's implement it as soon as possible." And still another said, "We'll knock the pants off our competition." After the discussion, Sloan said, "It's now time to vote on the proposal." The vote went around the table, and one by one, each board member voted "Aye." When the vote came back to Sloan, he said, "I, too, vote 'Aye' and that makes it unanimous. And for that reason, I am going to table the proposal until next month. I don't like what's happening to our thinking. We're getting locked into looking at this idea in just one way, and this is a dangerous way to make decisions. I want each of you to spend the next month studying the proposal from a different perspective." A month went by, and the proposal was brought up again at the next board meeting. This time, however, it was voted down. The board members had had an opportunity to break through the effects of groupthink.

Word Count: 746

Exercise

1. Summarize the reading selection in one paragraph.

2. Make a list of the times you have conformed with a group. Then put a G
   in front of those that were good and an N in front of those that were not
   good times to conform.

3. Explain what is wrong with groupthink.

Selection 4

Is every day a special day for you? Do you save things for special occasions? Do you put things off, planning to get around to it "soon"? How often
do you say to yourself, "One of these days . . ."? Read how the death of the
author's sister put a new slant on her own life.

ANN WELLS

WHAT ARE WE WAITING FOR?

My brother-in-law opened the bottom drawer of my sister's bureau and
lifted out a tissue-wrapped package.

"This," he said, "is not a slip. This is lingerie." He discarded the tissue
and handed me the slip. It was exquisite; silk, handmade and trimmed with
a cobweb of lace. The price tag with an astronomical figure on it was still
attached.

"Jan bought this the first time we went to New York, at least eight or
nine years ago. She never wore it. She was saving it for a special occasion.
Well, I guess this is the occasion."

He took the slip from me and put it on the bed with the other clothes
we were taking to the mortician. His hands lingered on the soft material for
a moment, then he slammed the drawer shut and turned to me.

"Don't ever save anything for a special occasion. Every day you're alive
is a special occasion."

I remembered those words through the funeral and the days that fol
lowed when I helped him and my niece attend to all the sad chores that
follow an unexpected death. I thought about them on the plane returning
to California from the Midwestern town where my sister's family lives. I
thought about all the things that she hadn't seen or heard or done. I
thought about the things that she had done without realizing that they
were special.

I'm still thinking about his words, and they've changed my life. I'm reading more and dusting less. I'm sitting on the deck and admiring the view without fussing about the weeds in the garden. I'm spending more time with my family and friends and less time in committee meetings.

Whenever possible, life should be a pattern of experience to savor, not endure. I'm trying to recognize these moments now and cherish them.

I'm not "saving" anything; we use our good china and crystal for every special event—such as losing a pound, getting the sink unstopped, the first camellia blossom.

I wear my good blazer to the market if I feel like it. My theory is if I look prosperous, I can shell out $28.49 for one small bag of groceries without wincing.

I'm not saving my good perfume for special parties; clerks in hardware stores and tellers in banks have noses that function as well as my party-going friends'.

"Someday" and "one of these days" are losing their grip on my vocabulary. If it's worth seeing or hearing or doing, I want to see and hear and do it *now*.

I'm not sure what my sister would have done had she known that she wouldn't be here for the tomorrow we all take for granted. I think she would have called family members and a few close friends. She might have called a few former friends to apologize and mend fences for past squabbles. I like to think she would have gone out for a Chinese dinner, her favorite food. I'm guessing—I'll never know.

It's those little things left undone that would make me angry if I knew that my hours were limited. Angry because I put off seeing good friends whom I was going to get in touch with—someday. Angry because I hadn't written certain letters that I intended to write—one of these days. Angry and sorry that I didn't tell my husband and daughter often enough how much I truly love them.

I'm trying very hard not to put off, hold back, or save anything that would add laughter and luster to our lives.

And every morning when I open my eyes I tell myself that it is special.

Word Count: 632

Exercise

1. Summarize the reading selection in one paragraph.

2. Do you think it's possible to live every day as though it were special? Explain.

3. Make a list of the things you have been putting off. Then pick one and actually do it today.

Selection 5

The following selection is from the author's autobiography. Dick Gregory is an actor, comedian, sometimes author, and frequent fighter for civil rights. On at least two occasions, Gregory has gone on long fasts to call attention to injustices of certain government policies or lack of policy. More recently he devotes much of his time with helping overweight people reduce and gain self-confidence. Here, he tells us about an experience that was to change his life.

DICK GREGORY

SHAME

I never learned hate at home, or shame. I had to go to school for that. I was about seven years old when I got my first big lesson. I was in love with a little girl named Helene Tucker, a light-complected little girl with pigtails and nice manners. She was always clean and she was smart in school. I think I went to school then mostly to look at her. I brushed my hair and even got me a little old handkerchief. It was a lady's handkerchief, but I didn't want Helene to see me wipe my nose on my hand. The pipes were frozen again, there was no water in the house, but I washed my socks and shirt every night. I'd get a pot, and go over to Mister Ben's grocery store, and stick my pot down into his soda machine. Scoop out some chopped ice. By evening the ice melted to water for washing. I got sick a lot that winter because the fire would go out at night before the clothes were dry. In the morning I'd put them on, wet or dry, because they were the only clothes I had.

Everybody's got a Helene Tucker, a symbol of everything you want. I loved her for her goodness, her cleanness, her popularity. She'd walk down my street and my brothers and sisters would yell, "Here comes Helene," and I'd rub my tennis sneakers on the back of my pants and wish my hair wasn't so nappy and the white folks' shirt fit me better. I'd run out on the street. If I knew my place and didn't come too close, she'd wink at me and say hello. That was a good feeling. Sometimes I'd follow her all the way home, and shovel the snow off her walk and try to make friends with her Momma and her aunts. I'd drop money on her stoop late at night on my way back from shining shoes in the taverns. And she had a Daddy, and he had a good job. He was a paper hanger.

I guess I would have gotten over Helene by summertime, but something happened in that classroom that made her face hang in front of me for the next twenty-two years. When I played the drums in high school it was for Helene and when I broke track records in college it was for Helene and when I started standing behind microphones and heard applause I wished Helene could hear it, too. It wasn't until I was twenty-nine years old and married and making money that I finally got her out of my system. Helene was sitting in that classroom when I learned to be ashamed of myself.

It was on a Thursday. I was sitting in the back of the room, in a seat with a chalk circle drawn around it. The idiot's seat, the troublemaker's seat.

The teacher thought I was stupid. Couldn't spell, couldn't read, couldn't do arithmetic. Just stupid. Teachers were never interested in finding out that you couldn't concentrate because you were so hungry, because you hadn't had any breakfast. All you could think about was noontime, would it ever come? Maybe you could sneak into the cloakroom and steal of bite of some kid's lunch out of a coat pocket. A bite of something. Paste. You can't really make a meal of paste, or put it on bread for a sandwich, but sometimes I'd scoop a few spoonfuls out of the big paste jar in the back of the room. Pregnant people get strange tastes. I was pregnant with poverty. Pregnant with dirt and pregnant with smells that made people turn away, pregnant with cold and pregnant with shoes that were never bought for me, pregnant with five other people in my bed and no Daddy in the next room, and pregnant with hunger. Paste doesn't taste too bad when you're hungry.

The teacher thought I was a troublemaker. All she saw from the front of the room was a little black boy who squirmed in his idiot's seat and made noises and poked the kids around him. I guess she couldn't see a kid who made noises because he wanted someone to know he was there.

It was on a Thursday, the day before the Negro payday. The eagle always flew on Friday. The teacher was asking each student how much his father would give to the Community Chest. On Friday night, each kid would get the money from his father, and on Monday he would bring it to the school. I decided I was going to buy a Daddy right then. I had money in my pocket from shining shoes and selling papers, and whatever Helene Tucker pledged for her Daddy I was going to top it. And I'd hand the money right in. I wasn't going to wait until Monday to buy me a Daddy.

I was shaking, scared to death. The teacher opened her book and started calling our names alphabetically.

"Helene Tucker?"

"My Daddy said he'd give two dollars and fifty cents."

"That's very nice, Helene. Very, very nice indeed."

That made me feel pretty good. It wouldn't take too much to top that. I had almost three dollars in dimes and quarters in my pocket. I stuck my hand in my pocket and held onto the money, waiting for her to call my name. But the teacher closed her book after she called everybody else in the class.

I stood up and raised my hand.

"What is it now?"

"You forgot me?"

She turned toward the blackboard. "I don't have time to be playing with you, Richard."

"My Daddy said he'd . . ."

"Sit down, Richard, you're disturbing the class."

"My Daddy said he'd give . . . fifteen dollars."

She turned around and looked mad. "We are collecting this money for you and your kind, Richard Gregory. If your daddy can give fifteen dollars you have no business being on relief."

"I got it right now, I got it right now, my Daddy gave it to me to turn in today, my Daddy said . . ."

"And furthermore," she said, looking right at me, her nostrils getting big and her lips getting thin and her eyes opening wide, "we know you don't have a Daddy."

Helene Tucker turned around, her eyes full of tears. She felt sorry for me. Then I couldn't see her too well because I was crying, too.

"Sit down, Richard."

And I always thought the teacher kind of liked me. She always picked me to wash the blackboard on Friday, after school. That was a big thrill, it made me feel important. If I didn't wash it, come Monday the school might not function right.

"Where are you going, Richard!"

I walked out of school that day, and for a long time I didn't go back very often. There was shame there.

Now there was shame everywhere. It seemed like the whole world had been inside that classroom, everyone had heard what the teacher had said, everyone had turned around and felt sorry for me. There was shame in going to the Worthy Boys Annual Christmas Dinner for you and your kind, because everybody knew what a worthy boy was. Why couldn't they just call it the Boys Annual Dinner, why'd they have to give it a name? There was shame in wearing the brown and orange and white plaid mackinaw the welfare gave to three thousand boys. Why'd it have to be the same for everybody so when you walked down the street the people could see you were on relief? It was a nice warm mackinaw and it had a hood, and my Momma beat me and called me a little rat when she found out I stuffed it in the bottom of a pail full of garbage way over on Cottage Street. There was shame in running over to Mister Ben's at the end of the day and asking for his rotten peaches, there was shame in asking Mrs. Simmons for a spoonful of sugar, there was shame in running out to meet the relief truck. I hated that truck, full of food for you and your kind. I ran into the house and hid when it came. And then I started to sneak through alleys, to take the long way home so the people going into White's Eat Shop wouldn't see me. Yeah, the whole world heard the teacher that day, we all know you don't have a Daddy.

It lasted for a while, this kind of numbness. I spent a lot of time feeling sorry for myself. And then one day I met this wino in a restaurant. I'd been out hustling all day, shining shoes, selling newspapers, and I had googobs of money in my pocket. Bought me a bowl of chili for fifteen cents, and a cheeseburger for fifteen cents, and a Pepsi for five cents, and a piece of chocolate cake for ten cents. That was a good meal. I was eating when this old wino came in. I love winos because they never hurt anyone but themselves.

The old wino sat down at the counter and ordered twenty-six cents worth of food. He ate it like he really enjoyed it. When the owner, Mister Williams, asked him to pay the check, the old wino didn't lie or go though his pocket like he suddenly found a hole.

He just said: "Don't have no money."

The owner yelled: "Why in hell you come in here and eat my food if you don't have no money? That food cost me money."

Mister Williams jumped over the counter and knocked the wino off his stool and beat him over the head with a pop bottle. Then he stepped back and watched the wino bleed. Then he kicked him. And he kicked him again.

I looked at the wino with blood all over his face and I went over. "Leave him alone, Mister Williams. I'll pay the twenty-six cents."

The wino got up, slowly, pulling himself up to the stool, then up to the counter, holding on for a minute until his legs stopped shaking so bad. He looked at me with pure hate. "Keep your twenty-six cents. You don't have to pay, not now. I just finished paying for it."

He started to walk out, and as he passed me, he reached down and touched my shoulder. "Thanks, sonny, but it's too late now. Why didn't you pay it before?"

I was pretty sick about that. I waited too long to help another man.

Word Count: 1813

Exercise

1. In one paragraph, summarize what Gregory became ashamed of.

2. Describe a time when you were made ashamed of something.

3. Summarize some of the reasons Gregory offers for why children are sometimes thought to be stupid in school.

4. Gregory says, "Everybody's got a Helene Tucker, a symbol of everything you want." Who or what symbol is your "Helene Tucker"? Explain.

Selection 6

The following article is based on a speech given by the author to the 1989 incoming freshman class at Duke University. Dr. Brodie, a psychiatrist, is also the president of Duke University. He makes some interesting observations about the hate, intolerance, and inhumanity towards those not like us that we too frequently exhibit.

H. KEITH H. BRODIE

WE'RE NOT TAUGHT TO HATE

A wide spectrum of group intolerance appears to be increasing on the nation's college campuses, including harassment on the basis of racial, cultural, religious and even sexual differences.

What is it that this racism and sexism and homophobia and religious and cultural intolerance have in common? They are all ways of denying that other people are of the same kind as ourselves. This denial can be blatant, as in the hurling of ugly epithets or the physical harassment or coercion of another. Or it can be subtle and even unconscious, as when the contributions of some members of a group are consistently ignored or belittled. Sadly, this is one of the basic characteristics that all of us human beings have in common: our tendency to categorize and stereotype other groups of people as inferior to ourselves, and to use them as convenient objects of blame and animosity.

But whatever the manifestation and whoever the target, group hatred and suspicion arise from a primitive psychological mechanism that has nothing to do with the race, color, creed, gender or sexual orientation of the excluded others.

Briefly, in terms of developmental psychology, here is how this mechanism of hate arises: An infant's first laboratory assignment in becoming a human being is to discover that it and its mother are two separate entities. Then comes the discovery of boundaries between self and others, along with the ability—for the sake of species survival—to form strong family ties.

Paradoxically, this process that creates our species' ability to love also is the source of our ability to hate. The most commonly used example of this connection is the so-called recognition sequence observed in infants. Before an infant learns to distinguish its own mother from all others, it shows no fear of strangers. It is only when it recognizes the mother bond that fear and rejection of other people develop, and the infant embarrasses the family by screaming with terror at the approach of kind old Uncle Sigmund.

In the formation of groups, you and I—all human beings—duplicate the earliest conditions of our lives by this instinctual bonding mechanism. But then, having formed groups for necessary and benign reasons, all too often—and for the most part unconsciously—human beings take the next step that fears and rejects, that differentiates between the beloved familiar and the stranger, between the in-group and the out-group, between us and them. To strengthen the bonding, the in-group identifies itself as superior to the out-group, even where significant differences between the people involved are virtually nil. Then, the in-group proceeds to defend this difference as though it were a vital, objective reality, rather than an inner, psychological choice.

Reprinted by permission of the author, Dr. Keith H. Brodie, President, Duke University.

Consider in this light the irony of Hitler's requirement that Jews wear the Star of David, without which these supposedly inferior others would have been indistinguishable from the rest of the German population.

Knowledge of the process of bonding and group formation allows us to see ourselves in the larger context of our history as a species. We psychiatrists depend on a very important axiom in our work: that what is unconscious is not within a person's control, but what is made conscious is available for human beings to understand, to change or to reinforce.

We as a species can no longer afford not to recognize our own infantile behavior. The human race has the power to blow up the world, and yet we continue to allow our actions, both personally and as nations, to be controlled by a psychological hate mechanism on autopilot. And all the while, we vigorously maintain our own innocence of any wrongdoing. Like warring children we fiercely insist that it wasn't our fault, that the envied or feared "other" stepped over the imaginary line, "got on my side," and "made me do it." We project onto others—of another color, of another creed, of another culture—our own fears, angers, imperfections; all the things about ourselves that we dislike, we attribute to someone else, to the members of the out-group—even, at times, to people who simply happen to be of the opposite sex.

The Swiss psychiatrist Carl Jung had a picturesque term for this psychological element commonly observed in human beings. He referred to it as the "shadow," the projection of each individual's darker side. Because it is so uncomfortable for us to acknowledge our own faults and recognize the possibilities for evil within our own natures, we repress the knowledge of our shadow, and with relief turn it outward. "You can then at least say, without hesitation, who the devil is," Jung wrote; "you are quite certain that the cause of your misfortune is outside and not in your own attitude."

It has been a troubling acknowledgment for universities and colleges to make, that in this privileged enclave where we talk about and think about and teach the lessons of humane learning, we have not necessarily been educating our community in attitudes of tolerance and humility. We have come to realize that we must be explicit, that the naturally broadening and civilizing process of a liberal arts education is not enough, by itself, to accomplish the goals of community we have set before us. We must engage intolerance and inhumanity openly and publicly, as a community, at every opportunity.

Word Count: 765

Exercise

1. Summarize the article in one paragraph.

2. Do you agree with Brodie's thesis? Explain.

3. Examine your own prejudices that come from your "shadow" or darker side. Where did they come from? What can you do about them?

4. Why does Brodie say that we "can no longer afford not to recognize our own infantile behavior"? Do you agree?

Selection 7

The following selection, originally titled "Whether to Fight or Flee," is taken from Jane Brody's *The New York Times Guide to Personal Health*. This passage deals with stress. As you can tell from the title, some stress may be good for us, but how well we handle stress is the problem. Read for some advice on how to cope with stress.

JANE BRODY

STRESS: SOME GOOD, SOME BAD

Stress is a factor in every life, and without some stress life would be drab and unstimulating. Too little stress can produce boredom, feelings of isolation, stagnation, and purposelessness. Stress in and of itself is not bad; rather, it's how you react to the different stresses in your life that matters.

Many people thrive on stress. They find working under pressure or against deadlines highly stimulating, providing the motivation to do their best. And they rarely succumb to adverse stress reactions. To slow such "racehorses" down to the pace of a turtle would be as stressful as trying to make the turtle keep up with the horse. Yet others crumble when the crunch is on or the overload light flashes. Some take life's large and small obstacles in stride, regarding them as a challenge to succeed in spite of everything. Others are thwarted by every unexpected turn of events, from a traffic delay to a serious illness in the family. . . .

Dr. Donald A. Tubesing, psychologist from Duluth, Minnesota, and author of *Kicking Your Stress Habits* (see "For Further Reading" . . .), likens stress to the tension on a violin string—you need "enough tension to make music but not so much that it snaps." . . .

There are many ways to cope with excess stress, and some methods are better than others. Too often people turn to the wrong solutions for stress relief, such as tranquilizers, sleeping pills, alcohol, and cigarettes, and end up further impairing their health while doing nothing to gain an upper hand on the causes of their stress reactions. Others resort to short-term solutions—shouting, crying, taking a hot bath—that help for a while. More lasting, "low-cost" relief could be obtained through regular exercise or talking with friends, Dr. Tubesing says.

How to cope with stress

Everyone should have a repertoire of stress-reducing techniques. Here are some that Dr. Tubesing and others have found helpful.

Set priorities

Divide your tasks into three categories—essential, important, and trivial—and forget about the trivial. Hire others, including your own children, to do the tasks that can be farmed out. Learn to say no when you're asked to do something that overloads your time or stress budget or diverts you from what you really consider most important. Be satisfied with a less than perfect job if the alternative is not getting a job done at all. Identify the activities you find satisfying in and of themselves, and focus on enjoying them, rather than on your performance or what rewards the activities might bring.

Organize your time

Identify the time wasters. Figure out when in the day you are most productive, and do your essential and important tasks then. Pace yourself by scheduling your tasks, allowing time for unexpected emergencies. If at all possible, leave your work at the office to reduce conflicts with the demands at home and give yourself time to recharge your batteries.

Budget your stress

The Metropolitan Life Insurance Company recommends taking a periodic glance at your schedule for the next three months to see what events may be coming up that may cause you to overdraw your stress account. Try to avoid clusters of stressful events by spreading them out.

Try "clean living"

Be more consistent in your living habits by trying to eat, sleep, and exercise at about the same time every day. Don't overindulge in alcohol or rely on pills to induce sleep (they're counterproductive). Be sure to get enough sleep and rest because fatigue can reduce your ability to cope with stress. Eat regular, well-balanced meals with enough variety to assure good nutrition and enough complex carbohydrates (starchy foods) to guarantee a ready energy reserve. Reverse the typical American meal pattern, and instead, eat like a king for breakfast, a prince for lunch, and a pauper for supper; you'll have more daytime energy and sleep better at night. . . .

Listen to your body

It will let you know when you are pushing too hard. When your back or head aches or your stomach sours, slow down, have some fun, take time to enjoy the world around you. Set aside some time each day for self-indulgence. Focus on life's little pleasures.

Choose fight or flight

Don't be afraid to express anger (hiding it is even more stressful than letting it out), but choose your fights; don't hassle over every little thing. When fighting is inappropriate, try fleeing—learn to fantasize or take a short break (do a puzzle, take a walk, go to a concert, or away for the weekend) to reenergize yourself. You can also give in once in a while, instead of always insisting you are right and others are wrong.

Learn relaxation techniques

These include deep breathing exercises, transcendental meditation, the relaxation response (a demystified form of meditation formulated by Dr. Herbert Benson, a Harvard cardiologist), religious experiences, yoga, progressive relaxation of muscle groups, imagery, biofeedback, and behavior modification. The last four may require professional help. On a tightly scheduled day, take a minute or two between appointments or activities for a relaxation break—stretching, breathing, walking around.

Revitalize through exercise

A body lacking in physical stamina is in no shape to handle stress. An exercise tune-up can increase your emotional as well as your physical strength. Exercise enhances, rather than saps, your energy; it also has a distinct relaxing effect. . . .

Talk it out

Problems often seem much worse when you alone carry their burden. Talking to a trusted friend or relative or to a professional counselor can help you sort things out and unload some of the burden. If things are really bad, don't hesitate to seek professional counseling or psychotherapy.

Get outside yourself

Stress causes people to turn into themselves and focus too much on their own problems. Try doing something for someone else. Or find something other than yourself and your accomplishments to care about. Be more tolerant and forgiving of yourself and others.

Finally, Drs. Robert L. Woolfolk and Frank C. Richardson, psychologists and authors of *Stress, Sanity and Survival* (see "For Further Reading" below), caution against "waiting for the day when 'you can relax' or when 'your problems will be over.' The struggles of life never end. Most good things in life are fleeting and transitory. Enjoy them; savor them. Don't waste time looking forward to the 'happy ending' to all your troubles."

For further reading

Benson, Herbert, M.D. *The Relaxation Response,* New York: William Morrow, 1975; Avon, 1976.

Carrington, Patricia. *Freedom in Meditation.* New York: Anchor/Doubleday, 1977.

Madders, Jane. *Stress and Relaxation.* New York: Arco, 1979.

McQuade, Walter, and Ann Aikman. *Stress: What It Is, What It Can Do to Your Health, How to Fight Back.* New York: Bantam, 1975.

Norfolk, Donald. *The Stress Factor.* New York: Simon & Schuster, 1977.

Selye, Hans, M.D. *The Stress of Life.* New York: McGraw-Hill, 1956; rev. ed., 1976.

———. *Stress Without Distress.* New York: Lippincott, 1974.

Steinmetz, Jenny; Jon Blankenship; Linda Brown; Deborah Hall; and Grace Miller. *Managing Stress.* Palo Alto, Calif.: Bull, 1980.

Tubesing, Donald A. *Kicking Your Stress Habits.* Duluth: Whole Person Associates, 1981. Available for $10 plus $1 for postage and handling from Whole Person Associates, Inc., P.O. Box 3151, Duluth, Minn. 55803.

Woolfolk, Robert L., and Frank G. Richardson. *Stress, Sanity and Survival.* New York: Sovereign Books (Simon & Schuster), 1978.

Word Count: 1105

Exercise

1. Summarize the techniques for coping with stress.

2. What solutions for coping with stress have you found are helpful to you when you feel under stress? Are they healthy solutions?

3. From what source does Jane Brody get much of her information on stress?

4. Go to the library and find one of the books on the "For Further Reading" list. Look through it to see if any of the techniques mentioned in the reading selection are covered more thoroughly. Read that section and summarize what it says.

Selection 8

It is no longer unusual in our society for children to be raised by single parents. There are, however, a growing number of women who are choosing to have children without a mate. The following essay explains why some women want to be single parents and reflects their irritation with those who feel they are wrong. Read their views and see what you think.

HOWARD HALPERN

SINGLE MOTHERS BY CHOICE

There's nothing new about an unmarried woman having a child. It's been happening for ages. But, in most instances, it was considered a scandal. The child was branded "illegitimate" and the mother a "fallen woman." And even when an unwed mother was not looked down upon, as has happened in the underclass in many societies, being a single parent was almost always considered an unwelcome burden.

Now a new phenomenon is occurring. An increasing number of women are choosing to have children without a mate. There are many reasons for this development. For one thing, more women now consider building their careers, not their families, top priority. As birthdays fly by, and they find themselves in their 30s, they become more concerned about approaching the end of their fertile years. They may have never married, or they were married but divorced before they had children.

But time is not the only important factor here. These women are also aware that there are few men around who are available, agreeable to having children (they may already have children from a previous marriage) and desirable as life partners.

Profile of unmarried mother

Many of these women refuse to let circumstances deprive them of the basic female experience of having and loving a child. So, they opt for single parenthood. What type of woman makes this decision? Here's how she is described in the brochure of an organization called Single Mothers by Choice, a support group based in New York City that has chapters in many major cities throughout the country: "She is a woman who *decided* to have or adopt a child, knowing she would be her child's sole parent, at least at the outset.

"We are many different kinds of people from many walks of life. Typically, we are career women in our 30s or 40s. The ticking of our biological clocks has made us face the fact that we could no longer wait for the right man to appear before starting our families.

"Some of us accidentally became pregnant and discovered we were thrilled. Some of us intentionally conceived with a man. Others went to a doctor for artificial insemination or found a child we could adopt.

"Single motherhood is for the woman who believes she has much to give a child and who has adequate emotional and financial resources to support herself and her child." (For more information about Single Mothers by Choice, the chapter nearest you or instructions on how to start a group in your area, write: Single Mothers by Choice, Box 7788, F.D.R. Station, New York, N.Y., 10150.)

'It really infuriates me'

There is considerable disagreement about the advisability and "fairness" of a single woman deliberately becoming a mother. Some disagree on moral or religious grounds. Others see it as an act of selfishness. Jennifer, a 36-year-old single social worker, said, "I want a child, and I know I have only a few years left to have one, but I would never have a child without being married. It just seems like such a selfish thing to do. What about the child? Isn't he entitled to two parents?"

Many single mothers would disagree with Jennifer. Elaine, a 43-year-old unmarried lawyer with a 4-year-old daughter, said, "It really infuriates me when people talk of us as selfish. I'm up at 6 every morning, dressing her, getting her breakfast, preparing her day, leaving instructions for the housekeeper, who will pick her up from nursery school. Then we have this great walk to nursery school when we talk about everything. I call her from work several times during the day, hurry home to have dinner with her, bathe her and get her to bed. Is this selfishness?"

The debate will go on for a long time. Some point to studies showing that children from single-parent homes are more likely to have psychological difficulties than those from two-parent families. But others note that these studies are mostly about mothers who did not choose to have a child without a husband, but in which the marriage ended, or in cases in which a single woman became pregnant and kept the child because she felt she had no choice. They suggest that the children in those studies lived in a home very different from the loving atmosphere provided by women who chose to have a child without being married.

It will be many years before we have clear and ample evidence of how these children of single mothers by choice fare in the world.

In the meantime, women who are considering having a child outside marriage must sort out their motivation, their feelings about the morality of the situation and whether they have the emotional and financial resources.

Word Count: 825

Exercise

1. Summarize the reasons some women want to be single parents.

2. Explain your views on the subject.

3. Do you think adoption agencies should allow a single person to adopt a child? Explain.

4. Is this a moral issue, a legal issue, or a religious issue? Explain.

Selection 9

Brian Rosborough, the author of the following essay is the president of Earthwatch, an organization "made up of scholars and citizens working together to increase public understanding of science and to expand our knowledge of the globe and its inhabitants." Frequently we can feel frustrated and helpless when we hear the dangers of global warming, the decimation of the world's rain forests, the depleting of the earth's resources. Here he calls our attention to something we can all do in our own way.

BRIAN A. ROSBOROUGH

PUTTING SOMETHING BACK

When was the last time you planted a tree? Five billion humans now live off the global commons. Our earth mother feeds, shelters, and clothes us—yet few of her children put something back. Imagine the good we could do if each of 100 million people, or two percent of humankind, made a commitment to plant and nurture a tree every year until the year 2,000: the air would freshen, birds might return, and we could see the mountains again. It should not require a crusade to put this across, just common sense and a better ethical compass.

Planting trees is more than a symbolic act. It is a manifestation of our need to manage the planet. Accountability for the global commons should be everyone's responsibility—not just the concern of property holders, resource economists, and government statisticians. What we take out of the global commons to meet today's needs dilutes the net global assets for our children. Putting something back is a form of insurance. We need to devise a simple system of economic equivalents so we can publish the natural resource base of *all* nations for world citizens to audit. National financial statements depicting "the wealth of our nation" should be distributed in schools so that children everywhere will understand net depletion and natural resource conversion. Only then will policies be encouraged to develop the global commons in less exploitative ways. Our children will insist on it.

Humans need to know how their individual behavior will affect the global environment in this crucial decade. Managing the planet calls on each of us to change the way we are overspending the global commons—the air, the seas, the diversity of life, nature's last resource. The great irony is that we are all guilty of poaching if we allow our lifestyles to interfere with this mission. The call to action is unambiguous. It should focus our

lives on the greater commons, not ourselves, and bond neighbors and nations in a rendezvous with destiny.

It is time to put something back.

Word Count: 370

Exercise

1. Summarize the author's thesis in one sentence.

2. Explain what Rosborough means when he says, "The great irony is that
   we are all guilty of poaching if we allow our lifestyles to interfere with
   this mission"?

3. What suggestions do you have for "putting something back"?

Index